THE STATE AND
HIGHER EDUCATION

THE WOBURN EDUCATION SERIES
General Series Editor: Professor Peter Gordon

The Victorian School Manager
Peter Gordon

Selection for Secondary Education
Peter Gordon

The Study of Education
A Collection of Inaugural Lectures
edited by Peter Gordon
Volume I   Early and Modern
Volume II   The Last Decade
Volume III   The Changing Scene

The Education of Gifted Children
David Hopkinson

Games and Simulations in Action
Alec Davison and Peter Gordon

Slow Learners – A Break in the Circle
A Practical Guide for Teachers in Secondary Schools
Diane Griffin

The Middle School – High Road or Dead End?
John Burrows

Music in Education
Malcolm Carlton

Teaching and Learning Mathematics
Peter Dean

Unequal Educational Provision in England and Wales:
The Nineteenth-Century Roots
W.E. Marsden

Dictionary of British Educationists
Richard Aldrich and Peter Gordon

History of Education: The Making of a Discipline
edited by Peter Gordon and Richard Szreter

Educating the Respectable: The Story of Fleet Road
School, Hampstead, 1875–1903
W.E. Marsden

Teaching the Humanities
edited by Peter Gordon

Education and Policy in England in
the Twentieth Century
Peter Gordon, Richard Aldrich and Dennis Dean

The Private Schooling of Girls Past and Present
edited by Geoffrey Walford

THE STATE AND HIGHER EDUCATION

Brian Salter
and
Ted Tapper

RoutledgeFalmer
Taylor & Francis Group

LONDON AND NEW YORK

First published in 1994 in Great Britain by
THE WOBURN PRESS
Reprinted 2004
By RoutledgeFalmer,
2 Park Square, Milton Park, Abingdon, Oxon, OX14 4RN

Transferred to Digital Printing 2004

Copyright © 1994 Brian Salter and Ted Tapper

British Library Cataloguing in Publication Data

State and Higher Education. – (Woburn
Education Series)
 I. Salter, Brian II. Tapper, Ted
 III. Series
 379.20941

ISBN 0-7130-0190-9 (cased)
   0-7130-4021-1 (paper)

Library of Congress Cataloging-in-Publication Data

Salter, Brian.
    The state and higher education / Brian Salter and Ted Tapper.
    p. cm. — (The Woburn education series)
    Includes bibliographical references and index.
    ISBN 0 7130 0190 9 (cased); 0 7130 4021 1 (paper)
    1. Higher education and state—Great Britain. 2. Educational
change—Great Britain. 3. Politics and education—Great Britain.
I. Tapper, Ted. II. Title. III. Series.
LC178.G7S25   1994
379.41—dc20   93–32137
                                                CIP

Typeset by Regent Typesetting, London

Contents

Abbreviations

ABRC	Advisory Board for the Research Councils
ACARD	Advisory Council on Applied Research and Development
ACC	Association of County Councils
ACSET	Advisory Committee on the Supply and Education of Teachers
ACSIR	Advisory Council for Science and Industrial Research
ACSP	Advisory Council on Scientific Policy
AFE	Advanced Further Education
AFRC	Agriculture and Food Research Council
AMA	Association of Metropolitan Authorities
ARC	Agricultural Research Council
ATOs	Area Training Organisations
AUT	Association of University Teachers
BEC	Business Education Council
BTEC	Business and Technical Education Council
CAT	College of Advanced Technology
CATE	Council for the Accreditation of Teacher Education
CBI	Confederation of British Industry
CDP	Committee of Directors of Polytechnics
CERN	European Organisation for Nuclear Research
CLEA	Committee of Local Education Authorities
CNAA	Council for National Academic Awards
CPS	Centre for Policy Studies
CSP	Council for Scientific Policy
CVCP	Committee of Vice-Chancellors and Principals
DES	Department of Education and Science
DFE	Department for Education
DPO	Departmental Planning Organisation
DSIR	Department of Scientific and Industrial Research
ERA	Education Reform Act
HEFCE	Higher Education Funding Council for England
HEFCs	Higher Education Funding Councils

ABBREVIATIONS

HELP	Higher Education and Labour Party Campaign
HEQC	Higher Education Quality Council
HMI	Her Majesty's Inspectorate
IEA	Institute of Economic Affairs
LEA	Local Education Authority
MRC	Medical Research Council
NAB	National Advisory Body
NAO	National Audit Office
NATFE	National Association of Teachers in Further Education
NC	Nature Conservancy
NCC	Nature Conservancy Council
NERC	Natural Environment Research Council
OPSS	Office of Public Service and Science
OST	Office of Science and Technology
PAC	Public Accounts Committee
PAR	Programme Analysis Review
PCAS	Polytechnics and Colleges Admissions System
PCFC	Polytechnics and Colleges Funding Council
PESC	Public Expenditure Survey Committee
PPB	Planning–Programming–Budgeting
PSHE	Public Sector of Higher Education
QAC	Quality Assessment Committee
RAC	Regional Advisory Council
RSG	Rate Support Grant
RSI	Regional Staff Inspectors
SEA	Socialist Education Association
SERC	Science and Engineering Research Council
SRC	Science Research Council
SSRC	Social Science Research Council
TEC	Technical Education Council
TUC	Trades Union Congress
UCCA	Universities' Central Council on Admissions
UFC	Universities Funding Council
UGC	University Grants Committee

Preface

On 1 April 1993, the Higher Education Funding Councils (HEFCs) for England, Wales and Scotland officially came into being. Their arrival has been heralded as a watershed in the history of the long and tangled relationship between the state and higher education. It has been argued that with the creation of the HEFCs the underlying logic of a single, united sector of higher education has finally been realised and that the institutional keystone for the future state funding of higher education is securely in place. After a decade of hectic activity in its organisational evolution, suggest the optimists, the state has reached a plateau of stability and the sunlit uplands of higher education are in sight.

Such a thesis ignores the continuing dynamic for change which fuels the institutions of the state. That it does so is not surprising. For while much has been written about higher education itself very little has appeared about the organisations of the state which, increasingly, determine its destiny. It is now more than thirty years since Berdahl's *British Universities and the State* was published. In the interim we have had only Carswell's *Government and the Universities in Britain* (1985), essentially an insider's view, to inform our understanding of the mosaic of state institutions which plan, fund or pronounce upon higher education. It is therefore inevitable, if regrettable, that discourses on higher education generally assume that 'the state' or 'the government', the terms are frequently employed interchangeably, has a single identity which can be taken for granted and wheeled out whenever the argument about a particular aspect of higher education so requires. While undoubtedly convenient as a rhetorical aid, such an approach merely masks the complex and powerful political currents at work within the state apparatus and, by omission, prevents the development of a proper understanding of change in higher education.

The objective of this book is to redress the balance by examining the issue of change in those organisations of the state which deal, and have dealt, with higher education. What forces have shaped the development of these organisations, what trends are observable in the way they have responded to the pressures for change, and what are the implications for higher education? In answering these questions, our intention is to provide a comprehensive and informed context for the current debate about the future of higher education.

Our analysis of this context is guided by the theory of educational change developed in our previous work. Within this we are concerned with the ideological struggle between the economic view of higher education and the traditional liberal ideal of the university (Tapper and Salter, 1978, Ch. 7; Tapper and Salter, 1992, Ch. 9), the independent bureaucratic drive of the central state (Salter and Tapper, 1981, Ch. 5) and the impact of the New Right on educational policy (Salter and Tapper, 1985, Ch. 7). In applying our theory to the problem of change in the institutions of the educational state, we have drawn extensively on a comprehensive range of primary sources to ensure that the empirical authority of the book is visible and secure.

The result is a study which a number of audiences may find of interest. For educational sociologists, political sociologists and social policy analysts, the exploration of changing patterns of state influence in higher education elaborates the view of policy-making contained in our previous work. For professional administrators in universities and colleges, the detailed analysis of all the major state institutions dealing with higher education provides an overview of the forces helping to shape the organisations in which they work. For the more general observer, the review of trends in the state's attitude towards higher education is an important counterbalance to the self-indulgence of some academic commentaries on the present condition of the universities.

The book begins with an overview of the perspective on higher education offered by our theory of educational change and identifies the main analytical themes to be pursued in the subsequent chapters, each of which deals with a particular part of the state. Chapters 2 and 3 take the political context and show how within both parties and Parliament there has been a steady decline in support for the traditional values of autonomous university education and a growing belief in the accountability of higher education to the needs of the economy. Historically, demands for accountability have been only occasionally expressed through the Privy Council, the Statutory Commissioners and the Visitor, and Chapter 4 discusses how these traditional mechanisms remained, until very recently, within the orbit of university influence. The same cannot be said of the central bureaucratic state. Chapter 5 analyses the successive contributions of the Board of Education, the Ministry of Education and the Department of Education and Science (DES) to the construction of ideological and administrative controls over higher education. For seventy years, however, the universities were protected by an arm of the state itself, the University Grants Committee (UGC) and Chapter 6 traces the many and varied conflicts within that body between the demands for accountability and the principle of university autonomy. In what was known as the public sector of higher education, the polytechnics and colleges, the state sought to extend its influence through its satellite agencies, the National Advisory Body (NAB) and the Polytechnics and Colleges Funding Council (PCFC). Chapter 7 explores how these bodies became the focus for a war of attrition waged by the central state against the local authorities.

Science in higher education posed a different problem for the state. Politically, the funding of science in higher education through the research councils has always formed part of a wider debate about civil science in all government departments. Chapter 8 therefore situates its analysis of the research councils in the context of the continuing attempts by the state to rationalise the organisation of science. Finally, Chapter 9 reflects on the implications of the changes in the organisations of the state for higher education and on the likely balance to be struck between the methods of central planning and those of the managed market.

Part of the research for this book was funded by the Economic and Social Research Council, and for that we are grateful. In addition we would like to thank Sir Christopher Ball, former chairman of the NAB; Mr Richard Bird, late of the DES; Mr John Farrant, University of Sussex; Mr N. Hardyman, former secretary to the UGC; Mr Frank Mattison, Registrar of University of Hull, and Mrs Barbara Holland, University of Kent.

BRIAN SALTER
TED TAPPER

1

The State and Higher Education

Writing in 1948, Sir Walter Moberly observed: 'Undoubtedly the machinery exists by which the State could, if it were so minded, apply almost irresistible financial pressure to the Universities. The basis of confidence is the conviction not that the State cannot but that the State will not want to do so; it rests in other words, not upon law but upon the convention of the Constitution' (Moberly, 1949, 16). Today that conviction is no more. State pressure on the universities, and on higher education in general, is a fact of life. With the passing of the 1988 *Education Reform Act* and the 1992 *Further and Higher Education Act* the pace of change in higher education has quickened immeasurably. After decades of incremental progress, of prod and nudge politics, of wait and see, the state has acquired powers which mark a qualitative shift in its relationship with the institutions of higher education. It is now in the position to orchestrate change on a scale and in a manner which knows no precedent.

The purpose of this book is to explain how the state achieved this ambition, to explore the nature of the power it now wields and to assess its ability to shape the future of higher education. In this opening chapter the analytical framework for achieving these objectives is developed through a dialogue with the theory of educational change contained in our previous work. The starting point, not surprisingly, is the definition of that part of the state which relates to higher education: what criteria should be used to determine where the state begins and ends? Furthermore, is it sensible, as some would have us believe, to regard the state as a monolith or should we be more sceptical in our conceptual approach and assume, to begin with at least, that it is composed of mutually suspicious elements? Second, what interest does the state have in higher education and, from this, what can we deduce about its long-term intentions in this field? Third, what political methods has the state used in pursuit of these intentions? Much of the discussion here centres on the ideological dimension of state power and the nature of the values which, for decades, it has employed to support its challenge to the universities' autonomy and to prise the polytechnics away from the control of the local authorities.

THE STATE AND EDUCATIONAL CHANGE

Arguments about what is, and what is not, part of the state have abounded for many years and have produced no generally accepted resolution. We have dealt with these arguments elsewhere and do not intend to rehearse them here (Salter and Tapper, 1981, Ch.5; 1985, Ch.2). Our own position is that the definition of the state should be related to the process of policy formation and implementation and, for reasons which we will discuss shortly, should be centred on the dominant government bureaucracy in any policy field. In the case of higher education that organisation is the Department for Education (DFE).

As the central state bureaucracy, the DFE deals with both the formation and the implementation of policy on higher education. In contrast to this, other parts of the state concentrate in the main on one policy function or the other. Thus the political parties and Parliament largely concern themselves with the formation of policy and the Higher Education Funding Councils (HEFCs) with its implementation. Obviously this distinction is not watertight. So, for example, Parliament's Public Accounts Committee (PAC) acts as a monitor of policy implementation and has produced numerous reports critical of particular policies. Equally, the old University Grants Committee (UGC) was never simply an instrument of policy implementation but in part acted as a lobby on behalf of the universities. But it is the Department which has the unique ability to hold the ring, define the rules of the game and allow some protagonists into the arena and exclude others.

Despite its centrality in the web of institutions which constitute the state and higher education, the DFE is not in a position to impose a uniformity of values and ambition upon the system. The once fashionable Marxist view of the state as a monolithic institution faithfully carrying out its function of reproducing the conditions required for capitalist production has long since proved inadequate. Tensions, hostility and conflict are as much a part of relations between the institutions of the state as they are in any political arena where a degree of plurality of interest exists. This is not to say that trends over time in the nature of these relations cannot be identified; indeed they

2

can. But what is clear is that the speed and precise direction of these trends is problematic.

As the trends become manifest, so the pressures for change in higher education emanating from the state increase. Despite their often difficult genesis, these pressures can be seen as the result of the interaction of three dynamics generated by the economy, the dominant state bureaucracy, and political institutions and interests. The modern economy, first of all, is fuelled by an ever-evolving mix of manpower and scientific knowledge and, ideally, would require the education system to train and research the appropriate educational products necessary for optimum economic advance. However, intervening between the economic dynamic and its potential impact upon education is the central bureaucracy of the state and the political institutions and interests, each with its own identity and concerns. To the best of its ability, each interprets and channels the demands from the economy in a way which suits the dynamic inherent in its own interests and policy preferences.

Much of this book deals with the interaction between these three dynamics. Depending on their response to these dynamics, and the response has varied from one part of the state to another, the institutions of the state have then created a further set of pressures for change on higher education itself. The importance of this analysis of the state is that it does not accept that the simple explanations of change in higher education, so beloved of academic commentators, are tenable. Instead, it promotes the view that a complex of forces are at work within the apparatus of the state, that many and varied political battles are fought before a visible result presents itself to higher education, and that change in the organisation of the state is frequently a necessary precursor of change in higher education.

THE STATE'S INTEREST

What, exactly, is the nature of the state's interest in higher education? If the answer to this question can be precisely stated then we should have identified the reasons behind the state's growing desire to orchestrate change in this area and the likely functions it expects higher education to fulfil. In the view of Halsey and Trow, the state's interest derives from the fact that the universities

> are a crucial foundation of the economy, conceived since Robbins as integral to a higher education system which supplies scientific manpower and technological innovation for economic

growth and widening opportunities to a rising proportion of the population. They are thus of crucial political importance and are in any case pressed into responsibility, or at least responsiveness, to the state as manager of economic growth, and the dispenser of individual opportunity for participation (Halsey and Trow, 1971, 60).

In the context of our theory of educational change, this can be interpreted as a description of the three dynamics of educational change: the economic (the demand for growth), the bureaucratic (the state as manager), and the political (in this case, the theme of 'equality of opportunity'). However, that said, rather more unpacking is required to understand why the state needs higher education and therefore why higher education possesses the power that it does.

Higher education offers a unique blend of two resources essential for economic and social development: knowledge and status. Furthermore, the history of the control of these resources has placed the universities, in particular, in a secure monopoly position so that, from the state's point of view, it makes strategic sense to seek to change them rather than close them down or create alternative, rival institutions. In this respect, the failure of the polytechnics to live up to the egalitarian and technological values invested in them by the Labour Party, and their subsequent 'academic drift' to become, in the jaundiced view of Pratt and Burgess, little more than 'bowdlerised universities', is a salutary tribute to the power of the universities and an example of why the state has to trade with them (Pratt and Burgess, 1974, 23–30 and 172–4).

Given that higher education is not the only social institution producing knowledge linked to status, the Church of England being another, how does it translate this activity into tangible power which the state has to respect? As the apex of the educational hierarchy, higher education makes the decision on how knowledge should be organised and what status should be attached to different knowledge areas. Likewise, any significant change in the content or boundary of a knowledge area has to be sanctioned by higher education if it is to carry lasting weight. Once sanctioned, the changes are then seen by the rest of the educational hierarchy as having received the higher education status stamp of approval. This can be described as the exercise of higher education's *educational* power.

Its translation into different forms of social and political power is a consequence of the vital part played by education in the process of social change and a further reason for the state's interest in courting, confining or directing higher education. Within higher education, universities act as what Halsey and Trow call 'the custodians of the selection process' through their control of much of the examination system (Halsey and Trow, 1971, 204). Society only accepts that an individual has acquired a particular body of knowledge if the possession of that knowledge has been certified by an appropriate institution and, as the dominant institutions in education, universities not only award the most prestigious certificates (degrees) but also strongly influence the form and content of certificates awarded by institutions lower down the education hierarchy. In effect, they thus define the context in which much individual social mobility takes place.

Equally, any occupational group wishing to enhance its social position has to pay due recognition to the universities' monopoly of the access to, and certification of, high status knowledge. In practice, this means requesting the universities to incorporate an occupation's certification procedure with the result that, historically, all ambitious occupations have sought the university stamp of approval for their ascent to professional status. In acquiring the mantle of university respectability an occupation also gains access to a high-status culture which, judiciously employed, will enhance its claims to professional respectability.

In its dealings with higher education, the state is obliged to recognise that universities perform a key social function by controlling the individual and occupational mobility necessary for social change. But this is not all. In addition, their monopoly of the union of high status knowledge and culture endows them with a third kind of socio-political power: the authority to promote particular sets of values. That is, it gives them ideological power. Since social and economic change has to be accompanied, if not preceded, by a corresponding shift in the ideology which legitimates the status quo, universities are frequently called upon by the state to use their ideological power to promote or resist such change. As we discuss below, their recent indifference to such calls has left them dangerously exposed as other sources of new ideas have rapidly emerged.

IDEOLOGY AND CONTROL

Given the nature of the state's interest in higher education, it is inevitable that it will seek to manage the process of educational change. Historically, it has used a variety of methods to achieve this objective: legal, financial, administrative and, most important of all, ideological. As the method of intervention has changed so higher

5

education has been obliged to relate to a different, and in some cases a new, part of the state. Writing in 1853, Sir William Hamilton, an energetic critic of the universities, remarked that:

> A university is a trust confided by the state to certain hands for the common interest of the nation; nor has it theretofore been denied that a university may, and ought, by the state to be from time to time corrected, reformed, or recast, in conformity to accidental changes of relation, and looking towards an improved accomplishment of its essential ends (Hamilton, 1852, 583).

According to this view, periodic legal intervention was sufficient to achieve the desired ends and throughout the nineteenth century the universities' relationship with the state was restricted to intermittent contact with Parliament and its temporary arm, the Royal Commission and the Statutory Commissioners. However, with the steady growth in public funding for the universities in the twentieth century the situation became more complex. Administrative mechanisms were required to determine and allocate the flow of moneys, beginning with the setting-up of the University Grants Committee (UGC) in 1919 and the various research councils soon thereafter. In effect, the boundaries of the state were expanding and assuming permanent form as a replacement for the ad hoc interventions of the previous century. As they did so, the nature of the state's power relationship with the universities changed from one of occasional legal fiat to one embedded in administrative and financial arrangements where the precise exercise of power was unclear and dominated by the prevailing ideological climate. Until 1964, both the UGC and the research councils remained on the periphery of the state: a situation which diffused the effect of any exercise of state power. The UGC received its money directly from the Treasury and, with its assistance, was able to resist the doctrine of accountability in general and Parliamentary scrutiny in particular. The research councils were funded via the Lord President of the Council and were subject to no coordinated control. But with the reforms of 1964, both UGC and research councils became the responsibility of the newly formed Department of Education and Science (DES). This meant that although both were still there as institutional 'buffers' between state and universities, their accountability to a single Department made them less peripheral and hence less able to fragment pressures for change on the universities. The process of consolidation of the state organisation in respect of higher education had begun.

However, to understand the implications of such structural shifts for the exercise of state power we need to place it in the context of our theory. This assumes that the objective of the state's interest in higher education is to change the way it organises knowledge and the knowledge-status hierarchy, transmits knowledge to occupational groups – new and old – through teaching and produces new knowledge through research. Educational change is therefore defined as change in the way in which higher education employs its educational, social and political power in achieving these ends. Naturally this change is reflected in organisational terms but the important conceptual point is that this is the result of demands for change in higher education's socio-political functions: that is why the state is interested in it. What our theory also makes clear is that change in these functions cannot simply occur but has to be legitimised by a parallel, or preferably a preceding, change in the values of higher education. Thus the exercise of ideological power by the state is essential if it is to wield any significant influence over the shape of higher education.

It is at this point that life becomes difficult for a state organisation bent on introducing change into higher education. How is it to achieve ideological supremacy over institutions which themselves have ideology creation as one of their inherited social functions? To make any progress whatsoever it clearly had first to develop its own ideological power base. Given the historical divisions within the state, the peripheral position of the UGC and the research councils, and the traditional dominance of university values within the state itself, this was never going to be easy. Memories are short, and it is as well to be reminded that it used to be regarded as axiomatic that the British elite was a unified, homogeneous group with a common value system and cultural identity. Since the leading members of both universities and state were happily included in this definition, the idea of a vicious, internecine conflict between the two, such as we have witnessed over the past decade, was never taken seriously. Now it is regarded as axiomatic that higher education and state exist in a situation of continuing ideological tension.

Writing in 1969, A.H. Halsey noted the 'historical continuity ... of de facto control of elitist institutions [the universities] by likeminded members of the elite' (Halsey, 1969, 137). This, he observed, in turn demonstrated 'the extraordinary stability of the British system of elite recruitment to positions of political, industrial or bureaucratic power' (ibid.). His view was not remarkable. Ever since the foundation of the UGC in 1919 it had been assumed that university life was part and parcel of the elite at cultural play. University and state were joined by a seamless web of shared understandings and values within which the UGC nestled comfortably and harmoniously. Hence, as one observer commented, 'the success of the UGC rests fundamentally upon unwritten conventions and the personal and social relations of a homogeneous community of university men, in and out of government, who share common tastes and a common outlook' (Dodds *et al.*, 1952, 73). Many of the members of the UGC and the Treasury officials belonged to the Atheneum Club and conducted a good deal of business in its convivial surroundings (ibid.).

In this situation it was difficult to envisage any disagreements between the universities and state which could not be resolved through gentlemanly discussion. Hence when in 1946 the Committee of Vice-Chancellors and Principals (CVCP) specifically requested that the universities should have 'a greater measure of guidance from the government than until recent days they have been accustomed to receive' on how they should 'devise and execute policies calculated to serve the national interest', it did so within a context of known possibilities (Niblett, 1952, 168). As Niblett points out, 'unless there had been fundamental trust that any British government would have a close understanding of what university ideals were, no such request for guidance could or would have been made' (ibid.). Part of that trust was that the state would never challenge the right of universities to decide for themselves whether to accept the advice given and certainly would never subject them to any ungentlemanly pressure. The assumption that a shared ideology existed of itself precluded the possibility of aggressive action by the state. In 1959, having examined the universities' relationship with the state in considerable detail, Berdahl summed up his own, and the general, view when he concluded: 'It is inconceivable that ... these people [of the Treasury] should ever initiate any state action hostile to the universities' (Berdahl, 1959, 168).

With hindsight, this view may appear blinkered and all too dismissive of the state's ability to form and propagate its own ideology of higher education. But thirty years ago it was a natural reflection of the prevailing hegemony and a measure of the task facing an ambitious state bureaucracy bent on expanding its power. In order to understand the size and complexity of this task we need first to explore the values which unified the universities and the state for so long. What are the primary components, what are the reasons for their long-standing dominance, and wherein lie the seeds of their decay?

The formulation of the traditional university ideal as we know it today took place in the second half of the nineteenth century when Oxford and Cambridge Universities were obliged by external pressure from the state and internal professional demands from a new breed of dons to justify their place in society (Rothblatt, 1968; Engel, 1983). In so doing, they drew selectively on two main traditions: the Christian-Hellenic, as Sir Walter Moberly described it, and the more recent liberal tradition. For Newman and Jowett 'the chief duty of the university is to produce good citizens. It should train an elite who are to be the future leaders in affairs and in the learned professions' (Moberly, 1949, 31). In so doing, the university must ensure that teachers and learners live together as a family. It must be, in Cardinal Newman's words, 'an Alma Mater, knowing her children one by one, not a foundry, or a mint, or a treadmill' (ibid., 33). Out of this experience would be forged a continuity of elite identity founded upon a common experience and shared values. Until the nineteenth-century Royal Commissions on Oxford and Cambridge, it was assumed that this experience would be not only fundamentally Christian but thoroughly Anglican. With the reforms that followed the commissions' reports, the Anglican stranglehold was broken and a broader, more liberal, and more secular education came into being.

None the less, although the educational experience had changed, its social purpose remained that of ensuring the maintenance of an elite identity. At the same time, the close-knit college community was seen to act as an effective vehicle for the 'conservation of the most highly prized beliefs and skills in the cultural heritage' and thus performed a vital cultural, as well as social function (Halsey, 1961). With the convenient, and efficient, integration of the social and cultural functions came the flowering of the liberal view of education as an activity concerned with much more than simply the transmission of knowledge. Within the liberal educational experience, high-status culture was absorbed as a natural part of college life and 'character' education was readily combined with the cultivation of social style and appropriate leadership qualities. But to be successful as a means for maintaining elite identity, liberal education also has to be exclusive: it has to foster a suspicion of non-elite forms of education and, in particular, of vocational education. So whereas it will applaud the importance of learning for learning's sake and 'the enthusiastic study of subjects for the love of them and without any ulterior motive' (Moberly, 1949, 37), it finds applied knowledge worthy of indifference at best.

9

In contrast to the preceding Christian-Hellenic tradition, the liberal ideal of education saw the pursuit of knowledge for its own sake as including the advancement of knowledge as well as its transmission. Interestingly, the ideological weight attached to the research function of universities has increased in proportion to the resources available. By the 1940s, an enthusiastic advocate of university values writing under the *nom de plume* of Bruce Truscot in *Redbrick University* expressed mainstream university opinion when he argued that the search after knowledge for the sake of its intrinsic value is paramount and all else subordinate to this objective. 'A university without research', he maintained, 'would be nothing but a super secondary school' (Truscot, 1943, 49).

The political durability of traditional university values was from the beginning enhanced by the claim that they possessed an absolute status which insulated them from the normal political round and from the indignity of having to reply to any ideological challenge. University autonomy, it was argued, is an essential precondition both for the disinterested search for knowledge and for the preservation of those values on which a civilised society depends. Furthermore, without this autonomy, universities would be unable to maintain the critical distance from society necessary for carrying out their onerous responsibility of 'focussing the community's intellectual conscience' (Moberly, 1949, 161). To question the right to this autonomy was therefore to question the basis of society's civilised existence: a nice conundrum which it was to take the state some time to resolve.

There was also the problem that the ideological power of the liberal university ideal was not unduly disturbed by post-war developments in higher education which, objectively speaking, seemed to question its relevance if not its validity. Essentially, it is an unashamedly elitist ideology yet, from the 1950s onwards, its ideas were employed to guide and justify progress towards a mass system of higher education. In 1956, for example, the UGC calculated that student demand would double from the then current figure of 85,000 places to 168,000 by 1968 – a massive expansion by the standards of the day (UGC, 1964, 70). Yet, as part of the response to this expansion, the Niblett Report on halls of residence in the following year is a pristine statement of traditional university values containing no recognition that these values might need in some way to adapt to a changing environment. The ideas of 'community', 'character training' and 'cultural transmission' were held as central to the educational experience. The fact that the raw university material was increasingly being drawn from a non-university background simply meant that the means for inculcating elite values had to be more assiduously applied. With an unconscious totalitarian flourish, the report maintained that such students would be required to accept that 'university standards should influence their whole personality, their range of interests and their social being' and that they should undergo 'a revolution of mind and attitude' (Niblett Report, 1957, 9).

More significantly, six years later in 1963, when the 1968 estimate of the student population had risen to 200,000, the Robbins Report on higher education was published and, in the words of the UGC, established 'publicly and authoritatively, the principles which should govern the scale and pattern of higher education in this country' (UGC, 1968, 49). Viewing Robbins from several decades distance, it is important not to underestimate the ideological significance attached to the Report at the time: so much so that Sir Robert Aitken, former chairman of the Committee of Vice-Chancellors and Principals (CVCP), could write, with no risk of caricature, that 'Robbins, like the Flood, is a watershed in history' (Aitken, 1969). Of the four aims of higher education laid down by Robbins, only one, 'instruction in skills', departs from the path of the liberal ideal. The others are the education of 'not mere specialists but rather cultivated men and women', the advancement of learning and 'the transmission of a common culture and common standards of citizenship' (Robbins Report, 1963, 6–7).

Despite the self-confidence of Robbins, it is significant that the report deems it necessary to mount an explicit defence of academic freedom. In the halcyon days when the liberal ideal reigned supreme and unquestioned, no such defence would have been required. The fact of elite homogeneity buttressed by ideological consensus would have rendered such protestations irrelevant and unseemly. However, once the universities are no longer an integral part of the elite, then the idea of university autonomy becomes an essential part of their ideological defence and the frequency of its use a measure of their insecurity. Thus when the Robbins Report stated that

> We are convinced also that such freedom is a necessary condition of the highest efficiency and the proper progress of academic institutions, and that encroachments upon their liberty, in the supposed interests of greater efficiency, would in fact diminish their efficiency and stultify their development (ibid. 228).

it signalled the beginning of elite fragmentation and the division between the universities and the state.

The power of an ideology can be measured in terms of its ability to ignore, or selectively interpret, reality and still be believed. By 1963, the move towards a mass higher education system was well under way and was justified by the commitment of the Robbins Report to the principle of 'social demand' which asserts that higher education should be available to all those qualified to receive it (ibid., 7-8). Yet at the same time, the Report insisted that the unlimited expansion to which this principle gives rise should be guided by a high-quality and expensive view of elite education. The fact that the reality and the ideology are fundamentally irreconcilable made no difference to the attempt to legitimate the former with the latter. The political need for policy legitimation was too great and the hegemony of the liberal ideal too strong. In the longer term, however, the relevance of the traditional values to a mass higher education system was bound to be questioned, but it would be a substantial challenge only if it was backed by an alternative ideology of higher education.

THE IDEOLOGICAL CHALLENGE

If the state was to bring higher education under its control, it had first to develop an ideology which not only justified the intervention required but also successfully challenged the dominance of the traditional liberal ideal. We have described the values used to perform these two tasks as 'the economic ideology of education' (Tapper and Salter, 1978, Ch.7). Its basic principle is that education is an economic resource which should be organised in a way that maximises its contribution to Britain's industrial development. From this premise it follows that socially relevant, or applied, knowledge is more important than pure knowledge, that higher education institutions should be responsive to economic needs, and that it is the responsibility of the state to ensure that these institutions are held accountable for carrying out their economic role correctly.

Although the economic ideology of education began to make inroads into the state bureaucracy immediately after the Second World War, it was not into that part of the state to which the universities related, namely the Treasury and the UGC, but into the Ministry of Education and the further education sector. The entry point is logical: the technical colleges in further education had traditionally been characterised by vocational training and links with local

12

industry, and in the economic stringencies of the post-war situation were the first to respond to the demands for the manpower to support Britain's international competitiveness. Numerous reports, beginning with the Percy Report of 1945 and the Barlow Report of 1946 had highlighted the need for Britain to produce more scientists and technologists, but by the 1950s the Ministry of Education was convinced that whereas the technical colleges understood and responded to this need the universities did not.

This view is clearly expressed in the Ministry's 1956 White Paper on Technical Education which begins with a warning of the dangers of Britain being outpaced in the production of qualified manpower by the USA, Western Europe and the Soviet Union and then spells out the implications for education: it must take on a 'national responsibility', be responsive to 'social need' and ensure that what it does is 'socially relevant'. There can be no shirking of education's economic duty:

> The management of full employment, with its much greater need for a responsible attitude to work and its challenge to greater output per man as the only way further to raise living standards, has brought a sense of dependence on education as the key to advance (Ministry of Education, 1956, 37).

Once it is assumed that education's primary goal is to serve the economy, all else is then subordinated to that goal. As an educational principle, the disinterested pursuit of knowledge is devalued. Knowledge no longer has an absolute status but its worth is contingent upon the yardstick of social relevance, so that applied knowledge is highly valued and pure knowledge regarded with suspicion. Education, or training, for occupations that will enhance economic performance is laudable and, conversely, education solely for the purpose of individual development is peripheral.

Although by the late 1950s the economic ideology of education had made inroads in some parts of the state bureaucracy, those dealing with the universities remained impervious to its charms and, apparently, securely in the grip of the traditional liberal ideal. The result was that two irreconcilable ideologies confronted one another across intra-state boundaries.

There was no logical reason why the ideological challenge should restrict itself to the manpower produced by technical colleges and, as its focus expanded, pressure grew for the Ministry of Education to concern itself with the production of highly qualified, degree-level

13

manpower as well. Since the universities were reluctant to bow to demands for a greatly expanded flow of scientists, engineers and technologists, and since the Ministry had no influence over them, the obvious solution was for it to create a new type of institution, cast in the appropriate mould. Hence the Colleges of Advanced Technology (CATs) were invented: a tangible tribute to the ideological divide within the state apparatus. Indeed, the Ministry's annual report in 1958 quite happily acknowledged the divide when it said of the CATs:

> The main justification for their existence, however, will lie not in their ability to copy the universities but in their success in marking out a distinctive place in the educational system. For this purpose, their principal instrument is their intimate link with industry ... the more strictly academic approach of most universities and the close association with industry that characterises the colleges of advanced technology can form a stimulating complement to each other to the national advantage (Ministry of Education, 1958, 57).

The report then makes it clear what it means by 'the national advantage' when it comments: 'one thing is certain: neither the colleges nor the universities (unless they were to be dominated numerically by their technological faculties) could alone produce the number of technologists which this country so urgently requires' (ibid., 38). Since the universities' traditional values rendered them inherently hostile to any suggestion that they should gear their activities to the production of economically relevant manpower, the Ministry considered the apartheid of 'separate but equal development' a necessary policy option.

As the ideology of education as the servant of the economy gained ground in the Ministry, it secured its position by establishing an identity of interest with the bureaucratic dynamic of the organisation. The theme which emerged was that if education is to serve the economy, then the state must ensure that it does so efficiently: education must be held accountable and managed for the economic good. Its emergence coincided with a growing political dynamic within the Labour Party, which drew together egalitarian and technological values and, in the period of Labour government between 1964 and 1970, reinforced the position of the economic ideology of education within the state apparatus. In practical policy terms, this overlap of values found expression in Labour's inauguration of degree-awarding polytechnics announced by Anthony Crosland, then

14

Secretary of State for Education, on 27 April 1965. His speech was a clear and unequivocal statement of the new educational ideology. It recognised that 'there is an ever-increasing need and demand for vocational, professional and industrially-based courses in higher education', that a 'public' sector of higher education, separate from the universities, was required to promote such courses, and 'that a substantial part of the higher education system should be under social control, and directly responsive to social needs' (*The Times Higher Education Supplement*, 1975, 15). The important political step had thus been taken to legitimise state intervention in higher education.

A major problem faced by the economic ideology of education was how to make convincing its claim that education should be linked to economic need. In the early 1960s, manpower forecasting was still in its infancy and the precise identification of the requirements of economic growth impossible, as they still are. Undaunted, the Department of Education and Science (DES), which succeeded the Ministry of Education in 1964, engaged in the general and largely undiscriminating encouragement of science and technology. To this end, the Committee on Manpower Resources for Science and Technology, chaired by Sir Willis Jackson, produced a series of reports in the late 1960s (for example the Dainton, Jones and Swann Reports) which championed the idea that one of the major weaknesses of the British education system was its failure to train and keep the quantities of scientists and technologists necessary for an expanding economy.

With the onset of the economic recession in the early 1970s, and a growing preoccupation with the efficient use of resources, it became clear that advocacy of the indiscriminate production of scientists and technologists was no longer a tenable strategy and that further refinement was required. Given limited resources, the DES argued, choices would have to be made according to known and rational procedures. Thus we see the Department's sponsorship of output budgeting and human capital planning emerging as an integral part of a more developed version of the new ideology and finding its first formal expression in 1970 in Educational Planning Paper No. 1 and Educational Planning Paper No. 2 (Department of Education and Science, 1970a and 1970b).

Whereas the legitimating power of the traditional liberal ideal relied heavily on ideas with an 'absolute' status – such as the preservation of civilised values – that of the new ideology rested on its claim to incorporate 'objectively necessary' goals – such as economic growth – which could be both identified and achieved using 'scientific' methods. In promoting economic growth, it was, after all, aiming at what was best for everyone. This 'inevitable' quality of the ideology was reinforced by its use of the 'impartial' sciences of economics and statistics in the construction of educational policy and, in this way, it legitimised itself by claiming to be value-free and, indeed, non-ideological.

The Department's sponsorship of the economic ideology of education provided it with an essential tool for the expansion of its bureaucratic power. In the same way that the traditional liberal ideal has been used by the universities as ideological protection, the application of economic values to education has been used by the Department as a form of ideological attack. If the socio-political power of the universities was to be harnessed and directed within an overall policy framework for higher education, state intervention had to be justified before it could be implemented. However, given the Department's inexperience in the business of generating educational values, it was inevitable that the DES would make slow progress. So it was not until the early 1970s that it began to address the specific changes required in the roles of institutions, staff and students if the universities were to be sensitive to the needs of the economy. When it did so it was immediately apparent that all the proposed changes were completely at variance with the traditional university values. The message was spelt out in the 1972 White Paper *Education: A Framework for Expansion* when it stated:

> ... at the same time they [the government] value its [higher education's] continued expansion as an investment in the nation's human talent in a time of rapid social change and technological development. If these economic, personal and social aims are to be realised, within the limits of available resources and competing priorities, both the purposes and the nature of higher education ... must be critically and realistically examined. The continuously changing relationship between higher education and the subsequent employment should be reflected both in the institutions and in individual choices. The Government hope that those who contemplate entering higher education, and those advising them, will the more carefully examine their motives and their requirements; and be sure that they form their judgement on a realistic assessment of its usefulness to their interests and career intentions (DES, 1972, 34).

According to the new economic values, students should base their decisions about their higher education on how it would contribute to their future employment and not, for example, on whether they would find it intrinsically interesting. This would enable them to become part of the 'efficient' distribution of human capital and so facilitate the linkage between economic demand and human supply. Equally, institutions should assist the process through the selection of appropriate students, by the manipulation of entrance requirements for particular courses and by internal restructuring. What they should not do is to resist the demands of the economy by seeking refuge in the traditional principle of university autonomy.

Unfortunately for the state this is exactly what happened, demonstrating that the convenient ideological marriage between the interests of the economic and bureaucratic dynamics was merely the first step, and that demolishing the power of the liberal ideal in higher education would require a long-term political strategy. For although by the early 1970s the economic ideology of education was firmly established in the Department, within higher education itself it had made few inroads; in fact, quite the reverse. Its vanguard and the embodiment of the new values, polytechnics and colleges of advanced technology, had allegedly all too readily been seduced and subverted by university values. In its 1976 report, the Select Committee on Science and Technology lamented:

> ... the transformation of the CATs into universities, and the present tendency of the polytechnics to seek 'parity' with the universities, reflect the distressing British habit of attempting to bestow status and prestige on institutions and individuals by changing their names rather than encouraging them to do well the things for which they are best suited (*The Times Higher Education Supplement*, 1976, 17).

The Committee correctly saw the incorporation of the CATs by the university system as an attempt 'to eliminate a potential threat to its traditional freedom and independence by turning that threat into an asset to be deployed in defence of the universities from direct state control'. Such was the power of the traditional university values that they succeeded, in the Committee's view, in rebuilding the CATs in 'the image of the institutions [the universities] which were regarded as having failed to provide the manpower which the nation required' (ibid.). So by the mid-1970s, after two decades of state sponsorship, the economic ideology of education had signally failed to make any inroads in the university sector and was having great difficulty maintaining its position in the polytechnic sector of higher education. The traditional values were as firmly ensconced in the universities as ever, and the prospects for state control in higher education seemed dim indeed.

CONCLUSIONS

Our theory of educational change is clear that in order to direct the socio-political power of higher education in the way which it considered fit and appropriate, the state had first to develop its own ideology and hence its own self-belief in its right to influence university affairs and then use this ideology to dominate the traditional liberal ideal in the public arena. By the mid-1970s the battle had been joined but the state was not yet in a position of being able to launch a sustained onslaught on the universities' view, with Robbins, that educational investment cannot be 'measured adequately by the same yardstick as investment in coal or electricity' (Robbins Report, 1963, 205). At that point it had not solved the riddle of how to out-manoeuvre an opponent with the kind of historic resources enjoyed by the universities.

It is also clear from our analysis that the pressures upon the state to control higher education's resources, and force it to respond to what we have called 'the economic dynamic', are overwhelming and inescapable. Modern economies require an ever-changing blend of new knowledge and educated manpower if they are to function effectively and no state can afford to leave its higher education system to its own devices. Such action would amount to an abdication of responsibility which no present-day government or its bureaucracy could tolerate either in terms of their internal organisational dynamic or in terms of the external demands upon them. This is not to say that the state will be able to translate the pressures upon itself into policies which produce the desired results. Indeed it may fail dismally because the policies are inadequate, or because it lacks the power to implement them, or because it is thwarted by the sheer institutional inertia of the higher education system. But it is inevitable that it will make the attempt.

In its bid to control change in higher education the state has had to operate within several constraints. Athough the economic ideology of education is what one might call its 'natural' ideology, in the sense that it legitimates the state's managerial role in the rational language of all bureaucracies, it has proved to be not alone as a set of values hostile to the universities. The rise of the New Right's view of education as a market place where educational products should be bought and sold and where supply and demand should be left to resolve distributive problems, directly challenged the universities' belief in their inherent right to state largesse. But it also challenged the right and the duty of state organisations to manage change in higher education in the light of the needs of the economy. A decade of Conservative government prepared to promote the market ideology has left the DES, now the DFE, with no alternative but to try and effect a compromise between the two value positions to produce a common front against the traditional university values. At present, the idea of 'the managed market' is the working solution (see pp. 202–12).

Moreover, the state does not have a single, homogeneous identity in terms of either organisation or values. The ability of the dominant bureaucracy, the DFE, to orchestrate the actions of its different parts will depend on its development of lines of financial and administrative control, its propagation of a unifying ideology of higher education, and the capacity of other parts of the state to establish and maintain a separate identity. The final outcome of this inter-institutional conflict is in no sense pre-ordained,and therein lies the fascination of the analysis. What can be identified are the trends in the conflict and the evolving positions of compromise and consensus.

2

The Political Parties

In our early work we have argued that the state's administrative apparatus was driven by a bureaucratic dynamic with its own broad policy preferences which it would pursue regardless of the party in office (Salter and Tapper, 1981). Then, in *Power and Policy in Education* we explored the nature of the party input to policy-making on private schooling, the important role of intellectuals and ideology in that process and the inevitable, but negotiable, tensions between party policies and the ambitions of the state bureaucracy.

In applying this perspective to the case of higher education, we analyse the shift towards the economic ideology of education which occurred in both of the political parties to have held office since 1945, the Labour and Conservative Parties, but resulted in different policies. To an extent these differences are the natural outcome of the parties' underlying values; but to an extent they are also the result of the persistence, organising ability and political acumen of particular groups of intellectuals who have tenaciously propagated their beliefs over a long period of time, often competing within the same party for influence over policy (see Salter and Tapper, 1985, Ch.5 and Ch.7). In both parties there has been the belated realisation that higher education is a difficult policy nut to crack; that its ideological and structural inertia renders it a quite distinct political animal from secondary education, where both parties have had their successes; and that policy alliances with the central bureaucratic state are a useful way forward.

THE LABOUR PARTY

The pre-war Labour Party was largely indifferent to the activities of the universities, seeing them as irrelevant to its major concerns (Berdahl, 1959, Ch.10). But with the experience of total scientific mobilisation during the Second World War its concerns changed and the post-war Labour Party became convinced not only of the vital importance of science but also of its perfect compatibilities with socialism:

> Science and socialism today are mutually dependent and inseparable ... it will be accepted by that growing body of scientists who realise that without a planned economy, science creates anarchy and endures frustration and becomes the instrument for destroying the civilisation it is seeking to enhance (Calder, 1949, 5).

In the drive to repair the ravages of war, the Party was emphatic that science must be harnessed to the economic needs of the nation and 'every refinement of modern technology must be applied in order to secure a positive trade balance and sustain the national standard of life' (Labour Party, 1949, 8).

Although the Labour Party was quite clear that science must serve the national economic interest and that the resources of science must be mobilised in the interests of greater productivity (ibid., 13), in the case of the universities it was much less clear as to how that goal was to be achieved and for many years exhibited an implicit deference to the principle of university autonomy. On the one hand, it accepted that the UGC should protect academic life from government interference and, on the other, argued that universities should help supply the qualified scientists required for industrial expansion; but it failed to deal with the critical policy problem of how the two objectives could be combined (ibid., 8). Its equivocal position was revealed again in its 1953 programme, *Challenge to Britain*, where it lamented the fact that universities 'are producing too few graduates educated in the human and technical problems of the modern world' and protested that 'it is high time that the teaching at our universities should take into account changes in our way of life and the community's needs' but had no positive reforms to recommend (Labour Party, 1953, 24). Instead, as an escape from its dilemma, it proposed that a Royal Commission be established to investigate the relation between the universities and the needs of society (ibid.).

Five years later the problem of how to reconcile the traditional ideal of a university and its commitment to institutional autonomy with a belief that universities be responsive to national need remained unanswered. In *Learning to Live* the Party stated that 'universities are for research, teaching and enlightenment' and that 'to do this work they must be free – not compelled by Governments or private interests to propagate particular doctrines, nor cajoled into giving their sole attention to immediate practical problems' (Labour Party, 1958, 63). But, the document emphasised, universities must also produce a higher proportion of scientists than in the past, expand their extra-mural work in adult education and keep in touch with the community. And once again, rather than confront the issue of how government could encourage the attainment of these goals without infringing the independence of universities, the document reiterated the proposal for the setting up of a Royal Commission into the universities.

Until the beginning of the 1960s the Labour Party had never directly questioned the traditional view of university education but had instead accepted the universities' right to determine their own future despite the paradoxical position in which this left party policy. But two developments served to heighten the paradox to the point where it became untenable: first, the party's policy towards the organisation of science became much more specific; and second, the principle of equality of educational opportunity was applied to higher education as well as to secondary education and comprehensivisation.

Science and the Future of Britain (Labour Party, 1961) foreshadows many of the ideas subsequently enunciated in the Trend and Zuckerman Reports regarding the research needs of particular sectors of industry and the way in which science should be organised in order to meet those needs and improve productivity (see pp. 163–5). The values of the economic ideology of education are boldly presented in terms echoing the Advisory Council on Applied Research and Development's (ACARD) *Exploitable Areas of Science* two decades later (see p. 177):

> To achieve the necessary foresight [for planning science] we need a body providing a continuous joint inquiry by economists and scientists, the economists contributing knowledge of the trends in the existing markets, the scientists and engineers an assessment of technological trends here and abroad (ibid., 4).

It is adamant that the 'present near-anarchy in the administration of science must end' and that government must take the lead (ibid., 39). The report proposed that a Minister of Science of Cabinet rank be created supported by a high-calibre secretariat and advised by a Scientific and Technical Planning Board which would replace the Advisory Council on Scientific Policy (ACSP). His task would be to review the programmes of scientific work of government agencies, stimulate work in neglected areas and expedite the application of science to industry.

In Labour's programme statement in the same year, *Signposts for the Sixties*, these ideas were accompanied by a pledge 'to broaden the present narrow apex of higher education at universities and technological institutes into a wide plateau' (Labour Party, 1961a, 29) and, as was to happen frequently when the Labour Party discussed the inadequacies of the universities, Oxford and Cambridge Universities were singled out for special mention:

> We believe the time has come to abolish fee-paying throughout the universities and to end the system of college entrance under which public schools still monopolise more than half the places at Oxford and Cambridge (ibid., 30).

The application of the principle of equality of opportunity to higher education at this time was almost certainly the result of the work of the Party's Study Group on Higher Education which subsequently reported in 1963. Fired by its egalitarian principles and by the burgeoning work of educational sociologists on inequality in educational opportunity and access, the Group took a much tougher line towards the universities and apparently ended the Party's equivocation over university autonomy. The 'evil of segregation', it maintained, must be ended in higher education as in secondary education and the invidious distinctions between Oxford and Cambridge, the other British universities, the Colleges of Advanced Technology and Teacher Training Colleges must be permanently removed (Labour Party, 1963, 9). The continuing 'academic and social snobberies' must be eliminated, the report continued, particularly with regard to the exaggerated prestige attached to Oxford and Cambridge universities:

> The false value attached to Oxford and Cambridge arises partly because it is still possible for parents to buy an increased chance of places for their children by sending them to public school. Only about one third of Oxford and Cambridge undergraduates come from maintained schools. This is good for nobody (ibid. 37).

As a short-term remedy, the Group proposed that universities should allocate their places in proportion to the number of A-level GCE passes in schools of each type and that Oxford and Cambridge be obliged to join the Universities' Central Council on Admissions (UCCA) (ibid., 37–8).

Its long-term solution involved a massive expansion of higher education and a considerable extension of state control. In justifying a much greater state involvement in university affairs the Group laid the principle of equality of educational opportunity side by side with the economic ideology of education. On the one hand it argued that 'higher education should no longer be a privilege but a right for all able young men and women, regardless of their families' class, incomes or position' (ibid., 7) and, on the other, that 'Britain's economic stagnation is a direct result of the neglect of higher education ... economic expansion is only possible if university and technological education expands rapidly and continuously to provide the necessary brain power and skills' (ibid., 8). To ensure that these goals were realised the Group was clear that efficient planning was necessary in order to make the best use of limited national resources. Under the new order, the privileged treatment of the universities as recipients of direct Treasury funding would no longer be appropriate:

> In a dynamic expanding society, this insulationist policy is good neither for society nor for the universities themselves. If they make large but legitimate demands, there is no Minister to plead their case with the Treasury. If they fail to meet public needs, there is no-one to prod them into action (ibid., 42–3).

Instead, an entirely new structure was required: the universities should be transferred to the Minister of Education and the UGC should be abolished and replaced by a National University Grants Commission with the task of developing a strategic plan for all of higher education. Beneath the Commission would be Regional University Grants Commissions with the financial control and executive responsibility for implementing the national plan.

Although these proposals were never implemented, the ideas and feelings which lay behind them indicate a growing lack of sympathy in the Labour Party for the traditional view of university education and a conviction that the universities should adapt themselves to the needs of modern society with some urgency. In a famous speech to the Party's Annual Conference at Scarborough in October 1963, Harold Wilson made it plain that the universities' contribution to socialism and the scientific revolution should be relevant and practical (Wilson, 1963).

But by 1965 the Party had decided that, rather than confront the universities directly, it would create two sectors of higher education: what it called 'the autonomous sector' (the universities) and 'the public sector' (the polytechnics). In his speech that year at Woolwich Polytechnic where he inaugurated the new binary policy, Anthony Crosland, then Secretary of State for Education, presented the polytechnics as the major vehicle for Labour's drive to link higher education with industrial and economic needs. The two sectors, he argued, must remain 'separate but equal in status'. But he had few kind words for the universities and concluded: 'Let us now move away from our snobbish caste-ridden hierarchical obsession with university status' (Crosland, 1965).

Exhortation is unfortunately no substitute for action and, in the years that followed the introduction of the binary policy, higher education did indeed remain obsessed with university status. By creating the polytechnics Labour had simply shelved the issue of what to do about the universities and allowed a segregated higher education system to continue. The policy also created confusion within the Labour Party once it became obvious that it was not going to advance the cause of egalitarianism very far. A second Study Group on Higher and Further Education was set up in 1967 but took 29 meetings and six years to produce a report. When it did finally publish the results of its deliberations it came down unequivocally in favour of a comprehensive system of post-school education of which the universities would form an integral part (Labour Party, 1973).

The work of the Study Group was dominated by a concern that higher and further education should be reformed to attack continuing social inequalities: the economic functions of education which so preoccupied its predecessor are not mentioned. The problem as the Study Group saw it was not only that the middle class had benefited disproportionately from the recent expansion of higher education but also that the institutions they attended gained more resources and were less accountable to the state. With nice phrasing the report commented that 'generally the status of the educational institution is inversely proportional to the extent of its subjection to local authority control and is directly proportional to the freedom of its senior academics to spend public money' (ibid. 20). At one end of the continuum were the universities, and at the other the much neglected further education colleges.

As a solution to the invidious distinctions in status and social class which pervaded the existing sectors of further, adult and higher education the report proposed the creation of a single sector: Adult Education. An Adult Education Commission should be established to take overall responsibility for education within all institutions catering wholly or in part for the over-18s. Following the line adopted by its predecessor, the Study Group also recommended the creation of a second tier of Regional Adult Education Commissions with executive powers and planning functions within the Adult Education Commission's overall policies. That the Study Group was expressing a view generally held within the Party is clear from the previous year's *Labour's Programme for Britain* which also advocated a comprehensive, post-18, adult education service 'to be provided by local authority colleges, universities and polytechnics, and voluntary bodies like the Workers' Education Association' (Labour Party, 1972, 58). If any reallocation of resources was required then the 1972 Programme was in no doubt that 'resources should be deliberately steered to those who at any stage are disadvantaged rather than automatically absorbed by expansion of the most expensive sectors of the education system' (ibid., 59) – a euphemism for the universities.

Although the 1972 Programme and the 1973 report once again apparently signalled the end of the Labour Party's tolerance of the universities as privileged institutions deserving of special treatment, in practice little was done to change the situation during Labour's 1974–79 term of office. As we have shown in the case of Labour Party policy on the private schools, there is a large gap between a study group's initial formulation of policy and its eventual implementation in legislative form when the Party is in government (Salter and Tapper, 1985, Ch.5). In fact, throughout the remainder of the 1970s there is a resounding legislative silence in this field and no evidence that Labour ministers had the will or the inclination to challenge the binary system. Occasional reiteration in Party documents of the need to end the 'current divisions and inequalities in control, funding and facilities within higher education' (Labour Party, 1976, 86) produced no practical policy result. Labour's 1974 Manifesto contains no mention of higher education, except for a ritual genuflection to the Open University, and its 1979 Manifesto talks vaguely of the need to increase opportunities for people from working-class background, particularly adults, to enter further and higher education (Labour Party, 1974 and 1979).

With the early 1980s came a resurgence of interest in post-school education policy. First, *16–19: Learning for Life* argued for a unified, comprehensive and continuing tertiary system of education for the 16 to 19 age-group (Labour Party, 1982) and then *Education After 18: Expansion with Change* applied this theme to the post-18 age-group and advanced a new principle to replace Robbins, which it regarded as too academically oriented, namely that, 'full-time and part-time post-school education should be available to those who wish to take up appropriate courses designed to meet their needs, regardless of age' (Labour Party, 1982a, 10). The reluctance of institutions to accept adults without traditional qualifications should be overcome, ex-perience of work should be recognised and valued, and new patterns of learning encouraged through increasing opportunities for part-time study, extending distance learning and developing modular course structures throughout all post-18 provision. The class bias and inequalities of the present system were attacked with the customary vigour and Oxford and Cambridge singled out for special mention:

> Oxford and Cambridge play a determining role in the formation of elites in Britain. Some critics have gone so far as describing them as 'a major cancer in the educational system'. In conjunc-tion with private schools, they perpetuate an unjust and divisive class system, their graduates obtain the most influential jobs in the civil service and numerous other professions; they constitute the widest freemasonry of all, with a disproportionate influence on the rest of higher education (ibid., 49).

Yet despite the rhetoric, *Education After 18* is strangely conservative in its proposals for the reform of the university system when compared with earlier reports and this probably reflects the emergence of a university lobby within the Labour Party. Although described as a 'secretive, unrepresentative and totally unaccountable' body requir-ing radical reform, the UGC was none the less to be retained as a separate funding agency and renamed the Universities Council.

The split between those intellectuals in the Party who wanted more resources devoted to a slightly revised version of the existing system of higher education, and those who wanted to introduce a comprehen-sive system of post-school education through the root and branch reform and unification of both higher and further education, was epitomised by the conflict between the Higher Education and Labour Party Campaign (HELP), founded in September 1985, and the Socialist Education Association (SEA). At the Party's Annual Con-ference in 1986, a resolution from the SEA calling for an end to the binary line was passed despite opposition from the leadership. Eric Robinson, then Director of Lancashire Polytechnic and vice-presi-dent of SEA, summed up the SEA's attitude to higher education when he called for the abolition of the binary line and said: 'I envisage a comprehensive post-eighteen education system in which part-time is the norm and we get rid of the idea of higher education as over-grown boarding schools' (*The Times Higher Education Supplement*, 1986a, 3). The feud resurfaced a few months later at the Fabian Society's winter conference when Robinson accused HELP of being elitist, lambasted the Party leadership for pursuing a highly conservative policy of 'minor tokenist change' and commented, with a flourish, 'It is as silly as asking people to join "Volvo owners for Labour"'. In his reply, A.H. Halsey, president of HELP, defended the Oxbridge approach to education but did concede that the UGC and National Advisory Body (NAB) should be merged and replaced by a Higher and Further Education Council (*The Times Higher Education Supplement*, 1987, 1).

This compromise position between the two groups had to an extent been presaged the previous year in the policy document *Education Throughout Life, A Statement on Continuing and Higher Education*, in which the Labour Party returned to the idea of a body responsible for planning across the whole of higher and continuing education (Labour Party, 1986). The difference was that in this formal policy statement it had been proposed that the university, polytechnic and adult and continuing education sectors, though planning jointly, should none the less retain their separate funding bodies; so the radicalism of the 1963 and 1973 Study Groups remained unfulfilled. It was not until 1989 that the policy review set up in the wake of the 1987 election defeat reported and recommended an end to the binary line and the creation of a 'Higher and Continuing Education Council' (*The Times Higher Education Supplement*, 1989, 2). Events in higher education itself had meanwhile moved rather faster than the Labour Party's policy-making machinery.

A casual observer of the dominant themes in Labour Party debates about higher education over the past forty years could be forgiven for concluding that, as part of the state's parliamentary arena, Labour Party policy and actions would unremittingly favour the values of the economic ideology of education and state intervention in, and coordination of, the higher education sector. These debates have been dominated by the belief that science should be harnessed to the needs of the economy; that education should be organised to provide comprehensive and equal educational opportunity for all social classes; and that, consequently, education should act as a vehicle for an attack on social inequalities. The early respect for the autonomy of the universities appeared by the 1960s to have been replaced by a conviction that more *dirigisme* by the state was required if equality of educational opportunity was to be achieved. Yet still more radical was the recommendation of the 1973 Study Group that, as part of the attack on social inequalities, higher education should be integrated into part of a unified system of adult education.

That the most significant achievement of the post-war Labour Party in office was the creation of the binary divide in higher education and, thereby, the consolidation of the universities' prestige and separateness, is a tribute to both the weak influence of its intellectuals and the divisions within their ranks. Elsewhere, we have charted the difficulties traditionally faced by Labour Party intellectuals in translating ideas into policy (Salter and Tapper, 1985, Ch. 5) but, in this case, their difficulties have been compounded by their internal conflicts. The older tradition of adult education as a vehicle for mass working-class mobility has, when applied to higher education, been opposed by a view that the distinctiveness of university education, an inherently elitist concept, should be preserved. The continuing tension between the two positions created an ideological impasse and little concerted pressure for genuine policy change.

THE CONSERVATIVE PARTY

For the Conservative Party the universities were effectively a non-issue until the late 1950s when the dawning realisation of the expansion required to meet the post-1945 bulge in the birth rate coupled with the need to respond to Labour's demands for 'modernisation' of the universities stirred the party into some action. The majority response was simply to assert that there was nothing wrong with the present structure. So, for example, a Conservative Research Department publication in 1959 protested that Labour demands for a Royal Commission were unjustified because

> The Universities have responded nobly to heavy demands. Why must they be subjected to a Royal Commission as recommended by the Socialists? What evidence is there that the Universities might be 'out of touch with the needs of the modern age' or in need of change? (Conservative Research Department, 1959, 20).

A forthright proponent of university autonomy during the 1959–63 Conservative government was Lord Hailsham who, as Lord President of the Privy Council and then as Minister for Science, had responsibility for the research councils. In his book *Science and Politics* Hailsham took the view that

> If Government sought to interfere with the scientist in the absolute freedom of his explorations, and the integrity and independence of his speculation, it would ultimately destroy his real source of vigour, or alternatively frustrate his purpose by undermining this confidence and his will to cooperate (Lord Hailsham, 1963).

Although Hailsham's view undoubtedly carried the day in the Conservative Party at this time, it did not go unchallenged. The Carr Report on science policy, published by the Conservative Political Centre in 1962, identified limited resources and the need for selectivity and coordination as the main issues faced by government policy on science. The report proposed the creation of a Minister for Science at Cabinet level supported by a Technical Policy Committee with cross-representation between the Office of the Minister and the University Grants Committee. Hailsham ignored it.

Once the rapid expansion of the universities began in the 1960s, and was legitimised by the Robbins Report, the Conservative Party simply followed suit and took the line that 'more is good'. It was not until the late 1960s that some Conservative intellectuals began to seriously question what was happening in education. Part of this concern was undoubtedly stimulated by student rebellion in the universities but for the most part the focus was on secondary education. A conscious attempt by New Right intellectuals to re-shape the nature of the dominant educational consensus began with the publication of a *Black Paper* in 1969 followed by four further editions between then and 1977. By 1971 80,000 copies of the first three *Black Papers* had been sold and their ideas were being propagated in the Conservative Party through publications such as those of Rhodes Boyson for the Conservative Political Centre (Boyson, 1973 and 1975).

The goal of the New Right in education was, and is, to create a social market where consumer choice can operate unfettered by state controls or professional resistance by teachers. Such a market, it is argued, will force up standards because the educational producers (schools, colleges) will have to compete for the business of the consumers (parents, students). Their first tangible effect on Conservative policy came with the inclusion of *A Charter of Parent's Rights* in the election manifesto of October 1974. The Charter had five components: the state and local authorities should take account of the wishes of parents; there should be a local appeal system for parents dissatisfied with their allotment of schools; parents should be represented on school boards; headteachers should be obliged to form a parent–teacher association, and schools would be encouraged to publish prospectuses about their record, existing character, specialities and objectives to allow parents to make a sensible choice. And in the 1979 manifesto parental choice was linked to standards: 'Extending parents' rights and responsibilities, including their right of choice will also help raise standards by giving them greater influence over education' (Conservative Party, 1979, 25). However, in neither manifesto were market principles applied to higher education.

Although the major part of the New Right's energy has, until fairly recently, been concentrated on the secondary education sector, some work was carried out in the 1960s and 1970s on how their principles could be applied to university education. Much of this work was sponsored, not surprisingly, by that well-known broker for free market values: the Institute of Economic Affairs (IEA). In two articles published by the Institute, Peacock and Wiseman (1964) and Prest (1966) examined in some detail how student loan schemes could be employed to finance university education and, in a third article, Ferns (1969) discussed the market principles which could be used to organise universities. Ferns's contribution is particularly interesting because it was commissioned by the IEA for a conference about the practicalities of setting up an independent university which, in turn, led to the creation of the University College of Buckingham.

Ferns's starting point is that the interposition of the University Grants Committee and the state between the universities and their customers has created a situation in which the universities can neither respond to the demand for their services nor tap directly into the resources required to meet it. Instead they are trapped within 'an elephantine system of centralised control' which 'is bound to engulf more and more university activity in the cobwebs of committee decisions primarily concerned with the system itself and only secondarily with the problems of education and research' (Ferns, 1969, 17). Because the universities are not directly accountable to the community through a market mechanism, he argues, there is no objective way of judging the quality of the education provided.

In a later paper commissioned by the IEA in 1975, Maynard, an economist, examines the feasibility of using student loans as the principal mechanism for funding universities. To the economic advantages conferred by a loans system – market responsiveness, lack of dependence upon the state, and the ability of the consumer (the student) to penalise inefficient producers (universities) by withdrawing his custom – Maynard adds the advantage of social equity:

> The main argument for the repayment by the student of part or all of the cost of higher education is distributional equity. It is regarded as contradictory to redistributive objectives that the potentially affluent student should receive subsidies from a society the majority of whose members have lower incomes than the beneficiaries of higher education (Maynard, 1975, 51).

Although this argument went largely unnoticed at the time, it was to surface with renewed vigour a decade later as the New Right switched its attention from secondary education, where the battle was largely won, to higher education, where for them it was just beginning.

The first signs that the universities were soon to feel the ideological heat came in a publication by the Conservative Political Centre in 1985. In the appropriately titled *No Turning Back* the main policy areas were reviewed in terms of what should be done next to carry the new Conservative radicalism forward. Under education the opinion is expressed that

> The same problem which afflicts our schooling, that of producer capture, is to be found in our tertiary education. Students have a nominal choice between universities and colleges, if they can secure acceptance. But the method of funding denies them any kind of input as consumers, and prevents their choices from having any serious impact on the system (Conservative Political Centre, 1985, 14).

The document is not reticent about what should be done. As with the schools, funds should be re-routed to ensure the operation of a consumer market in higher education in order to turn 'what are now the decisions of the bureaucrat into opportunities for choice by the consumer' (ibid., 17). Student loans are the preferred mechanism because they introduce economic and commercial calculations into the operation of student choice.

The competition between the New Right think-tanks for influence over Conservative Party policy-making is well illustrated by the rush of recent publications on how higher education can better be led into the market place. Forthright advice has come from the Adam Smith Institute, the Centre for Policy Studies and the Institute of Economic Affairs. In *University Challenge* Mason uses the concept of real student choice to link the demand for higher education, the supply of courses and the needs of the economy (Mason, 1986). If higher education is free and involves no cost to the student then demand is limited only by the available supply. If on the other hand, there is a cost to students when they choose to enter higher education – for example they receive a loan not a grant – then they will choose courses which will provide them with economic benefit when they graduate. (The assumption is that the higher-paid jobs will be those which the economy needs and is prepared to pay for.) As a result, the demand for higher education will be shaped by a student's cost-benefit assessment of taking a particular course. If, in addition, higher education institutions receive the majority of their income from student fees then they will be obliged to tailor their supply of courses to student demand and student purchasing power.

By waving its magic wand the market mechanism will, Mason maintains, remove the need both for those increasingly complex projections of student numbers used by bodies like the DES, UGC and CVCP and for the largely futile attempts to push student demand in one direction or another in order to satisfy the needs of the economy. Both will be rendered redundant by the operation of consumer choice. Then, of course, there is the moral case. 'It is clearly unfair', Mason argues, 'to subsidise one form of investment in a person's future when no other is so supported' (ibid., 39). It is even more unfair that those who leave school at 16 should subsidise through their taxes those who go on to higher education (ibid., 42). Similar arguments appear in the CPS's *Diamonds into Glass* (Kedourie, 1988) and the IEA Education Unit's *Higher Education: Freedom and Finance* (Letwin *et al*, 1988). Both emphasise the importance of shifting power away from the bureaucrats and into the hands of the consumers through the exercise of competition in the market-place. At the same time both recognise that this will not be easy. Officialdom has, through successive investigations, acquired 'an obsessive momentum' in 'its restless quest for new and better methods of controlling universities and their activities' and will not willingly loosen its grip (Kedourie, 1988, 20, 22). Secondly, as Sir Douglas Hague argues in *Beyond Universities*, universities are in a strong monopolistic position which is not easily challenged:

British universities represent a sheltered system, shielded from competitive pressure by two types of monopoly: natural monopolies of brain-power and of certain physical resources, like

33

THE STATE AND HIGHER EDUCATION

libraries or laboratories; and man-made monopolies, bestowed by government, first through restrictions on the power to confer degrees and, second, through the university cartel (Hague, 1991, 31).

Whether or not the New Right can influence the Conservative Party to implement policies which reduce the power of the central bureaucracy in higher education and remove the universities' monopolistic position, depends partly on the opposition it faces within the Party itself. Advocates of the social market in education have consistently been opposed by the paternalist wing of the Party, the One Nation Tories, who, although they agree with the goal of higher educational standards prefer state control as the means to achieve it – for example, through a national curriculum, which the social marketeers naturally abhor. In secondary education, the tension between the two positions is exemplified by the long struggle over the educational voucher, a policy idea quintessentially that of the market (Knight, 1990, Ch. 7). Clearly there is a natural affinity between the interests of the paternalist right and those of the central state bureaucracy, but in higher education the former have yet to reveal their hand.

The success of the New Right intellectuals in asserting and, to an extent, then implementing their values in secondary education have given them a confidence that a parallel victory can be achieved in higher education. After two decades of ideological conflict they have seen themselves move from the margins to the mainstream to the extent that Ferns's plea in 1969 that vice-chancellors should be 'inventing ways of selling their products to an ever-widening body of consumers' has changed its status from the muttering of an eccentric to a statement of, if not the obvious, then at least the acceptable. That the language of higher education is changing to include the concepts of the market is one indication of the New Right's impact at a general ideological level. But if this is to be reflected in changed institutional practice much depends on their ability to translate their general principles into practical and detailed policies and to convince ministers and their advisers that such policies are both acceptable and workable. In the case of student loans, for example, the assiduous work and lobbying of intellectuals such as Barr and Barnes has clearly had an impact, though the scheme eventually adopted departed some way from their original proposals (Barr and Barnes, 1988; Farrell and Tapper, 1992). As a result of the changed and increased importance of student fees, higher education institutions are having to become increasingly sensitive to their potential customers and to establishing a clear relationship between their internal costs and incentives and their external markets. However, whether this represents a genuine victory for the New Right or simply a more sophisticated version of the bureaucratic regulation of higher education through formula funding is a key issue and one we will return to in the final chapter.

CONCLUSIONS

The development of ideas to the point where they are formally adopted as party policy is a long and arduous business. Then when the party assumes office, there are further hurdles to be overcome before it can take legislative and administrative form. Both the Labour and Conservative Parties contain continuing ideological pressures for particular policies on higher education. In both parties, also, there are tensions between competing groups of intellectuals favouring competing policy options. But in neither party is there much evidence over the past decade of outright support for the traditional liberal ideal of the university. Despite their ideological differences, and adopting different routes, both parties have moved to embrace a version of the economic ideology of education.

Although inhibited for a while during the 1950s by the traditional view of university autonomy, the Labour Party's growing belief in science and technology as an essential ingredient of economic growth coupled with its analysis of universities in general, and Oxford and Cambridge in particular, as elitist and socially divisive institutions created an impetus for the reform of higher education. Then Crosland effectively diverted this impetus away from the universities with the creation of the polytechnics in 1965. Despite the recommendation of the 1973 Study Group that all institutions of higher education be unified under a single Adult Education Commission no threat to the binary divide and to the universities' privileged status emerged from the 1974–79 Labour government. When the policy debates on higher education resumed in the 1980s, a conflict was revealed between those intellectuals who wholeheartedly supported the unification of all aspects of higher and further education in pursuit of economic and social goals and a university-based group wishing to retain a separate university sector. With the creation of a single sector of higher education this debate can be regarded as an interesting, but redundant, ideological interlude as the Labour Party turns its attention to the issue of how the sector can be best managed.

In so doing the Labour Party is likely to find that it has much in common with the the patrician right of the Conservative Party. Both favour the more efficient management of higher education in pursuit of higher standards and national objectives, though of course their definitions of these objectives are different. Where the question mark arises is in the ability of the New Right to force its own version of the economic ideology of education on to the political agenda of higher education. In broad terms it can be said that whereas the Labour Party and patrician right prefer state management as the means for achieving economic and social goals, the New Right believes that the liberation of consumer power through the operation of the market is the appropriate mechanism to use. The long march of the New Right through secondary education policy is proof of its tenacity, its ability to translate ideology into policy and its familiarity with the bureaucratic institutions of the central state, and there is good reason to believe that higher education will continue to receive its interest and attention.

3

Parliament

Constitutionally, ultimate control of the formation and implementation of the state's policy towards higher education rests with Parliament. Those agencies of the state which allocate finance to higher education, that is the HEFCs, the research councils and government departments, do so within a legislative framework which is the product of party policy as expressed through the parliamentary arena. But Parliament's function extends beyond that of willing vehicle for the party policies discussed in Chapter 2. Its all-party select committees have shown themselves well able to take an independent line in monitoring the way in which the public's money is spent and to express a distinctive parliamentary view on many areas of policy, with at times embarrassing consequences for the government.

The powers and responsibilities of Parliament's select committees have not evolved in an orderly and logical fashion but have waxed and waned depending on the commitment of their members, the public response to the issues they have addressed and, most importantly, the attitude towards them of the governing party. Historically and constitutionally there has always been a tension between the legislature, of which select committees are the most independent part, and the executive. On the one hand, it is accepted custom and practice that Parliament should act as a check on the power of the executive and, on the other, no government is going to encourage challenges to its authority which limit its ability to control and manipulate Parliamentary procedure. In other words, it is not in its interest to extend or to rationalise the organisation of the select committee system and so it is not surprising that, as the Select Committee on Procedure observed in 1978, 'the system which we have inherited is unplanned and unstructured' (Select Committee on Procedure, 1978, ix). It is, none the less, as numerous ministers and civil servants have discovered, a system which can, on occasions, bite severely. But in general, the powers of the select committees are essentially ideological. Through the propagation of a particular view over time, they can help establish a climate of opinion in Parliament broadly in favour, or broadly against, a particular policy development.

In this chapter we trace the changing attitude of Parliament's committees towards higher education in the post-war period. The discussion focuses on the universities simply because, until relatively recently, the polytechnics were the responsibility of the local authorities and therefore seen as not part of the remit of the parliamentary select committees. Despite the different terms of reference of these committees, there has been a common shift towards a position which favours more accountability in, and more effective management of, the relationship between the state and higher education; though this has not necessarily promoted greater harmony between Parliament and other parts of the state. Over time, the values of the economic ideology of education have become more pronounced in select committee reports and those of the traditional liberal ideal of the university have suffered a terminal decline. In this chapter we show how this happened and consider the implications for higher education.

AUTONOMY OR ACCOUNTABILITY?

The most powerful select committee is also the oldest: the Public Accounts Committee (PAC). Established in 1861, the PAC's original brief was to check on the legality of expenditures already made, guided by the post-audit findings of the Comptroller and Auditor General and his Exchequer and Audit Office (later the National Audit Office). Technically, the PAC concerns itself solely with examinations into the economy, efficiency and effectiveness with which any department, authority or other body under its jurisdiction has used its resources in discharging its functions. It purports to avoid making criticisms of the policy objectives which lie behind the expenditure. In practice, as Griffith and Ryle observe, financial accountability procedures cannot be hermetically sealed in a box which has nothing to do with policy:

> Much depends, however, on its definition of policy and certainly much of the committee's criticism and that of the Comptroller and Auditor General raises questions whether the project was properly costed, whether alternative courses of action were considered, whether the project was effectively implemented, whether too much discretion was left to decision makers. Many of such questions could reasonably be called questions of policy (Griffith and Ryle, 1989, 443).

There can be no doubt that in its reports on higher education the Committee has now moved to a position very much concerned with what can be termed policies of accountability.

But to begin with, higher education was virtually invisible as an accountability issue. Before the Second World War, state spending on the universities was relatively small and there is no evidence that Parliament took any interest in this field at all. The arrangement whereby the universities received a minority of their finance from a non-statutory advisory body called the University Grants Committee set up by a Treasury minute in 1919 which, strictly speaking, was not accountable to anyone since it had no executive authority, went unchallenged. However, with the rapid rise in public expenditure on the universities in the post-war period, Parliament soon began to question their lack of accountability for the funds they received. In its 1946–47 report the PAC recommended that statutory authorisation should be obtained for all the continuing functions of government and pointed to three cases deserving particular attention: the National Savings Committee, the Department of Scientific and Industrial Research (DSIR), which funded university research, and the University Grants Committee (Committee of Public Accounts, 1947). Its argument was that without statutory authorisation there was no way of knowing what such bodies should be doing, how much money they should be getting and what criteria should be used to measure their performance in any accountability exercise.

Following further pressure from the PAC in the 1947–48 session the Treasury, the body responsible for allocating funds to the UGC and DSIR, agreed to give the DSIR a statutory basis but sought to protect the UGC from such a calamity. Sir Edward Bridges, Permanent Secretary to the Treasury, argued against the use of legislation in dealing with the universities in the following terms:

> The Government has always rejected the view that the state should control academic policy, and it believes firmly that it has found in the present arrangement the means of reconciling the maintenance of university autonomy with the need for the Government to ensure that the money provided by Parliament is well spent in the public interest (Committee of Public Accounts 1949, 33).

Having with some reluctance accepted the Treasury's argument that a statutory definition of the relationship between state and universities would ruin its unique quality, the PAC then switched its attack to a demand for fuller information on the universities' expenditure on the basic principle that Parliament is responsible for the spending of public money. The Committee maintained that 'While the last thing they wish to suggest is that University expenditure should be subject to detailed Treasury control ... that Parliament is entitled to expect assurances, based on some broad examination of the Universities' financial arrangements, that the grants are administered with due regard to economy' (Committee of Public Accounts, 1950, 28). At this point the Committee was demanding that it should have the right of access to the accounts of the universities themselves.

In effect it took the line that its responsibility to Parliament was more important than the concept of university autonomy, central to the traditional liberal ideal, which excluded the element of accountability. To have argued anything else would have been to deny the validity of its role in certain areas of public expenditure: a dangerous precedent. It was to be eighteen years before the Committee achieved the outcome it desired. For the majority of that time the Treasury was to act as the sponsor of traditional university values and, in that capacity, as the universities' first line of defence.

A staunch supporter of the PAC line on accountability was the Select Committee on Estimates, which in 1970 became the Select Committee on Expenditure. Founded in 1912, the Estimates Committee had the duty of examining the current annual Estimates and investigating the efficiency of projected expenditure in relation to policies. Its practice was to work through a network of sub-committees appointed for a specific purpose. In 1952 a sub-committee set up to examine the work of the UGC recommended that the fullest possible information should be supplied to Parliament 'especially whenever changes in the amount of recurrent grants were made, either as a result of the quinquennial review or at other times, showing the reasons for the change and the basis on which it was calculated' (Select Committee on Estimates, 1952, para 35). It further argued that the UGC should exercise a closer control over the spending of non-recurrent grants. In the following year the PAC reiterated these demands.

Although the Treasury strenuously resisted the idea that the Comptroller and Auditor General should be given the right to inspect either the UGC's or the universities' books, it did make a concession, which others might construe as a delaying tactic, by suggesting that the UGC appoint an ad hoc committee to report on the universities' methods of contracting, and of recording and controlling expenditure from

from non-recurrent grants. This the UGC duly did under the chairmanship of Sir George Gater but the PAC remained unimpressed. On receiving the Gater Report in 1956 it expressed its dissatisfaction observing that 'the report does nothing in itself to secure greater Parliamentary control over the expenditure of public money' (Committee of Public Accounts, 1956, para 14). Following further argument in 1957, the Treasury came up with a compromise which the Committee accepted: that the Comptroller and Auditor General should have access to the Treasury's files on the allocation of non-recurrent grants to the UGC.

At this stage, information on universities' expenditure of state money could be categorised as (a) recurrent or non-recurrent and (b) held by the Treasury, UGC or universities – that is, the information could fall into any one of six categories. After ten years of pressure Parliament had gained access to one category: non-recurrent and Treasury-held information. Furthermore, access to information is, of itself, a weak form of accountability unless it is supported by the ability to enforce recommendations for change in the way in which public funds are being used. In the case of the relationship between state and universities, such formal executive power did not exist until the formation of the Universities Funding Council (UFC) following the passage of the 1988 Education Reform Act.

That so little had been achieved despite the efforts of the senior parliamentary committee is a tribute to the political skills of Treasury officials and their commitment to the traditional value of university autonomy. Throughout the 1950s, the operation of the UGC's buffer role between universities and state in fact owed much to Treasury influence. With the transfer of ministerial responsibility for the UGC from Treasury to the Department of Education and Science in 1964 this first line of defence was removed and the UGC had to fight on alone. In addition, the rapid and state-funded expansion of the universities in the 1960s increased their political visibility considerably and made their exceptional treatment as a non-accountable area of public expenditure much more difficult to justify and sustain.

In 1965 the Select Committee on Estimates returned to the attack with an investigation into the Universities' Vote where it 'tried to discover not only ways of getting value for money, but ways in which the machinery of government could be altered to provide greater efficiency and greater incentives towards economy in the universities themselves' (Select Committee on Estimates, 1965, xxxix). This was the first example of Parliament recognising that it should consider the structure of the state–universities relationship as well as the financial arrangements employed within that structure. However, in the event the Committee avoided any radical suggestions and instead recommended substantial increases in UGC staff.

The PAC, meanwhile, continued with its long-standing campaign for access to information about universities' financial affairs and highlighted the unique position of the universities:

> When a grant in aid represents the major source of income of an organisation, the normal rule is that the organisation is required to render its accounts to the Comptroller and Auditor General for audit, or to grant him access to its books and records, so that he can report to Parliament on matters of financial administration and control. Parliament is informed of the position in which case by means of notes to the Estimates. *Expenditure by the universities is at present the sole major exception to this rule* (Committee of Public Accounts, 1967, v–vi, our stress).

Despite its recommendation that this exception should be removed, the Committee's respect for university values and its anxiety to reassure the universities that it was interested purely in the soundness of financial administration of the UGC and the universities, permeates its report. Likewise, in announcing the decision in the House of Commons that the Comptroller and Auditor General be given access to the books and records of the universities, the Secretary of State for Education and Science emphasised that the CAG's duty would be 'to comment and advise on the propriety, regularity and efficiency of the university grants and not on policy decisions reached on academic grounds' (Hansard (Commons), 1967, col. 749).

By 1972 CAG staff had visited all the universities, made recommendations to the UGC on a number of issues and reported back to the PAC. After considering the report the Committee pronounced itself satisfied and that the initial programme of visits had not caused any serious difficulties. It concluded:

> We trust that the arrangements will continue to work well. We welcome the interest shown by the UGC in the maintenance of a high standard of financial management at universities and trust that the UGC will encourage universities to seek ways of effecting improvements in their financial management procedures (Committee of Public Accounts, 1973, para 4).

This conclusion was to remain the basic opinion of the PAC throughout the 1970s despite, or because of, its investigation of detailed issues such as the adaptation and under-use of buildings at specified universities, unspent balances, and the choice of Coleraine as the location for the New University of Ulster. Having obtained its original 1940s' goal of access to financial information after two decades of pressure, the Committee for some time continued to regard sound financial procedures as its main criterion of university accountability and did not concern itself either with the structure of that accountability system – that is, the relationship between universities, UGC, DES, and Parliament – or with policy outcomes. Other committees, however, were less reticent.

FROM ACCOUNTABILITY TO INTERVENTION

Although the terms of reference of the PAC and the Estimates Committee technically precluded them from dealing with matters of policy, other committees were not so constricted and were able to examine the relationship between universities and state as they saw fit. In 1969 the Select Committee on Education and Science published a series of reports on student relations redolent with the themes of the economic ideology of education and highly critical of the role of the UGC which it regarded as far too passive. In particular, it criticised the UGC for having no view on the preferred type of accommodation at universities (collegiate or otherwise), students living at home, information provision by the UGC to universities, and staff–student ratios and for having no way of measuring or monitoring teaching standards. Nor did it believe the UGC should be non-interventionist but argued that more coordination was needed in the relationship between national manpower requirements and university policy and in controlling too great a proliferation of courses (Select Committee on Education and Science, 1969, 56–9).

Its scepticism about the right and the ability of the universities to define and regulate their own affairs is manifest and led it to conclude that a new way forward had to be found:

> In the university sector we have noted the failure of any national body to emerge as an effective organisation capable of generalising the best experience, providing a focal point for dicussion and guidance, and fostering the intelligent and informed anticipation of problems and issues which transcend the local interests of individual universities (ibid., 137).

As a solution the Committee recommended the setting up of a

Higher Education Commission with responsibility for all institutions of higher education which, it argued with some prescience, should all be financed in the same way.

Once Parliament no longer saw the state–university relationship as set in stone but as a policy field to be explored and judged like any other, the power of the liberal ideal of the university, which rests so heavily on the university's claim to unique status and exceptional treatment, immediately began to wane within the walls of parliamentary committees. Once the outer ideological defences had been breached committees looked with wonder, and some disbelief, at what they found. In its 1973 report on postgraduate education, an exasperated Expenditure Committee commented:

> These figures [on costs of postgraduates] are useless for public expenditure and control. We also find it difficult to comprehend how policy decisions can be taken without the basic data from which comparison can be drawn and trends observed. We think it essential that a suitable accounting system for postgraduate education should be introduced in both the university and further education sectors (Select Committee on Expenditure, 1973, xv).

The isolation of the university sector from the normal procedures of public accountability meant that it had never had to construct or justify its internal arrangements on a basis logically comprehensible to a parliamentary committee. As an examplar of the culture this produced, the Expenditure Committee chose, to quote this encounter in its report:

> When we asked Sir Brian Flowers, Chairman of the Science Research Council, about it [an aspect of postgraduate funding] he said: 'My answer to your question why we do it when perhaps it is a little illogical that we should – I quite agree – is that, if we had not, nobody would have done so' (Q1110). DES defended the policy (Q1571 to 1574) but admitted that, like Topsy, it had just grown: 'It is there because it works and it works not badly' (Q1572) (ibid., xxviii).

An unimpressed Committee commented acidly, 'We are not convinced that this accident of history should be perpetuated' (ibid.).

Nor was it convinced that the existing policy of simply responding to student demand was the appropriate method for determining the number and type of postgraduate places. Instead, it advocated the values of the economic ideology of education and maintained that postgraduate education shoud be shaped by the needs of the economy and of society as a whole, that the selection process for pre-work experience postgraduate students should ensure that only those who have settled on a career should be accepted and that post-experience training should be available at any stage in a career (ibid., xvii).

A concern for rationalisation, coordination and management is also clearly present in the parliamentary attitude towards science policy in general and university science in particular. In a series of reports at the time of the Rothschild Report in 1972 the Select Committee on Science and Technology made it plain it believed that central planning of the national research effort was essential. To this end it proposed a Minister for Research and Development, of Cabinet rank, who would be advised by a Council for Science and Technology which identified national research priorities and coordinated the R and D work of departments and research councils. University science would automatically be integrated within this general planning machinery (Select Committee on Science and Technology, 1973).

Further reports dealing specifically with university research followed in the 1974–75 and 1975–76 sessions of Parliament. Nowhere was any sympathy expressed with the traditional university view that science should be self-regulating, driven by the concerns of individual scientists and protected by institutional autonomy. On the contrary, the Select Committee on Science and Technology was quite clear that underlying its concern with university science were the beliefs that scientific endeavour 'should contribute to the social and economic wellbeing of the community' that scientific funding institutions should bear in mind the 'social and economic benefit of the community' and that politicians had a responsibility to ensure that 'a continuing and fruitful dialogue is maintained between the social and economic decision making machinery and the scientific decision making machinery' (Select Committee on Science and Technology, 1976, 10). In the difficult economic circumstances of the mid-1970s, such beliefs went hand in hand with the Committee's view that Britain's disappointing industrial performance arose partly

> from the extent to which pure science had been dignified as a profession – or an art – requiring no external justification and with no external aim [resulting in a] failure to integrate the process of scientific discovery into the process of industrial production (ibid., 15).

In the Committee's view, dealing with the problem of limited research resources meant establishing national priorities and, at this point, it was happy that the universities and research councils should put their own house in order provided, and this caveat was always present, 'that maximum possible support and encouragement is given to those areas of research which they consider to be of the greatest promise and to be in the national need' (Select Committee on Science and Technology, 1975, 26). Applied science was singled out for special mention and, in a forceful set of recommendations showing little regard for, or knowledge of, the state's limited powers in this field, the Committee urged that the UGC be instructed to regard engineering and applied science training as a privileged area for which additional earmarked funds and higher maintenance grants should be provided (ibid., 7).

There can be no doubt that, by the end of the 1970s, parliamentary opinion on higher education as represented by the Select Committee on Education and Science and the Select Committee on Science and Technology was firmly dominated by the values of the economic ideology of education. The Committee of Public Accounts, however, was more restrained and limited its criticisms to issues of financial administration and probity. Two events conspired which led the powerful PAC to adopt a much more proactive, and so far as the universities were concerned, less benign, stance towards the structure of the state–universities relationship: reform of the select committees and cutbacks in university funding.

In 1978 the Select Committee on Procedure reported that 'the essence of the problem ... is that the balance of advantage between Parliament and Government in the day to day working of the Constitution is now weighted in favour of the Government to a degree which arouses widespread anxiety and is inimical to the proper working of our parliamentary democracy' (Select Committee on Procedure, 1978, viii). Reorganisation and rationalisation of the existing structure was required, it maintained, to achieve 'the aim of enabling the House as a whole to exercise more effective control and stewardship over Ministers and the expanding bureaucracy of the modern state for which they are answerable, and to make the decisions of Parliament and Government more responsible to the wishes of the electorate' (ibid.). In particular, it stressed, priority should be given to strengthening the select committees, their powers to send for persons, papers and records, and the impact of their reports (ibid., xciv). The implementation of the Committee's recommendations gave the select committees a fresh assertiveness which, in the case of

46

the PAC, was given practical enhancement by the 1983 National Audit Act. This replaced the PAC's Exchequer and Audit Office with the National Audit Office (NAO) which, unlike its predecessor, was given statutory authority to carry out value for money studies, which previously had had to be conducted with the consent of the spending departments, and was strategically placed outside the Whitehall community as a means of increasing its independence.

At the same time as the PAC was relishing its new powers, between 1981 and 1984 the universities were experiencing a sea-change in their financial relationship with the state: for the first time in their history their UGC recurrent grants were being cut. Likewise for the first time in the UGC's history it had to manage a contracting, rather than an expanding, budget and had to make choices about the allocation of scarce resources rather than simply respond to university-defined demands for more funds. Part of the UGC's response was to encourage universities to shed staff using a state-sponsored redundancy scheme and it was this scheme which attracted the PAC's attention in 1986. Its report represents a very definite shift by the Committee from a position characterised by neutral accountancy procedures to one where issues of management and intervention are dominant.

Its conclusions were highly critical of the absence of positive direction from the UGC in its operation of the redundancy scheme and the laissez-faire manner in which university staff cuts were made. The Committee found it difficult to accept that the UGC should not have intervened when its early appraisals indicated the odd effects which redundancy cuts were having on the subject balance at some universities. As a case study, the redundancy scheme demonstrated to an astonished PAC that no one had effective responsibility for the system-wide effects of public expenditure cuts. Committee members found that some elementary questions had to be asked. Addressing Sir Peter Swinnerton-Dyer, chairman of the UGC, Mr Park asked:

> But since you allocated the money, does the UGC ever have any curiosity as to how the money is spent? Do you not think it might not be a bad idea to have a set-up whereby at given intervals there was an accounting to you as the person who allocated the money, for future guidance, as to how they spent the last lot? (Committee of Public Accounts, 1986, 30)

The PAC was not at all impressed by the UGC's reluctance to intervene and expressed itself unconvinced by the argument that the selective use of the power to withhold grant or the power to extend the period of contraction of an institution would have jeopardised the whole exercise (ibid., x). While it accepted that tenure had severely restricted both the UGC's and the universities' room for manoeuvre, it did not see this particular form of employment contract as an inalienable right of academic staff and called for its removal in the forthcoming legislation (ibid.). Nor did it regard the DES as having performed properly: 'when the system is under severe strain, as it was between 1981 and 1984, we regard it as unsatisfactory that the role of the department ultimately accountable for university funding should be confined to giving general guidance, particularly when the UGC in turn considers its executive powers to be limited' (ibid., xi). In the light of its findings, the PAC felt obliged to depart from its traditional 'hands off' approach to the universities and recommended that the respective roles and responsibilities of the DES and UGC should be reviewed to ensure that these were appropriate to 'effective control and management of university funding' (ibid.). It therefore welcomed the setting up of the Croham Committee by the DES which was to result in the replacement of the UGC by a statutory UFC.

For forty years the Committee of Public Accounts had concerned itself with the procedural details of the financial relationship between state and universities and had avoided the question of what should be done if the outcomes of that relationship were, in its view, unsatisfactory. It had, in effect, employed a weak form of accountability which excluded consideration of the mechanisms required to correct any faults identified. It was a formulation happily compatible with the principle of institutional autonomy which lies at the heart of the liberal university ideal. But with the 1986 report on redundancy compensation payments for university staff the Committee's position changed significantly as it discovered both unsatisfactory policy outcomes and the inadequacy of the state's powers to correct them. It moved to adopt a strong view of accountability which was soon further exercised by the problems of University College, Cardiff.

In 1985 an independent accountant predicted that, on current performance, University College would have an £8–11.5 million deficit by 1990 (Committee of Public Accounts, 1990, vi). In the subsequent attempts by the UGC and DES to rectify the situation it became abundantly clear that the state's powers of intervention in university affairs were too limited to provide a swift solution. In unravelling the reasons why, the PAC became more convinced than ever that the state–university relationship was creaking at the seams and reform was a pressing imperative. The Committee's examination of Sir David Hancock, Permanent Secretary of the DES, and Sir Peter Swinnerton Dyer, chairman of the UGC, revealed that the line of formal accountability between universities and Parliament was fragmented by the divided responsibilities of the DES and UGC. The accounting officer to Parliament for the payment of grants to the universities was the Permanent Secretary of the DES who was not allowed to interest himself in the affairs of individual universities. This was the responsibility of the UGC. The UGC, however, lacked the internal auditors necessary to carry out such an accounting task and relied instead on inspection of universities' annual published accounts (Committee of Public Accounts, 1988, 22). Sir David Hancock pointed out that under forthcoming legislation this problem would be resolved by the accounting officer of the proposed Universities Funding Council (UFC) becoming directly accountable to Parliament with the support of a team of internal auditors.

Despite eloquent evasive action by Sir David and Sir Peter, the Committee took the view that the UGC should have taken 'earlier and more positive action' to appraise and tackle the financial difficulties at Cardiff: 'We consider that they took too passive a role in concluding that they were unable to challenge the College's view that no staff reductions were necessary and that there would be no consequent financial problems' (Committee of Public Accounts, 1990, v). The UGC had also made an 'error of judgement' in not reporting the problems to Parliament in its annual report (ibid., vi). For the future, the PAC looked to the UFC to ensure a high level of accountability to Parliament for the financial control exercised over university expenditure and the economic, efficient and effective use of resources (ibid., vii). And as for the traditional values of the universities, the Committee was in no doubt that these now had a purely contingent status:

> We do not accept that their [the universities'] independence and autonomy, although undoubtedly valuable in many respects, is a valid argument against attempts to defend against shortcomings in realistic and effective management and control of the public funds on which universities are dependent (Committee of Public Accounts, 1990a, ix).

So far as the PAC was concerned, the Cardiff debacle had conclusively demonstrated that the universities' use of public funds had to be monitored, regulated and, where necessary, corrected.

In developing a much more stringent attitude towards university accountability to Parliament the PAC aligned itself with the position established in the 1970s by the Expenditure Committee and the Select Committee on Science and Technology. With the 1979 reforms, the higher education work of these committees was incorporated within the brief of the Education, Science and Arts Committee, one of the fourteen departmental committees set up to shadow the Whitehall bureaucracies. In addition, the House of Lords established the Science and Technology Committee in 1980 as one of only two permanent committees. The work undertaken by these new select committees in the 1980s has consolidated the parliamentary view of the universities already put forward by their predecessors. Thus the Education, Science and Arts Committee emphasised the desirability of the universities' responsiveness to economic and social demand, the need for the more efficient organisation of their teaching and research resources and their recognition that state intervention is, on occasions, justified while calling for a single funding and planning body for all higher education and a more selective allocation of the available resources (for example Education, Science and Arts Committee, 1980, 1982, 1985). Meanwhile the House of Lords Select Committee on Science and Technology called for the establishment of a Council for Science and Technology, a Minister for Science in the Cabinet, the consideration of a single research council for the universities, and its incorporation into a national priority setting system for science based on the identification of economically exploitable fields of research (Select Committee on Science and Technology, 1981, 1987, 1988, 1989).

CONCLUSIONS

If select committees had consistently taken the view that the principle of accountability to Parliament for public monies spent should be subordinated to the principle of university autonomy, the universities would have had at least some ideological protection within the parliamentary section of the state. Although, in the longer term, this would not have prevented the development of interventionist policies by the political parties and central bureaucracy, it would almost certainly have inhibited the pace of their implementation. Instead, there has been a steady, if different, progress of all the select committees dealing with higher education towards the espousal of the economic ideology of education with its associated themes of accountability and state management.

In the two decades following the Second World War, most of the arguments from the parliamentary side were put by the Committee of Public Accounts, ably supported by the Estimates Committee. Despite the relatively weak form of accountability embodied in its repeated requests for basic information on the UGC's and universities' administration of public money, the Committee ran into consistently strong opposition from another part of the state, the Treasury. The Treasury employed the values of the traditional liberal ideal to justify the treatment of university finance as a unique area of public expenditure so far as accountability was concerned. It was only when the responsibility for the universities passed from the Treasury to the DES in 1964 that the PAC's demands were eventually met and the Comptroller and Auditor General allowed access to UGC and university accounts in 1968. Once it had satisfied itself about the probity of the universities' financial administration, the Committee eased its pressure for greater accountability to Parliament until the events of the early 1980s caused it to reassess its position.

Other select committees were less readily appeased, mainly because their belief that higher education should serve the needs of the economy led them to examine both the structure and the goals of the state–university relationship. During the 1970s, the Select Committee on Education and Science and the Select Committee on Science and Technology advocated policies categorically opposed to the orthodox university values of autonomy, individual priority setting by individual institutions and the marginality of national economic need to university organisation and activities. Their reports consistently justify greater and more detailed intervention by the central state in university affairs as the means for achieving their desired ends.

With the reductions in the UGC budget in the early 1980s and the PAC's revived interest in the ability of universities adequately to manage their affairs in straitened circumstances, the relationship between Parliament and the universities came under detailed scrutiny. As the accountability flaws therein became steadily more apparent and as it became clear that universities were not always paragons of financial economy, the PAC's patience ran out and it joined the other parliamentary committees calling for significant changes to be made in the management of public expenditure in higher education. Whatever residual ideological credit had remained for the universities was now at an end. So far as state intervention in higher education is concerned, the issue for the future is not how far the select committees of Parliament will act as a check upon the executive, but how far the executive can meet their ambitions.

4

The Privy Council, Statutory Commissioners and the Visitor

In this chapter we focus upon the traditional channels of external intervention into university affairs; the Privy Council, statutory commissioners and the office of visitor. The intervention of these parties is essentially judicial in character. Moreover, their concerns have been very precise: either to grant would-be universities a charter or to interpret the meaning of their statutes. The emphasis is upon the formal rules within which the universities function. By its very nature, unless one can conceive of institutions changing their formal rules frequently, such intervention has to be spasmodic. Contemporarily the links between higher education and the state have been placed upon a legislative basis. In other words there is a firmer statutory framework to the nexus that binds the state to higher education. Although most of the details of these developments will be dealt with in later chapters, the traditional forms of external intervention in university affairs have also been affected by the legislation and, therefore, will be the subject of analysis in this chapter.

Most of the attention in this chapter will be directed at the old universities rather than at higher education as a whole. The reasons are obvious. The institutions in the public sector of higher education, while often the product of local and church interests, were not founded as independent corporations with a tradition of autonomy from the state. Unlike the universities, they lacked those trappings which historically directed and constrained the course of external intervention. As we will document, in this chapter as well as in those that follow, the relationship between the state and the public sector of higher education has changed dramatically over time. However, as the polytechnics and colleges lacked charters which assumed that they were autonomous institutions, the empirical focus of this chapter is irrelevant as far as public sector higher education is concerned. None the less, the formal amalgamation of the two streams of higher education, including the formation of a common funding council and the creation of procedures that enable polytechnics to acquire a university label, raises some interesting theoretical issues. Central to these is who is to control the idea of a university. As we will argue, the mystique surrounding the traditional forms of external intervention in university affairs has been stripped away. On the one hand, there has been legislation to place relationships that evolved conventionally on a statutory basis, on the other hand the perceived niceties that surrounded the traditional forms of intervention have been discarded to reveal what was always there – the reality of state power. While there may be political pressure to make higher education more responsive to society, and in particular the supposed needs of the economy, equally it is political pressure that has led successive governments to the conclusion that the definition of higher education needs to be determined by the state rather than by institutions which have respected – even been responsible for creating – the tradition of university autonomy.

CONTROLLING THE STATUTES:
INTERPRETING THE TRADITIONAL CONVENTIONS

In his seminal *British Universities and the State* Robert Berdahl wrote: '... universities, like other corporate entities in the body politic, must operate in a legal and constitutional frame of reference without which their ordered existence would be impossible' (Berdahl, 109). For the most part, that frame of reference consists of a Royal Charter and a set of statutes which Moodie and Eustace described as 'the instruments of their incorporation' (Moodie and Eustace, 1974, 45). Whether, in order for an institution to label itself a university, it needs to secure this or similar validation is a moot point. Ferns (1969) has argued that there is no legal requirement to fulfil this obligation, but it is required by 'the nature and structure of British society'. We can say that, until recently, without such backing any claim to university status would have been widely viewed as pretentious, even misleading. In the sense that charters have to be approved by the Privy Council, it is that body which controls the formal understanding of what constitutes a university. Although the Privy Council may be a very atypical organisation, in the manner typical of most organisations the business is delegated to a committee – the ultimate guardian, this side of parliamentary intervention, of the idea of the university.

The key consideration, therefore, is what factors have been most influential in determining the Privy Council's decisions. In view of the secrecy that shrouds the deliberations of the affairs of the Privy Council, it is impossible to answer that question with complete certainty. However, it does appear that throughout its seventy-year history (1919–89) the advice of the University Grants Committee carried most weight. Certainly this is the conclusion that Shinn reached in her study of the development of the UGC between 1919 and 1946. On the basis of three detailed case studies – Nottingham, Reading and Southampton – Shinn argued that the advice of the UGC was crucial both to ensuring that these three institutions remained on its grant list as university colleges, and subsequently to obtaining their own charters. Apparently the expanding role of the UGC was as much a consequence of the actions of the Treasury and the Privy Council as its own endeavours:

> In July 1920 the Chancellor of the Exchequer had explicitly asked the UGC to 'promote a continued advance in the standard of university teaching' and to nominate which activities under-taken by institutions were 'of university character'. For its part the Privy Council referred to the Committee every case of application for a charter or amendment to charter and statutes and the Board of Trade adopted a similar policy with regard to requests for incorporation (Shinn, 1986, 107–8).

It is evident that there was detailed consultation between the UGC and would-be universities *before* the submission of charters to the Privy Council and in the case of Exeter such consultation was con-sidered to be 'vital' (ibid., 111). Considering the apparent depen-dence of the Privy Council upon the advice of the UGC, it was obvious that early liaison made good political sense.

Given consistent criteria against which charter applications would be measured before they could receive the UGC's support, it can be argued that over time the initial judgements (gentlemen's agree-ments) were inevitably translated into a code of good practice. Shinn has written of a process of crystallisation which defined universities as centres of academic excellence, sustained by sound finances, with at least a reasonably sized body of students and faculty, with strong local community support, and committed to freedom of thought (ibid., 96–7). In 1963 the Privy Council issued its own Model Charter, which in effect formalised the codification process and offered an official view of the main characteristics of a university. Although charters could not be expected to pronounce on every aspect of the officially – that is the UGC's – sanctioned idea of a university, they could reflect the same broad pattern of values. For the purposes of this book the most significant fact has been the UGC's support for the wider representation of academic faculty in the decision-making institutions of the universities, and the willingness of the Privy Council to incorporate this input in its Model Charter. In the words of Moodie and Eustace:

> If account is also taken of the extent to which all charters, and particularly the Privy Council model, embody accepted (if often formal) practice rather than serve as 'ice-breakers', then it is indisputable that the century has witnessed a substantial move towards internal academic self-government in all major areas of decision-making (Moodie and Eustace, 1974, 36).

Wisely, Moodie and Eustace did not see this as an infinitely sustainable development for even the pronouncements of the Privy Council are amenable to the changing political context.

Once the Privy Council has approved a university's charter and statutes, then the question of subsequent statutory change arises. Historically the initiative for piecemeal change originated within the universities themselves. Thus the Privy Council has been in a position to intervene only intermittently in the process of updating university statutes, and then in matters that are not of its own choosing. Furthermore, only the most important statutes, known as Queen-in-Council statutes, need the sanction of the Privy Council to be changed. For example, it was one of the recommendations of the last royal commission on the Universities of Oxford and Cambridge (the Asquith Commission which reported in 1922) that many of the two universities' minor statutes should be transferred to the Ordinances (Cambridge) or Decrees and Regulations (Oxford) and made responsible to internal change procedures alone. In terms of the Universities of Oxford and Cambridge, the external commissions of enquiry that started in the mid-nineteenth century promoted the interests of the universities *vis-à-vis* their respective colleges, reshaped the patterns of university government, and promoted the interests of the resident dons against all other parties. Indeed, the donnish domination of university affairs probably owes more to external political intervention than any other single pressure for reform!

It is a common occurrence for institutions governed by statutes to experience occasional disruption because of internal disagreements over their interpretation, and educational institutions are no exception to the general rule. The statutes of most universities have provided for such an eventuality by creating the office of visitor. Although historically visitors exercised original jurisdiction, contemporarily their intervention is instigated by internal disputes. In the sense that the resolution of conflicting interpretations of statutes may bring about institutional change, the visitor can be regarded as another of the traditional external inputs into university affairs. Smith has argued that the university visitor has an 'overall supervisory function' that can be broken down into several constituent parts:

(i) to ensure that the statutes of the foundation are enforced, and that those who have duties to perform under the statutes are fulfilling their duties,
(ii) to expel and deprive members,
(iii) to supervise the administration of the property of the foundation,
(iv) to hear appeals from members concerning the foundation,
(v) to interpret the statutes in the event of any dispute as to their meaning (Smith, 1981, 611–12).

As the statutes of most universities invest the visitorial powers in the Queen (Farrant, 1987, 33), it is the Lord President of the Privy Council who usually exercises this authority. While at the time of his writing, Farrant may have argued correctly that '... this side of the Privy Council's business is not subject to political influence in the way that the granting of charters is ...' (ibid.), this must be a less certain judgement in the light of the more recent battles over academic tenure into which university visitors have been drawn.

Even if the visitor's office is not a channel along which external political pressure can penetrate the university, it does bring into very sharp focus the special legal status of universities and their claims to autonomy. There have been a number of court cases which have upheld the view that the visitor is the final arbitrator of domestic disputes, exercising a jurisdiction which is not subject to review by the courts. Sir Robert Megarry expressed the argument in forthright terms:

[There] is much to be said in favour of the visitor as against the courts as an appropriate tribunal for disputes of the type which fall within the visitorial jurisdiction. In place of the formality, publicity and expense of proceedings in court ... there is an appropriate domestic tribunal which can determine the matter informally, privately, cheaply and speedily, and give a decision, which, apart from any impropriety or excess of jurisdiction, is final and will not be disturbed by the courts (Patel v. Bradford University Senate [1978] 1 W.L.R., 1488–9; as quoted in ibid., 610).

While there may have been good reasons for granting the visitor what has been described as absolute power (in the sense that the visitor is the final court of appeal), the universities were as a consequence a special kind of corporate body. Sir Robert Megarry's judgment allowed the courts to intervene only in cases of 'impropriety or excess of jurisdiction' by the visitor, and this supervisory jurisdiction of the courts has been upheld subsequently (Regina v. Visitor of the University of Hull, Ex parte Page, as reported in *The Times* Law Report, 6 August 1991). It might be thought that dismissal from academic employment would be covered by the law of contract; however, the individual's contract of employment could be 'regarded as relating solely to the government and management of the corporation so as to be exclusively within the visitor's cognisance' (Smith, op. cit., 641). And this is a view that has been further upheld by the Law Lords in their judgment on 'the Page case' (Regina v. Lord President of the Privy Council, Ex parte Page, as reported in *The Times* Law Report, 15 December 1992). While these are matters that have been overtaken by the *Education Reform Act*, 1988 (see below), there remains a sizeable body of faculty whose tenure is still dependent upon the visitor's interpretation of university statutes.

Inasmuch as the Lord President of the Privy Council was fulfilling the tasks of the visitor on behalf of the Crown, this could have been perceived as an avenue for external intervention, even intervention by government and state, in the affairs of the universities. However, if the key purpose of the visitor was to ensure that the statutes were upheld, then this is a peculiar form of external intervention, for its purpose is not to impose new goals upon the institution but rather to make sure it did *not* veer from its original statutes. The office of visitor, therefore, is best viewed as a mechanism for maintaining the status quo. Whereas usually the external threat to university autonomy is not that they should maintain their commitment to founders' intentions, but they should be more amenable to the contemporary pressures of state and society.

If university visitors became increasingly involved in settling petty internal disputes (although the concerned parties may have seen them differently), while the universities themselves were in the business of proposing rather limited and piecemeal statutory change, then the question remained of how to undertake a major overhaul of a university's statutes. In the nineteenth, and to a much lesser extent, the twentieth centuries, the Royal Commission replaced the visitation as the means of initiating large scale statutory change. Although there was strong resistance in certain quarters within both Oxford and Cambridge to the Royal Commissions of 1850 (Clokie and Robinson, 1937, 82–3), it is widely recognised that Royal Commissions into the affairs of the universities have invariably resulted from a body of internal opinion in favour of their appointment. Ernest Barker went so far as to comment that, as a rule, a Royal Commission will be appointed only 'when there is already a strong demand from within in favour of some reform' (Barker, 1931, 14). While in the 1850s Oxford and Cambridge may have been split about the legality and wisdom of a Royal Commission, those in favour of reforms realised that they were more likely to succeed with the aid of such intervention. Thus, while a Royal Commission may be a means of putting into effect externally instigated innovations, viewed in this light the Royal Commission becomes a vehicle for resolving internal university conflict by deciding the future shape and direction of the university among its competing internal parties.

Once a Royal Commission had reported, the usual course of action was for the government to appoint statutory commissioners to act on its recommendations. In order to distance the statutory commissioners from the semblance of being constrained politically, there was a tradition that Parliament would not restrict them with specific terms of reference. For example, the members of the Cambridge Committee of the Asquith Commission (1920–22) agreed unanimously that women students should be admitted to full membership of the university but they were also evenly divided on how best to achieve this. Should the statutory commissioners be obliged to draft the necessary statutes? Alternatively, should the reformed university be trusted to undertake the required steps? Parliament left the statutory commissioners to make up their own minds, who in turn felt that it was a matter best left to the reformed university. As it turned out their trust was misplaced, for it was not until after 1945 that women students were admitted into full membership of the University of Cambridge! Although the outcome may be judged unfortunate, it could be argued that this was a price worth paying if it left the statutory commissioners unfettered.

The eventual terms of reference of the statutory commissioners appointed to implement the report of the Asquith Commission were typically very broad:

> [to] make statutes and regulations for the University, its colleges and halls, and any emoluments, endowments, trusts, foundations, gifts, offices, or institutions in or connected with the University in general accordance with the recommendations contained in the report of the Royal Commission ... (*Public General Statutes*, 13 and 14 Geo V, 1923).

They could modify those recommendations in the light of 'any representations made to them' but the only precise obligation with which Parliament saddled them was to have particular regard for 'the admission of poorer students to the Universities and colleges'. This directive reflected a continuing parliamentary concern with the exclusiveness of the social composition of Oxbridge undergraduates, and its inclusion in the terms of reference of the statutory commissioners represented a tactical concession to the more vocal parliamentary critics of the two universities.

Although statutory commissioners were invariably given a free hand in arriving at their decisions, Parliament required them to follow very detailed procedures in determining how they reached their recommendations. In the case of successive parliamentary interventions in the affairs of Oxford and Cambridge, it appears that the intention was to devise means of ensuring that the two universities and their respective colleges could participate as fully as possible in the redrafting of their own statutes. To achieve this they were given a period of grace in which to make their own changes and to submit them to the commissioners for approval; the commissioners were required to take into account representations from, and to communicate their proposals to, a number of named persons and institutions; and in revising college statutes the governing bodies of the colleges could 'elect three persons to be Commissioners to represent the College in relation to the making by the Commissioners of statutes for the College' (ibid.). If one also takes into account the fact that the Royal Commissions in the first place have been partly composed of several prominent university insiders, then the clear impression is created that Parliament is not directly responsible for the imposition of statutory change. This was a task for prominent academics even if they should be wearing a different hat.

The various channels by which external influence was brought to bear upon the universities before the twentieth century arose out of a very different set of interrelationships between state, society and the universities. There was no state apparatus in the sense that we understand it today, certainly not one that had the resources to influence the universities through continuous administrative inter- action. In terms of their financing, notwithstanding the fact that some institutions were founded by the Crown, they owed their continued existence to society and in particular to the Church (albeit an estab- lished Church). The focus for change was university statutes as if the actual character of an institution could be determined by its written constitution. The creation of new universities, and the reform of the ancient institutions, in the nineteenth century did not initially upset these assumptions. The Royal Commission was a setpiece event aimed at reforming statutes and could be likened to the medieval visitations. It is fascinating to realise the strength with which these assumptions persisted. In his evidence to the Asquith Commission, the Rev. Blakiston – former Vice-Chancellor of the University of Oxford – is purported to have remarked that when he learnt that it intended to give Oxford a block grant:

> ... he would have preferred to withdraw the whole application, as he felt that such a grant would lead to different kinds of control from what anyone had anticipated and would mean practically a fresh Commission every few years (Royal Commis- sion on Oxford and Cambridge Universities, 1992, Appendix 1, 5).

It appears that the Rev. Blakiston could not conceive of a continuous relationship between the state and Oxford, in which the latter would be free to distribute its block grant as, to use an oft-repeated phrase, it saw fit. But of course the university's distribution would be influenced by ties to the UGC, ties which became increasingly constraining over time. Perhaps Blakiston sensed developments that many of his con- temporaries preferred not to think about.

While visitations could be occasions on which the Crown brutally imposed its will upon the universities (notwithstanding that visitors were meant to uphold founders' prescriptions), the Royal/Statutory Commission route to change genuflected strongly to the universities. Although the primary purpose of the nineteenth-century commissions was to forge a new relationship between the universities and society, there were many within the universities themselves who believed that no alternative was possible if they wished to avoid a steady decline into intellectual and social ossification. Once the convention of powerful university representation among commissioners had been established, it is difficult to view this as a channel of external influence. The impression is that by the nineteenth century visitors were left with a role concerned essentially with resolving minor domestic disputes, and that the opportunities for an externally controlled and radical overhaul of university statutes had virtually disappeared. Moreover, the jurisdiction of the Privy Council was limited to approving either piecemeal change that emerged from within the universities, statutes drafted by statutory commissioners, or statutes drafted by those who wish to create a new university which had usually been constructed in consultation with the UGC – to which the Privy Council had a persistent habit of deferring!

The disadvantages – from the perspective of the state – of the traditional channels by which external pressures could influence the universities are obvious. Their focus, university statutes, was often an inappropriate target for it is evident that universities on occasions have been able to function only by evading them. The process of change was protracted and costly, both timewise and possibly also politically. Moreover – as we have gone to some length to illustrate – it was a process that by convention was not fully under the control of the state, and thus its outcomes could not be guaranteed. Essentially these were channels of influence that had evolved before the twentieth century, and were inappropriate for handling the kinds of problem that were likely to emerge once the Exchequer had become the major underwriter of recurrent university costs and the state had felt compelled to take an increasing interest in the nature of higher education. While Oxford's former Vice-Chancellor (Blakiston) was expressing to the Asquith commissioners his fears of perpetual investigation by commission, so the Oxford Reform Committee, in the same body of evidence, remarked:

> We think that is to the advantage of the nation that the University should be in a large measure autonomous, but that the attempt to provide the necessary elements of external control by Statutes, assisted by periodic Royal Commissions, has proved unsatisfactory. So far as external control is necessary, it should be continuous, not intermittent (ibid., 10).

In fact the UGC, which between 1919 and 1989 was to serve as the most important conduit between the state and the universities, was already in place by the time these words were written, and was in the process of working out how it was to relate to both the universities and to other state institutions. It was obvious that if the Exchequer was to make funds available to the universities to meet their recurrent costs, then the state–university nexus had to be placed on an orderly administrative basis. The old channels of interaction were increasingly irrelevant in the changed circumstances.

FROM GUIDANCE BY CONVENTION TO THE MANAGED MARKET: REVAMPING THE LEGAL FRAMEWORK AS AN INSTRUMENT OF STATE CONTROL

There is widespread agreement that in recent years the law has intervened more forcefully in the regulation of university affairs. In their introduction to the excellent text, *Universities and the Law*, the editors, Farrington and Mattison, remark that

> ... the last three years have seen a great move into prominence and contemporary significance of legal principles as they affect universities: the jurisdiction of the Visitor, tenure, formation of contract, variation of contract, personal legal liability of offices and members of governing bodies (Farrington and Mattison, 1990, xv–xvi).

But the change of direction goes far beyond the restructuring of the essentially internal university business listed by Farrington and Mattison. The broader concern has been to place the key institutional relationships that bind the state to the universities on a statutory basis. In the words of Henderson and Mattison:

> The *Education Reform Act* 1988, however, has the effect of placing much of the relationship between universities and the source of the instrument of government of most of them, the Crown, on a statutory basis (Farrington and Mattison (eds.), 1990, 13).

The key university clauses in the Act are those which replaced the UGC by the Universities Funding Council (UFC), and provided a framework to regulate its relations with the universities and the Secretary of State. With the passage of the *Further and Higher Education Act*, 1992, and the amalgamation of the UFC and the

Polytechnics and Colleges Funding Council (PCFC) into the Higher Education Funding Councils (HEFCs), the intervention of the law has been reinforced. What we need to understand is the significance of these changes, that is both the interference with the traditional channels of external influence and the broader thrust to place the state–university axis on statutory foundations. In a nutshell, how are we to interpret this new situation?

The last significant commission of enquiry into the affairs of higher education produced what is colloquially known as the Robbins Report (Robbins Report, 1963). Although it would be absurd to claim that we have seen the last of such massive setpiece enquiries, the fact that the Robbins Report appeared some thirty years ago suggests they will be used very sparingly in the future. Of course this depends partly on the political style of the government, and the four recent governments of Mrs Thatcher were convinced that their disadvantages greatly outweighed their advantages.

While the use of Royal Commissions may have fallen into disrepute, the *Education Reform Act*, 1988 contained very important clauses that established statutory commissioners. The task of the commissioners was laid down very precisely: to amend university statutes so that persons appointed or promoted after 20 November 1988 (the date the Second Reading of the Education Reform Bill began in the House of Commons) could be dismissed by virtue of redundancy, in addition to the customary 'good cause' clauses that were usually to be found in university statutes. It is almost as if the government, while accepting the convention that legislation should not apply retrospectively, was doing its best to limit as severely as possible the consequences of staying with conventional mores. Five statutory commissioners were appointed, a model statute covering these matters was produced, and negotiations with the concerned organisations and individual universities eventually led to new statutes.

Does this represent a different use of statutory commissioners than was customary in the past? Certainly the commissioners included some very well-known insider names (for example, Lord Butterworth, former Vice-Chancellor of Warwick University, and Professor David Williams, currently Vice-Chancellor of Cambridge University). However, their appointment was not the result of a prior general enquiry into the affairs of one or more universities, and the specificity of their brief contrasts remarkably with the scope granted to most previous commissioners. It would be difficult to argue convincingly that the commissioners were required to do anything other than to put into effect the government's policy on a very particular matter. This is not to say that the commissioners have performed the task other than scrupulously, and it is conceivable that the universities now have statutes that are more sympathetic to the interests of their academic faculty than if they had been redrafted by government bureaucrats. There is simply no way of resolving this conundrum. One is reminded of the dilemma that the UGC faced in the early 1980s. Was it to impose the cutbacks in university expenditure necessitated by the decline in its recurrent grant? Or should it resign and leave others (most probably the DES) to do the government's bidding? The two situations are different inasmuch as the statutory commissioners were appointed knowing full well the nature of their task, but in both cases we have parties that traditionally have been regarded as removed from (although not independent of) the state being required to implement government policies with remarkably little discretion available to them.

Besides appointing statutory commissioners to act on tenure, the *Education Reform Act*, 1988 also removed from the jurisdiction of university visitors their rights 'in respect of any dispute relating to a member of the academic staff which concerns his appointment or employment or the termination of his appointment or employment' (Section 206), although the visitor retains the right to hear and determine appeals, and hear and redress grievances. The employment of academic staff is now fully subject to the courts' jurisdiction, although this did not come into effect until the new statutes were approved. Moreover, the differing positions of faculty appointed and/ or promoted before or after 2 November 1988 needs to be kept in mind. There remains a range of possible domestic grievances that may well come before university visitors (for example, student appeals against their examination results), but undoubtedly the 1988 legislation represents a severe limitation on visitors' powers by removing responsibilities which had been consistently supported in law, and over which, as late as 1992, the Law Lords had asserted only a supervisory jurisdiction. The ambience that surrounds the visitor's traditional role is not one that accords easily with either the world of industrial tribunals or legislation designed to outlaw sexual discrimination in employment and to promote equal opportunities.

Perhaps more remarkable than the above changes, is the *apparently* new position in which the Privy Council finds itself. This is very significant because, if our earlier interpretation is correct, it is the

Privy Council which formally controls the definition of what it means
to be a university. Only the most politically naive could believe that
the Privy Council had ever been able to function without taking into
account the prevailing climate of political opinion, and above all the
wishes of the government of the day. As Farrant points out, the
decisions to create the Open University, and what was to become the
University of Buckingham, were determined politically, and the Privy
Council was in no position to have exercised a veto even assuming it
had wanted to do so (Farrant, 1987, 32). Under the terms of the
Further and Higher Education Act, 1992 (Section 77) institutions in
the higher education sector can apply to the Privy Council 'to include
the word "university" in the name of the institution', and the only
discretion which the Privy Council can exercise is to 'have regard to
the need to avoid names which are or may be confusing'. Within a few
months of the Act's passage, 31 former polytechnics had successfully
applied to the Privy Council for titles which incorporated university in
them (*The Times Higher Education Supplement*, 19 June 1992, 1).
Overnight, therefore, we witness the largest expansion ever in the
history of the nation's university system. This is *not* to say that the new
universities are undeserving of their new titles (and it should be
recognised that not everyone from within the polytechnics approved
of the change), but to point out that this is a very different process of
university creation from that experienced in the past. Under political
direction the Privy Council applies its rubber stamp and, at least
formally, the transformation process is completed.

Of course to acquire the label is not the same as acquiring the
substance. There are other, less tangible, but in all probability more
hazardous, bridges which have to be crossed before many of the
former polytechnics are likely to be recognised universally as universities. But there have always been layers of prestige within the British
university system and, for example, no other universities – at least in
England – have been able to compete with the fact that Oxbridge
retained its collegiate exclusivity, notwithstanding some imitations.
But the speed and ease with which these polytechnics were able to call
themselves universities, once the political decisions had been taken,
contrasts remarkably with the painstaking progression of, for
example, Exeter, Reading and Southampton to full university status.
The reasons for the different treatments are obvious. The UGC had
developed a particular model of the university to which institutions
had to conform if they were to receive a charter from the Privy
Council. The university label had a relatively precise meaning

(despite layers of prestige) and the substance had to match the label. Now the political pressure is in favour of a system of higher education with a wide range of internal diversity, and there is no one model of the university to which the former polytechnics have to conform. The Privy Council, at least with respect to handing out the university label, has become no more than a rubber stamp. And it should not be thought that these particular developments reflected only a narrowly partisan political perspective. The debate on the Second Reading of the *Further and Higher Education Bill* generated little discussion in the Commons on the higher education clauses. So marked was the political agreement that Tim Eggar, the Minister of State, was able to observe: 'It is fair to say that there has been a consensus in welcoming the higher education provisions in the Bill' (Hansard (Commons), 11 February 1992, Volume 203, Column 901, 11).

Throughout the 1980s, as it sought to defend academic tenure, there were repeated attacks by the AUT (Association of University Teachers) upon both the government's expressed intention to appoint statutory commissioners to revise terms of employment, and the Privy Council's advice to universities that, when seeking a revision of their statutes, they should introduce clauses which sanctioned the termination of contracts on the grounds of redundancy. In an interesting article in the Association's *Bulletin*, John Akker argued that the government's proposed appointment of statutory commissioners to revise tenure clauses represented a significant break with established practice (Akker, 1984). The essence of Akker's case is that the Secretary of State, who at the time was Sir Keith Joseph, was not, as he asserted, following precedent in his proposed course of action. Having claimed that he intended to proceed by precedent, it is fair to argue that the Secretary of State should have been aware of precisely what that entailed, and ensured that his proposed actions matched his words. Although the facts of the case may support Akker's interpretation of what following precedent necessitated (although surely Sir Keith – or his advisers – would disagree), the more interesting point is that Sir Keith felt obliged to make the claim and that Akker wanted him to fulfil it. Another way of interpreting the situation is that the Secretary of State knew that he was breaking precedent (or possibly was unconcerned, one way or the other) but made the claim for political reasons – on the grounds that is is more difficult to criticise something if it can be argued (and, ideally, demonstrated) that it has all been done before.

Akker concludes his article with the words:

The appointment of Commissioners, whether they be High Court Judges, as seems likely (with no doubt a sprinkling of ex-senior academics), marks a very pronounced encroachment by the State. *No precedent exists for this* and it is another reason why the AUT is totally opposed to the proposed changes in tenure (ibid., our stress).

Undoubtedly the real intentions of the Secretary of State were to bring about changes to university statutes which made it possible to dismiss academic staff on the grounds of redundancy. In similar vein, the real purpose of the secretary of the AUT was to resist this change and fight for the maintenance of academic tenure in as pristine a form as possible. It is not that the arguments about 'following precedent' are irrelevant, but it is evident that they are serving different political ends. The only obligation that the Secretary of State was required to fulfil in the appointment of statutory commissioners was to act constitutionally, and whether or not he followed precedent was a political consideration. Perhaps in the past statutory commissioners had been university insiders, perhaps they had been appointed to enact the broad recommendations of a commission of enquiry instigated by internal university pressure for change, and perhaps their attention had been directed towards reform in specific universities – all requirements Akker argued that had to be fulfilled if the claim to be following precedent was to be substantiated. But the Secretary of State was not required to perpetuate any of these traditions. It can be asserted with some conviction that the Thatcher governments were intent on breaking the conventions that had governed the relationship between the state and the universities. In order to do this it was to be expected that they would break with the past for the conventions had grown out of established procedures, and inevitably they were reinforced through adherence to a traditional way of doing business.

The Privy Council's recommendation to a number of universities that they should change their statutes to permit dismissal for reasons of redundancy came about as the Thatcher governments in the 1980s made it increasingly clear that they intended to end academic tenure. Various institutions, (for example, the University College of Wales at Aberystwyth, the University of Sussex, and the University of London's Institute of Education), were caught up in this process long before the government took action in the *Education Reform Act* of 1988. In a letter to Aberystwyth, the Privy Council wrote:

Ministers have now concluded that all new and Supplemental

Charters for University institutions which contain provisions on tenure must include in such provisions an explicit mention of redundancy as a reason for dismissal, and I have been asked to invite the College to submit a suitable redraft of Statute 22 accordingly (as quoted in AUT, 1983, 3).

Not surprisingly the AUT had expressed its concern at this development and in an earlier exchange of letters, the Clerk to the Privy Council wrote to the General Secretary of the AUT that

You will of course know what the Secretary of State for Education and Science said about this [the government's wish that university statutes protecting tenure should be revamped] in March in reply to a Parliamentary Question *and since the Privy Council is part of the machinery of government*, it is, I suggest, natural that the advice given from this Office should reflect his views (as quoted in AUT, 1982, 3, our stress).

So, although in the past the Privy Council may have been strongly influenced by the advice of the UGC in making its decisions whether or not to grant a university charter, it is clear that the formal responsibility has always resided with ministers. In the penetrating observation of Wade and Bradley this responsibility has tended 'to be obscured by the dignified façade of Privy Council formality' (Wade and Bradley, 1985, 245). What we have seen in recent years is a stripping-away of this dignified façade, with the Secretary of State and the DES clawing back their authority. Whereas the Treasury may have promoted the interests of the UGC in these matters (see above), the DES evidently had its own interests to buttress.

While recognising that the Privy Council 'has always been an instrument of Government', the AUT claimed that 'never before in granting Charters and Statutes to universities or in approving amendments, has this body tried to impose aspects of day-to-day Government policy' (AUT, 1983, 1). Even if this is a correct interpretation of previous Privy Council behaviour, there was – as with its proposed use of statutory commissioners – no legal obligation why the government should not break with the past. Moreover, and more significantly, it is unclear why government policy should contain any less a vision of the future than recommendations from the UGC or royal commissions. Again it is difficult to escape the conclusion that the AUT's concern is with the nature of that vision, rather than the way the government was prepared to use the Privy Council. As the AUT reflects: 'Charters and

Statutes have always been intended to shape universities over the long term' (ibid.). It is our contention, however, that to bring about long-term change was precisely the purpose of government action on charters and statutes.

What institutions such as the UGC and the Privy Council succeeded in doing was to give the appearance of not being integrated into the state apparatus. Perhaps it was an image which was sustained most ardently by those interests concerned to preserve university auto-nomy, rather than one which they consciously strove to sustain themselves. What we have witnessed in the past decade is the willing-ness of governments to enact legislation which ties the previous margins of the state apparatus more closely into those parts of the state that traditionally have been more immediately responsible for the implementation of government policy. Thus, in spite of the continuing potential for internal conflict, the state has become a less fractured body over time.

Of course the above development is not immune from the pressures of the political process. The *Education Reform Act* received a rough passage in Parliament and, mainly as a result of opposition in the Lords, the government was forced to amend the terms of reference of the statutory commissioners. In exercising their functions the commis-sioners have

> to ensure that academic staff have freedom within the law to question and test received wisdom, and to put forward new ideas and controversial or unpopular opinions, without placing them-selves in jeopardy of losing their jobs or privileges they may have at their institutions (*Education Reform Act*, 1988, Section 202).

Some may feel that the future of academic freedom in Britain is indeed precarious if its well-being is dependent upon such guarantees being built into legislation. But we have seen that it is not entirely unknown for Parliament to direct statutory commissioners, and the debates have all the hallmarks of a political struggle in which the purpose of the opposition is to embarrass the government, and of the government to resist for as long and as hard as possible. Just as the government made concessions when the commissioners were appointed in 1923 to revise the statutes of the Universities of Oxford and Cambridge, so it was sensible politics for the government to make concessions in 1988.

Given that the state had relied increasingly upon financial and administrative controls to direct university policy, then why did the

Thatcher governments feel compelled to place the institutions responsible for exercising those controls on a statutory basis, and to undermine the conventions which had grown up around the traditional channels of external influence? We have argued that over time the UGC assumed a central planning role within the British university system, and its replacement by the UFC represented a shift from a planned to a managed market model of higher education. The planned model was inconsistent with the main ideological thrust of the Thatcher governments, especially as the institution with the key planning role (the UGC) was perceived to be dominated by producer interests (the universities) and had secured considerable autonomy within the state apparatus. If the universities were to be responsive to market demands (not to forget cuts in the Exchequer's recurrent grant!) then they required a more flexible labour force. In government eyes, tenure was not so much a bulwark against the erosion of academic freedom as tangible evidence of professional self-interest and proof that the dons had established a privileged position in the labour market.

Given the scale of the changes that were contemplated, the government had little choice but to proceed through the legislative process. It can also be argued that the prior arrangements by which the Exchequer made resources available to the universities were anomalous (the UGC was created by a Treasury Minute), and became increasingly so as the state underwrote an ever higher percentage of the universities' recurrent expenditure. Legislation has not only broken the old conventions (and created the opportunity for new conventions to evolve) but it has also tied the universities more closely to the state apparatus (section 134 of the *Education Reform Act* empowers the Secretary of State to 'confer or impose on either of the Funding Councils such supplementary functions as he thinks fit . . .'), and drawn the further shores of the state more closely into the making of government policy (note the role assigned to the Privy Council in the *Further and Higher Education Act*, 1992). In an amazingly short space of time the relationship between the state and the universities has been placed on a footing that discards much of its traditional trappings – whether they be medieval, or forged in the nineteenth century (the great age of the Royal Commissions), or evolved in the days of the UGC, the high watermark of donnish domination. At present the state controls the use of the university label and, given its wide-ranging sources, who is to say that it will not also determine the future idea of the university?

5

The Board, the Ministry and the Department

The index of Berdahl's landmark text *British Universities and the State*, published in 1959, contains no references to the Board of Education and precious few to its 1944 successor, the Ministry of Education. While Carswell, in his sparkling insider's view of *Government and Universities in Britain* (1985), is prepared to devote a chapter to the Treasury, neither the Ministry of Education nor the Department of Education and Science (which succeeded the Ministry in 1964) warrant such prominence. For both Berdahl and Carswell their analysis of the relationship between the state and the universities is directed primarily at the changing role of the UGC, its links to a tolerant Treasury and its response to political – especially parliamentary – pressures.

Our enhanced focus upon the state's central educational bureaucracy is a consequence of three considerations. Most obviously, this is a book about higher education rather than the universities alone, and the development of the Public Sector of Higher Education (PSHE), as it is invariably labelled, has been strongly influenced by a powerful input from the central bureaucracy. Second, the time spans of the respective observations are different. Berdahl's work takes events no further than the late 1950s, and Carswell is concentrating upon the period 1960–80. This book, however, pays considerable attention to changes in the 1980s; the decade in which state pressure so intensifies that even the most elevated universities find it more difficult to pretend to be autonomous institutions, and in which the UGC is transformed from either a buffer or coupling link between the state and the universities into, in the eyes of many, little more than an agent of government policies.

While the above two reasons are essentially pragmatic justifications of our somewhat different focus (the reader will have noticed that we also pay considerable attention to the UGC, Parliament and the Treasury!), there is another, more substantive point. In all of our previous research we have given considerable prominence to the increasing role of the DES in the orchestration of educational change. It is not simply that we feel the need to maintain the continuity of our previous work, but rather – as we argued in Chapter 1 – the pressures which the Department brought increasingly to bear upon the other sectors of education have been experienced ever more sharply by higher education institutions in recent years. Thus it is our contention that the process of change in higher education cannot be fully understood without a serious analysis of the input of the bureaucratic dynamic and its interaction with the evolving political context. Carswell has rightly observed that the ties between the state and the universities have been intimate throughout much of this century (Carswell, 1985, 159), and what has changed is the nature of the links – from the personal and social to the bureaucratic and formal. But, as presumably Carswell would concur, that is not all that has changed, as the most cursory observation of the shifting balance of power between the respective parties would demonstrate.

Integral to our chapter on the UGC is the idea that the Committee was much more than a convenient mechanism by which the Treasury distributed state monies to the universities, that its very existence became a symbol of university autonomy. The conventions by which it fulfilled its key function were perceived as a guarantee that there was a buffer between the state and the universities. The UGC provided a protective ideological shield for the idea that the universities were self-governing institutions that determined their own purposes. The PSHE, on the contrary, was managed mainly by the local authorities and reconstituted over time by the direct intervention of the central state. There is, therefore, no legacy to suggest that its institutions are in any sense autonomous. Moreover, the PSHE was directly responsive to societal pressures, many of them local in nature. Thus it provided a range of vocational qualifications for a variety of professions, as well as courses geared to the interests of the local or regional industrial base. While the universities were funded by the Treasury on the understanding that they would be responsive to national needs, it was tacitly agreed that the universities – at a later date with more guidance from the UGC – would determine how that should be done. By way of contrast, either the state or voluntary associations determined the purposes of institutions in the public sector (note especially the training of prospective teachers) or interests could buy into institutions on more or less their own terms (thus the provision of professional qualifications). It is impossible, therefore, to see the PSHE institutions as controlling their academic destinies.

The purpose of this book is to understand how this admittedly simplified bi-polar model of British higher education was radically transformed by the cumulative intervention of first the Ministry of Education and subsequently, and much more significantly, by the DES. In this chapter certain key developments will be analysed. The first part examines some of the important historical bench-marks in the relationship between the universities, the UGC and the state which culminated in the transfer of responsibility for the UGC from the Treasury to the DES. Second, we trace in broad terms the development in the Ministry of Education of an ideology of education which posed a direct challenge to the idea that universities should define their own academic purposes, and we couple that with some consideration of the planning procedures that evolved in the DES so enabling it to have a more effective input into the policy-making process. Although it is widely recognised that the UGC was steadily drawn into the state apparatus, and became increasingly a vehicle for the transmission of government policy, this did not secure its preservation. The third part of the chapter discusses the demise of the UGC and outlines the new relationship between the Secretary of State, the UFC and the universities. Fourth, we look at how the DES preserved the public sector of higher education from a university take-over by the creation of the polytechnics and the binary system of higher education, and how later in the 1970s it ensured that this second tier of higher education was not seriously undermined by the mass transfer of colleges of education into the universities. The state in effect established a stratum of higher education that provided an alternative tradition to the university model. Finally, we return to our analysis of the interaction of the political and bureaucratic dynamics in the process of educational change, and in so doing posit an understanding of the contemporary relationship between the state and higher education which will be further developed in our final chapter.

ASSUMING FORMAL RESPONSIBILITY FOR THE UGC

In our analysis of the changing relationship between the universities, the UGC and the state, we allude to the apparently rather peculiar arrangement whereby the body responsible for distributing state monies to the universities was placed in 1919 under the auspices of the

Treasury rather than the Board of Education. It may be true, as Owen contends, that the prime reason 'was, in the end, purely practical' since the Committee was to administer grants throughout the United Kingdom and the Board of Education's writ covered only England and Wales (Owen, 1980, 258). The fact that this may have also better safeguarded the autonomy of the universities was noted as 'a *consequential* advantage, but this was not a prime consideration' (ibid., his stress). On reflection, however, it surely would not have been beyond the administrative capabilities of the persons most intimately involved to have solved the conundrum to the Board's advantage if the political will had supported its case? Moreover, while the issue of autonomy may not have been a prime consideration to either Chamberlain (the Chancellor of the Exchequer) or to Fisher (the President of the Board of Education), as Owen argues, it certainly figured prominently in the contemporary debates and *was* a major cause of concern for many in the universities.

However we interpret the historical evidence as to the UGC's origins, it is clear that its very presence was later perceived as a guarantee of university autonomy, and it was integral to its symbolism that it nestled in the warm and undemanding embrace of the Treasury. Besides creating an interpretation of current realities, ideological symbols also have built into them an implicit understanding of the nature of alternative realities. Thus the UGC under the Treasury umbrella would protect university autonomy, whereas if it were to become one of the Board of Education's responsibilities it would not. And no matter how much the Board's President sought to win over university opinion, he could not overcome the prevailing perceptions. The correspondence between Fisher and the University of Oxford's Vice-Chancellor, concerning the University's request for public money, illustrates perfectly how easy it was to offend the fragile sensibilities of the University in spite of the President's exceedingly deferential tone. It is almost as if the Board were the supplicant and the University the provider of largesse (Royal Commission on Oxford and Cambridge Universities: 1922, Appendix 4).

There has never been a definitive statement as to what autonomy means for the simple reason that its meaning has been dependent upon the conventions that evolved over time to sustain the relationship between the state, the UGC and the universities. It can be argued that as the conventions evolved so the relationships changed, and the meaning of autonomy was transformed. None the less, a strong, consistent theme is that the universities should control their own academic development, that the state should not use its financial leverage to impose upon the universities its own preferences. In his correspondence with Oxford's Vice-Chancellor, Fisher wrote:

> I may say in conclusion that no one appreciates more fully than myself the vital importance of preserving the liberty and autonomy of the Universities within the general lines laid down under their constitution. The State is, in my opinion, not competent to direct the work of education and disinterested research which is carried on by Universities, and the responsibility for its conduct must rest solely with their Governing Bodies and Teachers (ibid.).

In view of subsequent developments, perhaps the Vice-Chancellor was right to remain suspicious. Even at the time, however, it could be expected, notwithstanding Fisher's reassurances, that the Board of Education would have a more clearly defined view as to the desirable course of university development than the Treasury – at least one would have hoped so!

It was not simply a question of the potential pressure of the Board's view of university development but also that the universities would be coupled with the Board's other concerns. The fear was that in any internal struggle there was no guarantee that the university interest would prevail. If one were of the opinion that a planned system of education required the Board to evaluate claims and set priorities then this would appear reasonable, but the political support for a centrally planned educational system was not strong, and in any case the universities may have felt that to relinquish their autonomy to further the apparent progress of the educational system as a whole was a price they had no wish to pay. So the Board's view did not prevail in 1919 and, although it may have been very pragmatic in administrative terms, the UGC ended up as the responsibility of the Treasury, which could scarcely pretend to know very much about higher education and, furthermore, was placed in the peculiar position of overseeing a spending department (that is the UGC) while its primary function was to control and coordinate the demands of other spending departments. Whether Fisher and Asquith were able to perceive any logic, as well as pragmatism in these arrangements, Owen did not reflect upon. But for the UGC and the universities it was the perfect settlement: sponsored by the highly prestigious and undemanding Treasury and unencumbered by the potentially unwelcome attentions of the very lowly Board of Education.

The first serious threat to the 1919 settlement emerged towards the end of the Second World War, and it also centred on the interrelated questions of university autonomy and the overall planning of the educational system. In view of the understandable feeling that all the nation's energies had first to be devoted to bringing the war to a successful conclusion and then to the pressing demands of post-war reconstruction, coupled with the belief – strongly enhanced by a Labour government after 1945 – that a critical ingredient in the pursuit of this end should be centrally planned government action, it was scarcely surprising that these issues re-emerged. Interestingly, it was the wartime coalition government's President of the Board of Education, the Tory grandee R.A. Butler, who staked a vigorously renewed claim for control over the universities on the grounds that he had

> ... never felt happy that the Board should be responsible for education, and yet have nothing to do with the universities, whom it is our duty to feed from the schools. In fact I do not think one can be a successful minister of education and have no contact at all with the universities (R.A. Butler, President of the Board of Education, to Sir Maurice G. Holmes, Permanent Secretary of the Board of Education, 12 February, 1943, PRO ED 136/560, as quoted in Price, 1978, 359).

Whereas the Butler quote raises again the spectre that the Board needed to consider the educational system as a whole if planning were to be effective, the big question after the war was that of university expansion, and whether the universities could train the ever-increasing supply of scientists and technologists that many believed were vital for the regeneration of the economy. There were powerful sentiments in the Labour government that the universities could not deliver the goods, and that matters would not improve until responsibility for the UGC was removed from the Treasury. These sentiments were expressed most forcefully by Herbert Morrison, Lord President of the Council, and Ellen Wilkinson, the Minister of Education. There was the possibility of transferring the UGC from the Treasury to the Ministry, to the Lord President of the Council or even to a newly constituted department with responsibilities for a variety of matters including higher education and research (Benn and Fieldhouse, 1993). In the end the balance of political forces in the government (Attlee, the Prime Minister, and Dalton, the Chancellor of the Exchequer, were reluctant to upset the status quo) was weighted against new institutional arrangements.

In essence the outcome of this struggle was a typically pragmatic compromise. The changes in institutional relationships were marginal: it was agreed in 1944 that the Permanent Secretary of the Ministry could attend UGC meetings, and a Cabinet committee – which proved to be largely inoperative – was set up to advise the Cabinet on university policy. The UGC was given new terms of reference which suggested that henceforth it would provide the universities with closer guidance, its chairman was made a full-time post, its committee structure was extended and its secretariat enlarged. Perhaps most significantly, with respect to the maintenance of the established state-university nexus, the UGC was prepared to accept the expansion targets set by the Barlow Committee, albeit somewhat reluctantly at first. It seems that Attlee in particular was very persuaded of the necessity of expansion, and as long as the UGC and universities felt that they could achieve the Barlow targets, he was prepared to sustain their autonomy. Although in the short run the 1919 settlement had been preserved, the UGC's hesitant acceptance of the Barlow targets opened up a constant source of post-1945 pressure upon the universities – could they meet the manpower needs of the British economy? As we will see, the test as to whether they were indeed meeting national needs was defined increasingly in these very narrow, and contentious, terms.

Although there was clear political, indeed government, pressure in the mid- to late 1940s for the relationship between the universities and the state to be restructured, and that this was supported by many eminent persons – including R.H. Tawney, Sir Ernest Simon and Sir Henry Tizard – who had strong links with both government and higher education, it seems that there was less sympathy within the civil service itself for radical structural change. Benn and Fieldhouse, with references to a memorandum prepared by the Ministry of Education for the Cabinet, a Ministry minute paper and correspondence between Ministry and Treasury officials, have written that while both Morrison and the Minister, Ellen Wilkinson,

> ... were inclined to put the universities under the control of the Ministry of Education ... both the Ministry mandarins and the Treasury were opposed to this, and managed to quietly bury the idea (ibid., 302).

Regardless of what the civil servants may have felt in 1946, this was an issue that was not going to disappear, and by the early 1960s it was back on the political agenda.

Among its all-encompassing range of interests, the Robbins Report proffered advice on how state-university relations should be revamped (Robbins Report, 1963, Ch. XVII). The Report, after evaluating the alternatives, argued that the UGC should become the responsibility of a Ministry of Arts and Science. In the Committee's opinion the autonomous institutions of higher education required the separate articulation of their interests (that is, as opposed to the expression of their interests in a department with responsibility for the educational system as a whole) with their own direct line to the Cabinet. In an equally critical set of related proposals, the system of higher education would þe unitary in character and the Ministry of Arts and Science would also take responsibility for those institutions in the public sector of higher education which successfully acquired autonomous university status. As is all too evident, this is yet another of the Robbins proposals that failed to materialise. The Report contained a 'Note of Reservation on Administrative Arrangements' (ibid., 293–6) by H.C. Shearman in which he expressed his preference for bringing the UGC into the orbit of the Ministry of Education. His reasons were twofold: the need to establish closer links between higher education and the rest of the educational system, and in particular to ensure that at some point in the administrative hierarchy the concerns of the universities and the public sector of higher education could be evaluated in relation to one another. If the Robbins proposals had carried the day, a situation would have been created in which the public sector institutions steadily escaped the clutches of the local authorities to join the self-contained university sector.

In the event the Ministry of Education was incorporated into a newly created Department of Education and Science which also took under its wing the UGC and the research councils. Although this move was vehemently opposed by the UGC and many prominent university figures, it was virtually unopposed politically and appears to have met little resistance, indeed quite the contrary, in either the disappearing Ministry of Education or the slightly denuded Treasury. On the political front, this was the time of the first Wilson government which combined a faith in the expansion of higher education with the efficacy of national planning. It was not altogether surprising, therefore, that an administrative change which appeared to make sense in planning terms, and in this respect note the long-expressed belief that the educational system would perform more effectively if the needs of its component parts could be evaluated in conjunction with one another, would find government support. In his review of the workings of the DES, Sir William Pile, the Department's Permanent Under-Secretary, 1970–76, is annoyingly coy on the departmental view of the change-over. He does, however, articulate the planning argument with particular reference to the expansion of secondary school numbers, the increased demand for higher education, and thus the necessity of providing more university places (Pile, 1979, 156). Whether it was beyond the wit of the involved parties to resolve such problems without changing the machinery of government is another question, but they appear to be reasonable legitimations for change. Perhaps as significant was the remorseless expansion in university expenditure, which must have made it more difficult, as Lord Bridges, a former Treasury head, implied, for the Chancellor of the Exchequer to double as a departmental and Treasury Minister (ibid.). Regardless of the reasons, the change-over was effected and the obvious question was what differences, if any, it would make.

DEVELOPING IDEOLOGY AND PLANNING PROCEDURES: THE DES CLIMBS THE WHITEHALL TOTEM POLE

In view of the fact that the UGC's move from the Treasury to the DES was not accompanied by legislation to place the new relationship on a statutory basis, it is not surprising that the conventions that had evolved between the UGC and the Treasury should continue to flourish, at least initially, in this new situation. In his evidence to the House of Commons Estimates Committee, John Carswell – at the time a DES functionary – is reported as saying:

> In the last four years that I have been dealing with this kind of work, first in the Treasury and then, when the work was moved, in the Department, I have not felt that I was duplicating any of the functions of the UGC; *it was and still is a question of acting as the joint between the UGC and the Government* (Fifth Report from the Estimates Committee, Session 1964–65, as quoted in Owen, 1980, 269, our stress).

And Sir Eric Ashby, one of the more ardent defenders of university autonomy, claimed in 1968 that, although there was almost continuous consultation on policy issues between UGC officers and Curzon Street civil servants, 'the prime initiative for these proposals lies in the UGC, not in the DES' (Ashby, 1968; see Owen, ibid., 269). However, it is not inappropriate to note that the UGC officers were in fact seconded Curzon Street civil servants, which may have made the flow of policy initiatives somewhat more equivocal than Ashby implies!

The manner in which the new responsibilities were integrated into the Department must have also reassured the universities. Their interests were to be taken care of by a new universities branch; in other words they were not amalgamated with the public sector of higher education, although coordination could occur at a higher departmental level. Furthermore, the DES was to have two permanent secretaries, one of whom would be responsible for the old Treasury commitments. This gave the universities a direct line to a departmental head, and through him to a Minister of State who was to oversee the affairs of higher education. Although the arrangement of two permanent secretaries was quickly abandoned, and the Minister of State was to be downgraded to a Parliamentary Under-Secretary, it is reasonable to argue that in the latter years of the 1960s university autonomy was under greater threat from Parliament, and especially from the persistent demands of the Public Accounts Committee that the accounts of the UGC and the universities should be available for inspection by the Comptroller and Auditor General. The Wilson governments were committed to the binary system, and the Department's administrative arrangements reflected the divide in British higher education.

If, in its relations to the universities, the DES initially continued in the same diffident manner as its predecessor, the Ministry, then what forces changed this situation? In our opinion there were three key developments. First, the Department needed to establish an understanding of the purpose of higher education that would enable it to challenge the deeply entrenched idea that universities were autonomous institutions. Second, if the Department were to have a critical impact upon government policy, one that reflected the concerns of its internally generated ideology, then it was vital that it developed cogent planning procedures. As the DES was not overburdened with direct managerial responsibilities – most of formal education outside the universities was under the auspices of the local education authorities, the UGC gently guided the universities, and the research councils distributed the civil science budget – it was obviously very important for it to act on this front for if it was to direct the course of policy-making, then it could scarcely be effective if it lacked the necessary tools.

This third factor that has changed the relationship between the Department and higher education, is that external pressures – from other departments, government, Parliament and the political parties – have encouraged the DES to move in this direction. Indeed it could be argued that some of these pressures were ahead of the Department in demanding that it adopt a more positive posture. There is considerable irony in the fact that, although both the political left and the political right have been more than convinced of the malevolent machinations of the British civil service, when in government they have invariably helped to expand its influence. Governments that wish to make a mark have to use the tools available to them, and they have few viable alternatives but to make use of the civil service for both policy formation and policy implementation.

In this book, and elsewhere, we have analysed at some length the development in the Ministry of Education of what we have termed 'the economic ideology of education' (Tapper and Salter, 1978, 148–71; 1992, 8–18; Salter and Tapper, 1981, 198–208; 1985, 23–30). This posed an alternative understanding of the purpose of higher education to that contained in the traditional university ideal, and at the same time seriously threatened the independence of universities, for it implied quite explicitly that their purpose was to fulfil societal – above all the economy's – needs, and that the state had a legitimate interest in trying to ensure that they achieved this goal. The evidence that the ideological challenge developed in the Ministry is dependent upon the numerous reports it issued which espoused this ideological theme. However, it can be reasonably argued that government departments do not issue reports unless there is ministerial support for them. But it is not our argument that the Ministry was acting contrary to the wishes of government ministers (or even trying to manipulate them!) – indeed quite the opposite – for the bureaucratic and political dynamics had mutually reinforcing incentives to sustain an ideological challenge to the traditional university ideal. For the Ministry there was the defence of further education and the public sector of higher education which, to put it merely at the level of resource distribution, needed to be planned in conjunction with the university sector. For government ministers, and politicians in general, there was the realisation that investment in higher education was increasingly costly, and thus it became steadily more difficult to accept the idea that university expenditure should not be subject to close scrutiny. Furthermore, as one government after another grappled with Britain's relative economic decline, seemingly with little success, it was obviously politically attractive to argue that education, including higher education, should be in the forefront of economic regeneration (a return to postwar reconstruction after a brief interlude in the 1950s).

Support for the argument that a potent economic ideology of

education developed in the Ministry of Education is provided by John Carswell, although not surprisingly he expresses it in different terms. With reference to the Ministry, Carswell has written:

> Psychologically the CATs were very important because they arose out of the womb of the educational system as it had been fertilised since 1944. That system had always been kept at a distance from the universities. The CATs were consequently the pride and joy, the favoured children, of the Ministry of Education ... (op. cit., 20).

And later we read:

> There were, however, certain parts of the Curzon Street machine where such pressures [for departmental intervention] had already found a friendlier reception. The creation of the directly administered colleges of advanced technology and the 'master-minding' of the Council for National Academic Awards were striking instances of Curzon Street initiative. Two zones of the Department were especially active in this forward policy. The inspectors concerned with further education had for some time formed a distinct corps within the Inspectorate as a whole, and the developments in technical education just mentioned had been very much of their making: and they exercised a very detailed control over the approval of courses and the distribution of scientific equipment (ibid., 69).

Within the Ministry, therefore, there appears to have developed a critical element in favour of positive action on behalf of technical education, and it does not require too great a leap of the imagination to hypothesise that this element overlapped closely with those officials who also believed in centralised planning:

> If the Ministry of Education had little administrative or direct financial power, it nevertheless had a clear duty to plan for the future. ... In this sense it was very much the heir of the post-war reconstruction and the Attlee years, during which most of its ablest officials had been recruited: and in the fifties it was very much a department of officials. Not all the officials approved of this tendency ... but it nevertheless had great intellectual appeal in a department which was sedulously denied access to the substance of education (ibid., 21).

Ranson has argued, somewhat contrary to the evidence offered by Carswell, that 'a broad consensus about policy objectives for the service and for 16–19 education in particular' (Ranson, 1985, 61) took root in the DES *after* 1975 in response to 'the developing economic crisis and the structural revolution in employment driven by new technologies' (ibid., 69). This consensus was allegedly centred on the three 'underlying presuppositions' of 'rationalization, vocationalism and stratification'. Ranson saw this development as in contradiction to the guiding ethos of an earlier period (1955–75) in which the organising principle was 'personal development, child-centred education', the code was 'one of opportunity, of raising expectations and lifting horizons', and the key actors were the LEAs and the teachers, with the DES's role confined to winning resources and 'reinforcing the overriding principles' (ibid.).

The Ranson and Carswell viewpoints can be reconciled by the proposition that the influence of the economic ideology of education, within first the Ministry and then the Department, waxed and waned over time as external circumstances changed. Generally it has been stimulated by Labour governments, economic crises, and the emphasis upon planning in, for example, the wartime years and the post-1945 period of reconstruction. However, for more than a decade we have experienced a succession of Conservative governments, which have attacked explicitly the efficacy of planning, and yet it would be hard to deny that education is now seen as essentially an economic resource. Ranson's claim about the post-1975 period is particularly significant as he sees the new values emerging out of economic crisis and technological change, the very pressures that one would expect to give rise to demands that education should be more closely linked to the needs of the economy. Moreover, these are pressures which, if anything, have intensified in the 1990s.

As we have already indicated it is not an easy process to translate ideology into policy, even assuming that the means exist to do this, which many believed the DES lacked. Perhaps the clearest expression of the belief that the primary purpose of education is to service the economy is to be found in the manpower planning lobby, frequently associated with the former Labour junior minister in the DES, Lord Crowther-Hunt. Given the complexity of the occupational structure, the fact that technological change can rapidly date specialist skills, and disputes as to whether it is better to maximise vocational training or aim for more broadly based educational experiences, it is not surprising that the lobby has had only a limited impact upon higher education policy making (Maclure, 1987, 12). But it would be wrong to write off its influence completely. In a variety of fields, with the teacher training programmes providing the longest running example, the Department has monitored student numbers very closely and institutions have been given specific targets in, for example, medicine, dentistry and architecture. Besides the general post-1945 exhortation to increase the output of science and technology graduates, the universities were under increasing pressure to plan their student numbers by ever more precise categories. Earmarked grants were used in the 1980s to provide the universities with the incentive to enlarge their undergraduate populations in engineering and technology, and as the UGC's recurrent grant was cut in the early 1980s, so the government injected additional resources into 'new blood' (directed overwhelmingly to science, pure and applied) and information technology posts. It may be that deep-seated cultural biases against entrepreneurialism and technology make such endeavours rather marginal, but it could also be argued that the change process has to start somewhere, and that such initiatives constitute part of a wider struggle to modify the cultural horizons of the nation. Whatever form the economic ideology of education may take, and however contentious the evaluations of its impact may be, it would be difficult to deny that in the 1990s the overwhelming sentiment – in government, Parliament and the parties – as well as popular sentiment at large, perceives higher education as primarily an economic tool.

Kogan has written that:

> The assimilation of the DES to central planning styles as they were pressed on the departments by the Treasury did not prove easy ... the Department found it difficult to provide quantifiable information on the objectives and output of the education service, and to apply such briefly fashionable techniques as planning-programming-budgeting (PPB) to the field of education (Kogan, 1987, 232).

Moreover, as Kogan goes on to note, the existing power balance within the educational system did not help the Department's cause. But, in spite of these problems, our previous analysis of the increased effectiveness of the Department's planning procedures (see especially, Salter and Tapper, 1981, 100–14) is now widely accepted. Lawton sees 1976 as a watershed, arguing that since then DES officials 'have been more willing to develop central policies and pursue them vigorously' (Lawton, 1986, 26).

Inasmuch as the DES had to respond to two critical assessments in the mid-1970s of the effectiveness of its policy planning procedures (OECD, 1975; Select Committee on Expenditure, 1975–76), Lawton may be correct about the significance of 1976, but the planning techniques, rudimentary as they may have been, were already taking shape. Since the early 1960s government departments, as part of the inter-departmental competition for resources, have had to conform to the demands of the Public Expenditure Survey Committee (PESC). Inevitably any attempt to review the following year's expenditure plans would lead to some evaluation of policy goals (especially if the Treasury were intent on curtailing expenditure), however cursory. Although planning strategies such as PPB and Programme Analysis Review (PAR) may have been only briefly fashionable, as Kogan suggests, they did have the merit of pointing to the need for the longer term analysis of alternative policy options, coupled with their projected costs, in contrast to the essentially short-term, and at times crisis management, perspective associated with the annual negotiations of the PESC. In 1970 the DES brought out two planning papers (DES, 1970 and 1970a) which gave expression to its sponsorship of output budgeting and human capital planning. More significantly, the Department set up in 1971 the Departmental Planning Organisation (DPO) and a review of its activities constituted the core of the Select Committee on Expenditure's Tenth Report, 1975–76. The DPO is serviced by a small Planning and Programmes Branch whose membership, like that of the DPO, is entirely in-house. In 1980 the branches dealing with further and higher education were reorganised so that the interests of the public sector of higher education and the universities could be coordinated at a lower level in the departmental machinery. Not surprisingly, a key input into all the planning exercises has to come from the Finance Branch, because policy proposals need to be costed, and because this is the channel which controls access to the Treasury.

Several major criticisms have been levelled at the Department's approach to planning: it is too secretive, it is too cautious – what Crowther-Hunt has termed 'an essentially passive concept of planning – reacting to events', it is 'not sufficiently concerned with the role of education in meeting the needs of a modern industrial society' (Crowther-Hunt, 1983, 49–50), and – what may be a reiteration of the second objection in a different form – it has been so centred on the projection of student/pupil numbers that Maclure can argue 'Student numbers provide the main focus of public policy discussion for higher education' (1982, 269). While such criticisms may be valid, a key and widely agreed point that needs to be kept in mind is that for all its apparent protracted passivity the Department's planning procedures have become more sophisticated over time and, as this has occurred, so the Department's ability to manage the system from the centre has become more assured. The extent to which these developments brought about a change in the overall balance of education power (see Kogan, above) is open to debate, but it cannot be denied that the post-1945 partnership of which Ranson is enamoured has been destroyed, and the Department remains as chief master of the ring.

As with the development of its economic ideology of education, it is important to note that the more active planning role of the DES had strong political support, and was not simply a consequence of its own internal bureaucratic logic. As much as the Department may have instinctively rejected the critique of Lord Crowther-Hunt, it can be imagined that he stimulated internal departmental thinking about its planning role (Saville, 1983, 1). Both the Expenditure Committee's Tenth Report (1975–76) and the 1979–80 Report of the Education, Science and Arts Committee (*The Funding and Organisation of Courses in Higher Education*) contained a variety of recommendations aimed at improving the Department's management and planning of higher education. In view of this stimulus to action, coupled with an economic context which made the resourcing of higher education more precarious (note the quinquennial funding arrangements collapse early in the 1972–77 cycle), it is not surprising that observers should discern the Department as taking a more active role after 1975. The arrival of Mrs Thatcher's first government, with its deep suspicion of bureaucrats and professionals which put both the DES and the UGC respectively in the firing line, posed a challenge to this new-found central *dirigisme* which raises the question of why the Department was able to prosper but the UGC came to grief.

FROM THE UGC TO THE UFC: REFORMULATING THE BUFFER'S RELATIONSHIP TO THE STATE

In a formal sense the UGC was always a part of the state apparatus and its position between the state and the universities could be analysed in terms that went beyond the buffer imagery (Moodie, 1983). However, it never perceived itself, and in its heyday was never perceived by the universities, as belonging to the state. Moreover, it is the buffer model which most strikingly conjures up the longest-lasting impression of its role. In spite of the fact that government policy became more intrusive from the late 1960s onwards, and some interventions – notably the government's decision in 1967 to raise the fees of overseas students (that the universities set their own fees was a symbol of their autonomy) – caused a considerable political stir, most of the additional *dirigisme* was directed through the buffer, the UGC. To many within the universities it seemed as if the UGC was being increasingly absorbed into the state, to the point that it became little more than a conduit for government policy. The real crunch came in 1981 when the UGC accepted the responsibility for distributing a recurrent grant that had been substantially cut by the government. A strongly expressed body of university opinion felt that the Committee was now little more than a blunt instrument of government policy, and it should have resigned *en masse* rather than accept such an igno-minious fate (Kogan and Kogan, 1983). There are others, however, who believe that the UGC had little choice in the matter, and it was in the best long-term interests of the universities for the Committee to perform the odious task rather than a DES-led committee, which presumably would have occurred if the UGC had resigned. Indeed Shattock and Berdahl have claimed:

> Nevertheless the vigour and snap with which the UGC tackled the task greatly restored its prestige within Whitehall where government departments were wrestling often ineffectually with similar cost-cutting exercises (Shattock and Berdahl, 1984, 491).

Unfortunately the authors fail to offer any evidence in support of their claim, and the universities particularly disadvantaged by the UGC's proposals may have felt that the Committee's action smacked of qualities other than 'vigour and snap'! None the less, Shattock and Berdahl confidently predicted a bright future for the UGC:

> Nevertheless, we believe that the wide range of its functions – not only acting as broker but also adapting, co-ordinating and reconciling university plans; arguing for funds and then distri-buting them; assisting institutional development and interpret-ing national needs – gives the UGC a power base which will prove difficult to erode unless it chooses to do so itself by abandoning the more active role it has pursued since 1979 (ibid., 498).

In view of the fact that scarcely five years after this was written the

UGC was consigned to the scrapheap of British institutions deemed to have outlived their usefulness, we have to reflect upon what went wrong.

While agreeing with Shattock and Berdahl's conclusion that the UGC had no choice but to grasp the nettle in 1981, and that under the leadership of Sir Edward Parkes it had assumed a more dynamic role, Sizer is more equivocal about the effectiveness of the Committee's part in the events leading up to the 1981 cuts (Sizer, 1987, 359–60). The question is whether the Committee could have prevented, or at least mitigated, the cuts by a more effective defence of university interests. Taking an interestingly different line, Maclure has argued that the way the cuts were distributed reflected values that were not in tune with those of the government. Thus Aston and Salford were very badly hit, while those universities with a less pronounced applied science/vocational bias seemed to come off better. The government was apparently horrified, and determined to have a funding body in which the academics lost their in-built majority, and thus their ability to defend the traditional values of academe (Maclure, 1989, 92). Berdahl and Shattock could argue that their prediction was undermined by the UGC itself for, far from continuing in its more active role, it crept back into its shell. The National Audit Office not only objected to the way the UGC had permitted some universities, following the 1981 cuts, to run their redundancy schemes but also called for a review of the UGC. Moreover, while the UGC may have felt itself constrained from intervening in the affairs of University College, Cardiff, because of the conventions surrounding university autonomy, others had reached the conclusion that it was time for the government to bring those conventions to an end.

While the above arguments are each in their different ways plausible explanations of why the government decided that the UGC needed to be replaced, it is our contention that the time had come to place the relationship between the Secretary of State and the universities' funding body on a different basis. Part of that different basis had to be determined by legislation so that the government could define more carefully the lines along which the future state-university relationship would evolve. It is not that statutes can be so detailed and precise that no conventions are necessary, but that the government wanted new conventions, ones that would be shaped by its legislation and by its values. The legislation itself, that is the relevant clauses of the *Education Reform Act,* 1988, were preceded by the White Paper, *Higher Education: Meeting the Challenge* (DES, 1987), certain aspects of which were extremely distasteful to a wide body of university opinion. Kogan wrote of the White Paper that it can

> ... leave academics in no doubt that self-government by collegium is on the way out and that they must now begin to consider their places within an objectives-led and centralised system (Kogan, 1987a, 349).

And in a mood far less bullish than when he was optimistically predicting the continuing saga of the UGC, Shattock remarked: 'What we are witnessing is the absorption of a publicly financed university system into the structure of civil government', and 'it looks as if the Department of Education and Science is at last firmly in the driving seat and the buffer principle, so widely admired by other countries, has had to give way to the requirements of the modern state' (Shattock, 1987, 485).

There were three aspects of the White Paper to which academic opinion strongly objected. The first was the government's intention 'that payment of grants to institutions should be replaced by a system of contracting between them and the body to succeed the UGC' (DES, 1987, 37), accompanied by the quite explicit threat that 'Any serious failure to meet the terms of a previous contract may result in revised terms or a failure to renew' (ibid., 32). This was the language of the commercial world; universities were reduced to the status of mere firms providing services for their customer, the government. Second, the new funding body apparently would not have the right, like the UGC, to give advice to the Secretary of State, with the implication that it would simply receive its orders and pass them on to the universities. Third, there were no proposals in the White Paper to protect academic freedom, which was considered as very significant within the universities as the government intended to restrict, even abolish, academic tenure. What was wanted were guarantees that individuals could not be dismissed because of their opinions.

A fierce, and protracted, political struggle ensued from the time the pressure was on to revamp the UGC. While the Jarratt Report recommended that the UGC should be restructured, the Croham Review was given the official responsibility of presenting reform proposals. The 1987 White Paper represented in part the government's reaction to those proposals, and presumably the *Education Reform Bill,* 1988 took into account responses to the White Paper. The end result was the passage of the *Education Reform Act,* 1988 (ERA), which was the product of Parliament's response to the Bill, including of course the government's tactical concessions made in the light of the parliamentary manoeuvres. In spite of the anxiety generated by the White Paper, and to a somewhat lesser extent by the Bill itself, it could be argued that the Act's final form took into account the objections raised within university circles. There was no reference whatsoever to the effect that the UFC (or the Polytechnics and Colleges Funding Council (PCFC) for that matter) had to make its funding available on the basis of contracts: 'The Council shall have power to make grants, *subject to such terms and conditions as they think fit* . . . ' (ERA, Clause 131, 6, our stress). The councils also had the right to make their views known to the Secretary of State: 'to provide the Secretary of State, in such manner as he may from time to time determine, with such information and advice relating to activities eligible for funding under this section as they think fit' (ERA, Clause 131, 8b). Finally, there was a specific guarantee of academic freedom. The University Commissioners, established by the Act for the purpose of removing from university statutes clauses which guaranteed tenure, were required 'to ensure that academic staff have freedom within the law to question and test received wisdom, and to put forward new ideas and controversial or unpopular opinions, without placing themselves in jeopardy of losing their jobs or privileges they may have at their institutions' (ERA, Clause 202, 2a). The government, therefore, appeared to have shifted somewhat from the position it adopted initially in the White Paper, forced to change tack thanks primarily to pressure exercised by a potent university lobby in the House of Lords (Crequer, 1989).

The question of whether the changes were sufficient to scotch the worst fears of Kogan and Shattock, and to fulfil the hope expressed by Moodie (1987) that the UFC could grow into a body that was respected by both universities and government, can never be answered. The UFC, along with the PCFC, was wound up by the *Further and Higher Education Act*, 1992, and both councils were amalgamated into a Higher Education Funding Council for England, with separate funding councils for the Welsh and Scottish universities. The UFC existed for too short a time to make definitive judgements on its role. However, it is evident that the UFC was meant to be a different body from the UGC in terms of its composition, its links to the Secretary of State and the universities, and how it performed its functions. Moreover, the HEFCs, at least in statutory terms, will follow the precedent set by the UFC/PCFC – rather than the UGC – models.

With respect to composition, the striking distinction between the UFC and the UGC was the smaller size of the former and, more importantly, the explicit requirement that in appointing part of its membership the Secretary of State 'shall have regard to the desirability of including persons who appear to him to have experience of, and to have shown capacity in, industrial, commercial, or financial matters, or the practice of any profession' (ERA, Clause 131, 3). Even if the members who were currently academics should be the largest wedge on the Council, there was meant to be a substantial leaven of lay representation. While the Secretary of State was not empowered to establish conditions that could be attached to a grant made to a specific institution, he could 'make grants to each of the Funding Councils of such amounts and subject to such conditions as he may determine' (ERA, Clause 134, 6). In other words he could require the councils to impose general conditions that the higher education institutions had to meet if they wanted to be funded. In fact the Secretary of State took to issuing general memoranda of guidance, and the councils were expected to take these into consideration when making their funding decisions. The potentially most draconian powers were to be found in what appear to be two reserve subclauses: 'The Secretary of State may by order confer or impose on either of the Funding Councils such supplementary functions as he thinks fit' (ERA, Clause 134, 1); and 'In exercising their functions under this Part of this Act each of the Funding Councils shall comply with any directions given to them by the Secretary of State' (ERA, Clause 134, 8). Presumably such powers would only be used in exceptional circumstances but, at least on the surface, it seemed that the Secretary of State had the potential power to order the councils to do precisely what he wanted them to do, and subject to the constraints of the law, there was no authority to resist his diktat.

How much the above differences changed in practice the relationship between the Secretary of State, the UFC and the universities from the days of the UGC is open to question. Before its demise the UGC was accustomed to receiving guidance from the Minister, which Booth has likened to statements of 'ministerial priorities' (1987, 62). Obviously these could become more elaborate, precise and demanding over time. Second, DES officials attended UGC meetings as observers but presumably such a seemingly quiescent role could become ever more assertive. Booth refers to the increasingly close links between the officials of the UGC and the DES (ibid., 62–3), with the implication that policy could be initiated as much by departmental officers as those of the UGC, contrary to what Ashby alleged was the case in the 1960s. In this respect the independence of the UFC may actually have been greater than that of the UGC for it could appoint its own staff, rather than have its secretariat composed of seconded departmental officials. However, again the changes may be superficial, for UFC staff had civil service terms of reference and senior appointments were approved by the Department (Farrant, 1992). Although what we have termed the 'reserve' powers of the Secretary of State, may appear overwhelming, it could be argued that it is hard to imagine circumstances in which they are likely to come into play.

There is some evidence from the short history of the UFC that it was actually rather unsuccessful at imposing its will upon the universities, which could suggest that if it was designed as a smooth channel of departmental influence something was amiss. However, it is clear that the Council was moving towards establishing a different kind of relationship between itself, the universities and the Secretary of State which the HEFCs are in the process of building upon. This is most clearly seen in its failed attempt to require universities to determine the size of their undergraduate numbers in terms of bids made according to guide prices fixed by the Council (UFC, 1989, Annex D [revised]). The obvious intention was to set up a system in which universities competed with one another for their teaching income. In the process it was hoped that student numbers would expand while unit costs would be driven down. The scheme was scotched by the universities' failure to make many bids below the guide prices; in effect they acted as a successful cartel. In response, the Council adopted the strategy of seeking the same ends by rewarding universities who accepted a disproportionate percentage of 'fees-only' students with additional 'fully-funded' students. In other words the target of 'expansion-on-the-cheap' (as its critics have called it) was set by the state, the UFC developed the appropriate managerial strategy to accomplish the goal, and the universities had to decide how they were to respond. The end result is the evolution of what we term 'the managed market'.

It is not our contention that the changing relationship between the state and the higher education institutions can be understood merely in terms of the statutory framework. It is crucial to examine the prevailing political and ideological context, in particular to understand how government is prepared to use the statutory framework. It may be true that in its short existence the UFC did not live up to government expectations (which possibly explains why it was superseded and additions were made to the statutory framework), but a longer time period is needed to reach a more conclusive judgement on the evolving state–university nexus than the very short life-span of the UFC. However, the relationship between the Secretary of State and the funding bodies is now on a statutory basis, and it is widely agreed that this gives the Minister more authority than he possessed in the days of the UGC. Moreover, regardless of the formal prescriptions, neither the UFC nor the HEFCs could be seen – as the UGC came to be seen – as institutions for keeping the state at bay. The idea that higher education should be autonomous may still carry some weight, but what is meant by autonomy has changed enormously over time. It is no longer a question of keeping the state at a distance, but how much influence it will seek to exert, and the manner in which it will exercise that influence. Not only do we have a statutory framework (the *Education Reform Act*, 1988 and the *Further and Higher Education Act*, 1992) but a new political context – dominated by a succession of Conservative governments – within which the conventions for the future are being formed.

THE DES AND THE PUBLIC SECTOR OF HIGHER EDUCATION

The central state did *not* create the public sector institutions of higher education; they were a product of action by local authorities and voluntary associations, notably the churches. But it is fair to argue that neither the history nor the contemporary shape of the sector (including what can be construed as its abolition by the *Further and Higher Education Act*, 1992!) can be understood without due consideration given to the almost continuous intervention of central government. As our analysis of the DES's role in the restructuring of the university sector is somewhat circumscribed by our subsequent examination of the UGC, so our later study of the shifts in the control of the PSHE has ramifications for this section of the chapter. Moreover, given that the purpose of this book is to examine how the state has gradually extended its controls over higher education in Britain, then the traditional non-university sector of higher education is intrinsically less interesting to us for the simple reason that historically these were institutions that have been closely managed by the state, albeit the local state. They never had a strong tradition of self-government, of the autonomy from state control which was considered to be part of the definition of a university. Thus the key development was the erosion of local control as opposed to the undermining of the idea of autonomy, which was historically absent.

The full analysis of the relationship between the state and the public sector of higher education would need to consider at least four key changes: the creation of the polytechnics in the mid-1960s, the relocation of responsibility for the teacher training institutions in the 1970s (which led to a more complex PSHE model), the emergence of the National Advisory Body (NAB), and the replacement of the NAB by the PCFC (the amalgamation of the PCFC and the UFC into the HEFC is part of a wider political struggle). This part of the chapter will concentrate upon the first two developments; it will examine, therefore, how the DES in effect restructured the shape of the public sector of higher education. In doing so it had to resist the potential absorption of this sector by the universities, and is, therefore, an appropriate topic to consider alongside the evolving relationship between the Department and the universities. It was upon this basis that the subsequent struggle for control between the centre, and those forces which favoured continuing local responsibility, took place. But, unless the state had first secured the independence of this stratum of higher education from the universities, then this later struggle could not have occurred, for substantial parts of the PSHE would have already been merged into the world of the universities and the UGC. Of course, merger was eventually to take place but by then the UGC had disappeared, pristine interpretations of university autonomy were on the wane, and the polytechnics and colleges had secured their own national funding council. In a formal sense polytechnics may have become universities, but in a real sense perhaps the reverse has come true.

We have already considered how there developed within the Ministry of Education a strong sympathy for the cause of technical education. In concrete terms the Ministry helped to fund, and gave formal approval of a variety of courses that were run by technical colleges. The Robbins Report had urged that the colleges of advanced technology be given university status, and had proposed one route into higher education: through the acquisition of a university charter and thus membership of the UGC. If this unitary model of higher education had been established, then the Department risked losing its direct influence in the most ambitious technical colleges: those which wanted to be recognised as higher education institutions. This is not to suggest that the binary model, within which the polytechnics became a second tier of higher education, was created with the sole purpose of enabling the DES to retain its direct influence upon the technical colleges (note that the local authorities also had much to lose), but rather to make the point that this was not an inconsequential consideration.

That the DES was the main architect of the binary model is beyond dispute. Crosland, as Secretary of State, formally announced the government's intentions to establish the second tier of higher education in his famous speech at Woolwich Polytechnic on 27 April 1965. Sharp records: 'According to Crosland, senior civil servants at the DES wanted to get the binary policy "on the record" as soon as possible' (1987, 42). This Crosland did in spite of his own reservations and apparently 'before he had fully mastered the topic . . .' (ibid.). Although it can be argued that the White Paper, *A Plan for Polytechnics and Other Colleges* (DES, 1966), which followed his speech, 'provided little more than a statement of intention and was inadequate in both educational and organisational terms' (Nixon, 1987, 58), it is clear that the negotiations leading up to its publication were orchestrated by the Department. For better or for worse the polytechnics were the brainchild of the DES.

Having ensured that the leading technical colleges would not be absorbed into the universities, the major concern of the DES was with their machinery of government. Indeed Locke has maintained that there was scant departmental attention paid to little else (Locke, 1974). The major thrust was to loosen the reins of the local authorities over college government. The guidelines appear to have been established by the Report of the Study Group on *The Government of Colleges of Education* (DES, 1966a). Significantly the Study Group took as its starting point one of the prescriptions of the Robbins Report:

> We share the conviction of the Robbins Committee that academic freedom is a necessary condition of the highest efficiency and of the proper progress of academic institutions (ibid., 3).

In concrete terms this was translated by the Study Group to mean that the governing body should *not* be dominated by local authority representatives, that there should be an academic board with substantial representation of the junior members of the teaching staff, that the chief education officer should not be – as he typically was – the institution's chief administrative officer, and that within the approved budget there should be considerable scope for virement. It is hard not to form the conclusion that the thinking of the Study Group was strongly influenced by a model of university government and, to conclude, with Locke, that 'The schemes of government of the polytechnics do not define an educational development but seek to establish the status of institutions' (Locke, 1974, 171). But the other consideration, which should not be overlooked, is that many of the local authorities resisted these moves, and that this is part of a long struggle between national and local government for control of the public sector of higher education. While at this stage the centre could not expect to replace the local authorities in the management of that sector, it could weaken their influence. None the less, it may appear somewhat ironic that in the public sector greater institutional independence serves the long-term interests of the Department, while in the university sector the opposite is the case.

Having been instrumental in establishing the second tier of higher education through the creation of the polytechnics, it is not surprising that the Department should wish to further that sector's interests, especially if to do so also coincided with the interests of the Department! The Department provided direct funding for the training of teachers and was responsible for controlling the numbers who entered the teaching profession. With pressures to diversify the academic programmes of the colleges of education (as a method of expanding higher education), and the moves towards upgrading teacher training programmes into degree courses, the question inevitably arose as to where this evolving segment of higher education belonged – with the polytechnics, with the universities, or as a third force. It appears that opinion in the DES as to the most appropriate location was initially divided. Sharp has claimed that in 1970, when the discussion of these matters was coming to a climax, argument shifted substantially in favour of the link with the polytechnics:

> ... Herbert Andrew, the Permanent Secretary of the DES who was sympathetic to the university/college connection in teacher training, was due to retire at the end of July [1970], and it had already been announced that his successor was to be William Pile who had worked in the Teacher Supply Branch of the DES in the early 1960s. In Pile's time this Branch had been strongly opposed to the Robbins solution for teacher training and had favoured local authority retention of the colleges (Sharp, 1987 105–6).

In June 1970 Hugh Harding, who was currently in charge of the teaching training branch at the Department, had presented a paper at

York which left his audience with the clear impression that the DES did not see the future of the colleges as belonging with the universities (ibid., 107). As architect of the binary policy, it was inevitable that Toby Weaver would also throw his considerable weight behind the claims of the public sector. For the government, the key argument in the last analysis appeared to be financial – the belief that it would be easier to contract programmes of teacher training (the demographic trend pointed to the need for fewer teachers) if the colleges of education were amalgamated with the advanced sector of further education. In the event a more complex patchwork of public sector higher education emerged as the colleges of education took different routes, but with few exceptions the universities were kept at bay.

Although the DES may have been instrumental in establishing in a formal sense an alternative tradition of higher education to the universities, the critics of the Department argued that the failure to engage in academic planning would end by the polytechnics 'undermining the policy they are meant to express' (Pratt and Burgess, 1974, 109). The argument is that in the absence of purposeful direction from the centre that built on grass-roots support, the polytechnics would inevitably succumb to the wiles of the established academic tradition powerfully expressed by the university model. Indeed, in its insistence on a wide measure of institutional self-government, the Department itself had helped to encourage this drift. In other words, in spite of appearances to the contrary, there was an emerging unitary model of higher education, and it was underwritten by university values. The thesis is not without its attractions, but perceptions of change are heavily dependent upon the viewer's vantage point. To Pratt and Burgess it may have seemed as if the polytechnics were selling their souls; to the Oxbridge don the chasm may have appeared unbridgeable for, no matter what, glass simply cannot be turned into diamonds. Moreover, and more significantly, the Pratt/Burgess thesis implied an unchanging university model which clearly has *not* been the case. So perhaps the reverse process could occur and diamonds be turned into glass with the Department prepared to act as the catalyst.

THE DEPARTMENT AND THE PROCESS OF CHANGE IN HIGHER EDUCATION

Much of the literature that has examined the changing system of higher education in Britain, places considerable stress upon the input of key individuals. Not unexpectedly this is very pronounced in the work of the ex-insider, John Carswell, who has given us several illuminating insights into the personalities of many of the departmental mandarins. Shinn, in her study of the UGC, has emphasised the central part that Sir William McCormick played in the development of British higher education in the early decades of the twentieth century, both before the establishment of, and as the first Chairman of, the UGC. For Berdahl, it is Sir Walter Moberly, Chairman of the UGC during both the war years and the important post-war reconstruction period, who merits special favour. Owen has even claimed that it may have been Lloyd George's suspicion of the Anglican influence in the Board of Education that led him to insist that the Treasury, and not the Board, should retain responsibility for making grants to the Welsh colleges in the 1911–19 period (Owen, 1980, 257)! We have not been above this ourselves, noting – along with literally everyone else – the pivotal role of Toby Weaver in the creation of the binary system. But it is evident to all, including the authors to whom we have just referred, that any serious understanding of the process of change in higher education must go beyond an analysis of individual inputs, significant as they may appear at the time.

Central to our research has been the claim that the process of educational change is increasingly controlled by a bureaucratic dynamic located in the DES. But as this book will have also made clear, this change dynamic unfolds in a political context to which it has to relate in a sophisticated manner if it is to prosper. This is not to deny the input of broader social and economic trends which set the context for political struggle. Clearly demographic trends have influenced the development of the British educational system at all levels, to such an extent that planning allegedly has meant little more than how to meet the expanding or declining demand for educational services. Education in Britain has felt the force of relative economic decline in two different but equally important ways: recurrent economic crises have meant frequent oscillation in the provision of resources, and the educational system is seen increasingly in terms of its ability to stimulate economic growth. But the social and economic forces have to be interpreted before their policy impact is felt, and it is the bureaucratic and political dynamics which make the interpretations.

Historically the central educational bureaucracy was in a weak position to influence the policy-making process for it exercised few direct managerial controls over educational institutions; there was a powerful traditional ideology against centralised intervention, most keenly felt in relation to university education; and it lacked sophisticated planning procedures. We have seen how at all levels of the educational system these established barriers to intervention have been eroded. In part this was a product of internally generated change, and in part a consequence of external political pressure; there was widespread agreement that the Department should have a firmer grasp of the educational system and a stronger input into the policy-making process. Once it had been agreed that the Department needed to adopt a more positive role, and it had developed the appropriate planning mechanisms, it was only a matter of time before more direct managerial controls would emerge. Thus in the case of the schools the days when the curriculum could be referred to as 'a secret garden' are long past, and even before the demise of the UGC it was evident that the state was pressing successfully for a clearer separation of research and teaching responsibilities, so undermining one of the central planks in the self-image of a university don.

One of the interesting aspects of these developments is that they in fact speeded up in the 1980s when the major political force, that is the government of the day, was manifestly deeply suspicious of its own civil service. As it turned out, it curtailed both university autonomy and academic influence in the policy-making process by increasing the authority of the central state apparatus. How is this conundrum to be explained? In terms of their broad ideological commitments, the Tory governments of the 1980s believed that goods and services were supplied most efficiently by the market. Could a market be constructed given that the Exchequer would continue to underwrite the overwhelming bulk of educational expenditure in Britain for the foreseeable future? Sir Keith Joseph, as Secretary of State, explored the possibility of introducing educational vouchers, but although he found the idea intellectually attractive he was persuaded that such a move would be impracticable (Seldon, 1986). Moreover, even a voucher scheme would presumably have been constructed in a manner that advanced the government's policy goals, for it is difficult to conceive of a commitment of public resources unconnected to the pursuance of official policy. A policy compromise was required, and it emerged in the form of the managed market.

If the demise of the educational voucher signified the termination of official efforts to create an educational market, then the DES remained as the only serious immediate mechanism available to the government in the pursuit of its policy goals. The Department was supposedly the instrument of government policy, and the obvious reaction to its suspect loyalty was to allay those suspicions rather than try to bypass what could be a very potent power base. Clearly the other traditional partners in the educational system, that is the local authorities and the teachers' unions, were – from the perspective of a radical Tory government – politically suspect. Matching the government's faith in market mechanisms has been its concern to both limit public expenditure, and to require of institutions greater accountability of their public funding. The Treasury has inevitably applied the pressure which, ironically, has led Beloff to claim that this erstwhile friend of the universities now poses the severest threat to their independence, and that it is a threat which persists regardless of the political make-up of the government (Beloff, 1990, 4–5). However, the DES has also proved to be a very useful government ally. While it was political pressure that led to the capping of the common financial pool from which the polytechnics were funded, it was the Department which led the discussions on creating formulae to determine both inputs into the pool and withdrawals from it. Moreover, while the Department's initial response to the deep governmental suspicion of quangos was to withhold its pressure for a national board to assume responsibility for the public sector of higher education (thus outflanking the local authorities), it was soon able to resurrect the idea and sell it to the government on the grounds that such a body would be able to manage the sector more effectively, including a more efficient use of resources. The arrival of the NAB is striking testimony to the sophisticated accommodation of the political and bureaucratic dynamics. Its demise demonstrates yet again the long-term political will of the DES, and is another manifestation of the evolving relationship between the two dynamics.

In spite of the general recognition that the DES has steadily increased its hold over the institutions of higher education, there are those who remain sceptical as to the real extent of its influence. Kogan, among several others, has been at pains to stress that the Department is not 'a monolith' (1987, 227–8). But surely the key consideration is not whether there are different policy positions in the Department, indeed it would be amazing – and very worrying – if there were not, but how significant is the departmental input into the policy-making process? It is our contention that this can be decisive even if there are internal departmental conflicts. The questions to consider are whether the Department sees an issue as falling within its jurisdiction, whether it can construct a consensus on policy, and whether it has the resources to implement its preferred options. While one can expect departmental differences at all three stages, this will not of itself negate its policy input.

100

The difficulty with much of the analysis in this field is that it is heavily determined by the very contemporary historical context, which not only denies the role of theory in favour of self-evident empiricism, but also in a rapidly changing situation can be caught out by the march of events. Writing in 1987, Booth offered a number of possible alternatives for the future development of integrated planning in the field of higher education, with an exceedingly cautious prognosis (1987, 72). But it was already very clear – as Booth also noted – that the government was determined not, as some were advocating, to cede its planning responsibilities to an 'overarching body', but to accept 'its own responsibilities for higher education policy and planning as these may be enhanced by the absence of such a body' (DES, 1985, 35). If this were to happen, it is evident that the planning responsibility would go to the single higher education planning branch that the DES had created in 1980. Booth may be correct when he was writing that the DES did little more than 'maintain the existing relationship between the department and the NAB and the UGC' (1987, 69), and (more contentiously) that the desire to extend the planning system was lacking, but government intentions were plain and this may well be a case of the political dynamic enabling the Department to realise its potential. Moreover, it can be argued that by amalgamating planning responsibilities for the two sectors of higher education into a single branch, the Department in fact preceded commensurate political action on the funding agencies by over a decade, and it was not until government action had caught up with departmental change that the latter could realise its full potential.

If the nation had experienced Labour, as opposed to radical Conservative, governments in the 1980s it is possible, if unlikely, that the bureaucratic and political dynamics would have reached a somewhat different accommodation. However, while the UGC might have survived longer, and perhaps the interlude of the UFC would have been avoided, a common funding body for the two sectors of higher education would have emerged. Indeed the Parliamentary Labour Party did not oppose the amalgamation of the UFC and the PCFC into the HEFCs in the passage of the *Further and Higher Education Act*, 1992. Labour governments have been more enamoured of state planning than Conservative governments, and have been very convinced of the need for close links between education and industry. It is likely, therefore, that whatever the funding mechanisms for higher education, the state under a Labour government would have been as *dirigiste* as when under Conservative governments, with much the same goals in mind. At present we have likened the pattern of control to that of a managed market. By that we mean the state controls the parameters within which the higher institutions function (through control of the legislative framework, issuing memorandum of guidance, and devising, through the funding bodies, mechanisms to achieve policy goals), while the institutions have to develop the appropriate strategies on how to respond to these constraints. It seems unlikely that Labour governments would have given the higher education institutions a freer hand, and equally, in view of past experience and the balance of political forces within the Labour Party, that they would have allowed the state to be more explicitly interventionist. On all the long-term broad policy fronts the outcomes, therefore, were unlikely to have been substantially different, although we would see this as the consequence of political and bureaucratic forces interacting within particular social and economic constraints, and not – *pace* Beloff – the apparent machinations of malevolent, and indeed allegedly incompetent, Treasury mandarins.

But, as we will discuss more fully in our final chapter, to manage a market requires constant attention to detail, both to modify the controlling parameters that regulate institutional behaviour, and to counter the potential incursions of other parts of the state apparatus. The UFC's first Chief Executive (Sir Peter Swinnerton-Dyer), in response to fears of the Public Accounts Committee that several universities were on the verge of bankruptcy, protested that the Council had no powers to intervene as the universities remained autonomous institutions, able to spend their grants as they saw fit (*The Times Higher Education Supplement*, 14 September, 1990, 1 and 3). After the débâcle of University College, Cardiff, the Committee undoubtedly felt that the Council should have had the authority to step in and take action before matters got out of hand. Lo and behold, we find in the *Further and Higher Education Act*, 1992 a clause which enables the Secretary of State to give explicit directions to the HEFCE about its provision of funding for institutions suspected of such mismanagement. We have made several references to general Treasury pressure upon the government machine. But besides facing pressure from on high, the Department also risks incursions upon its terrain from other spending departments. The emergence of the Manpower Services Commission, and a plethora of training programmes for the young unemployed, provide an excellent 1970s illustration of this. That this process is capable of being taken further is seen in the very recent decision to remove from the DES its responsibilities for civil science and leave it as the Department For Education. That the state will attempt to manage its commitment of resources more effectively is not in doubt: the key issues are what institutions and mechanisms it will employ to achieve this end. In all these changes there is undoubtedly one development that stands out, and that is the seemingly indeterminable decline in both the administrative responsibilities and the political influence of the LEAs. Power gravitates to both the centre and to the periphery as the middle levels of the old educational establishment evaporate.

6

The University Grants Committee

The story of the University Grants Committee's (UGC) development from its foundation in 1919 to its demise in 1988 is the story of how the state came first to believe and then to insist that the middle ground between itself and the universities should be state territory, owned and ruled. Obviously the universities did not agree and the UGC became the crucible in which the ideological and political struggle for control took place. Under the pressure of numerous and diverse events, the UGC adapted both its values and its structure in a continuing, and eventually vain, attempt to reconcile the two sides.

The pattern of that struggle was not uniform. The boundaries of the conflict moved forwards and backwards as conditions and strengths changed. Advances were not always held and the same ground was sometimes fought over more than once. General trends are none the less present and in this chapter are dealt with in terms of four phases in the UGC's development:

Phase One: Cultural Consensus and the Liberal University Ideal, 1919–39
Phase Two: War and the Nation State, 1939–52
Phase Three: Challenge and Response, 1952–74
Phase Four: Management or Martyrdom, 1974–88.

This chapter takes the reader up to the 1988 Education Reform Act and the creation of the Universities Funding Council (UFC). Developments since that time and the short but varied life of the UFC are dealt with in Chapters 5 and 9.

CULTURAL CONSENSUS AND THE LIBERAL UNIVERSITY IDEAL, 1919–39

The UGC was established on 14 July 1919 by a Treasury Minute. It had no statutory basis or powers, no bank account, no income-generating capacity, and no grant was made to it. And so it was to remain for the next 70 years. As an advisory committee, a common enough device, its terms of reference were 'to enquire into the financial needs of University Education in the United Kingdom, and to advise the government as to the application of any grants that may be made by Parliament towards meeting them'. Of itself this was nothing new. Several other advisory committees on university grants had preceded it beginning in 1889 with the ad hoc Committee on Grants to University Colleges in Great Britain, also created by a Treasury Minute. As an ex-secretary of the UGC, John Carswell, observes, 'The UGC was invented as a device in recognition of the autonomy of the universities, which was then financial as well as constitutional' (Carswell, 1985, 12).

From this inauspicious beginning the UGC was to evolve into one of the dominant influences in British higher education. Though its terms of reference were to change they remained fundamentally vague. Likewise its formal powers and constitutional status were to continue feeble and indeterminate throughout its long life. In their absence, an accumulation of custom and practice emerged to guide the development of the universities. Effectively a political vacuum was created in which ideology could operate unhindered by any precise definition by the state of the universities' purposes and responsibilities. Whoever controlled the dominant ideology would also control government policy on the universities.

Although to begin with some universities were sceptical of the state's intentions and of their ability to control the way in which the university–state relationship should develop, this scepticism soon faded. Throughout the first two decades of the UGC's existence it came to be considered axiomatic that the universities themselves should enunciate the guiding framework of values since they were, demonstrably, independent institutions. The UGC, after all, supplied only one third of universities' total income, the remaining two-thirds coming equally from endowments and local authorities, and it was thought essential by all concerned that this balance should be maintained. Statements about university self-determination during this period were seen as simply reflecting the reality of financial autonomy. Thus the UGC's 1921 *Report* urges universities to regard endowment funds as their central source of revenue: 'it was indisputable that only by a consolidation of a stable and substantial income from independent sources could the autonomy and progressive development of a University be assured' (UGC, 1921, para 18). Other

UGC reports of the 1920s and 1930s echo this sentiment and stress that the role of state money should be to stimulate other finance not act as a substitute for it (UGC, 1936, 49). The implications of this view were made clear in 1936 by Neville Chamberlain, Chancellor of the Exchequer, in a letter to Lord Crawford, Chancellor of the University of Manchester: 'If this [autonomous] character is to be maintained, it is necessary that economic independence of the universities shall also be maintained ... this condition places a limit upon the extent to which the universities should look to the State as a principal source of Revenue' (TES, 7 March 1936, 86).

Not only was the state a minority shareholder in the universities, it also provided its contribution in a manner guaranteed to minimise its influence over the way in which the money was spent. The mechanisms for funding the UGC were exceptional in two ways. First, until 1963 the UGC's money was obtained through the Parliamentary Vote on Treasury expenditure. Not surprisingly, the Treasury had neither the desire nor the expertise to develop a policy on how the money was spent but simply followed UGC advice. Much has been made of this arrangement: it has frequently been portrayed as a deliberate construction to protect university autonomy. However, like other aspects of the modern myth about the university–state relationship this may be a post-hoc rationalisation of an arrangement that was arrived at, at least partly, for practical reasons following a long argument between the Treasury and the Board of Education as to who could administer the university grant most efficiently (Owen, 1980, 257–8; Shinn, 1986, 29–41). (Between 1911 and 1919 the university grant had been administered by the Board of Education on the advice of the Advisory Committee on University Grants.) Owen maintains that the Treasury won the argument because it had a UK remit and could therefore administer money to all universities. The Board of Education dealt with England and Wales only.

Second, the UGC, or rather a deposit account which the UGC then allocated to individual universities, received its income as a grant-in-aid. A grant-in-aid is an exception to (a) the rule that expenditure within a Parliamentary Vote must be accounted for in detail to Parliament through the Comptroller and Auditor General and is subject to his audit and, (b) the rule that monies voted by Parliament that are unspent at the end of the financial year must be surrendered to Parliament. This technicality placed the UGC in an unusually privileged position *vis-à-vis* the state since it meant not only that it could build up reserves but also that it could dispose of its funds with little interference from its parent department and with the maximum of virement between heads of expenditure (Shinn, 1986, 50–51).

Up to 1939 the universities dictated the terms of the ideological climate within which any discussion of the universities took place. Academics, civil servants and politicians alike considered it perfectly natural that the state should be very much the subordinate partner in its relationship with the universities and that the administrative arrangements should reflect that subordinate position. As a result, the UGC was able to propagate without interference, albeit through suggestion rather than direction, its own values regarding the appropriate direction of university development.

These values were essentially those of the traditional liberal ideal of university education (see pp. 9–12). Deliberately formulated in the mid- and late-nineteenth century as an integral part of the Oxford and Cambridge reforms and the rise to power of the college don, the traditional ideal placed a premium on the democracy of collegiate life, the transmission of civilised values through the character education of students, close tutor–student relations and pure rather than applied or vocational knowledge. It served well as an ideological instrument of the newly self-conscious academic profession since, as Rothblatt points out, 'by creating men who would influence the direction of social change, they [the dons] hoped to affirm their own importance and authority and regain their independence' (Rothblatt, 1968, 247). Once the ancient universities had taken the initiative and pronounced a new set of educational values the civic universities were obliged to follow. In part this was a result of the fragility of the bourgeois culture of the provincial classes when confronted by the culture of Oxbridge and in part the simple fact that the civic universities recruited Oxbridge graduates (Halsey, 1961; Perkin, 1969, 20).

There was therefore no doubt in the collective mind of the UGC between the wars about the kind of university education they should be encouraging and their uncomplicated enthusiasm for the task before them illuminates the reports of that period. Much of their zeal centres on the quality of the experiences available to the student. Clearly, they argue, he should be concerned with much more than just vocational training.

> Has he also received that stimulation and enrichment of the whole mind which will enable him to lead a fuller and more interesting life and to play more adequately his part as a member or leader of the community? (UGC, 1936, 11)

How can arrangements be made to ensure that the student lives in an atmosphere of intellectual argument, daring and adventure so as to evoke in him 'an energy of the soul in the pursuit of excellence', asks the Committee rhetorically. Quotations from Bacon and Newman are used to support their reply that opportunities for fellowship are the best means available (ibid., 13). From a statement of principle the Committee then moves to a detailed and practical discussion of how student unions, sports facilities, a health service and halls of residence ('a great humanising force') can contribute to the realisation of that principle (ibid., 14–18).

Equally important to the UGC was the ideal of the student–teacher relationship: 'Educational administration is merely a device for bringing pupils face to face with the right teacher and so giving them an opportunity to catch fire from one who is himself aflame' (ibid., 19). For such a relationship to produce the kind of educated man the UGC considers desirable it must have an appropriate knowledge base to work with: the curriculum must not respond too readily to the pressure for more vocational and specialised knowledge. In its 1925 *Report*, for example, the Committee makes one of its frequent defences of liberal education when it emphasises the necessity of broadening the basis of university curricula so as to establish a proper relationship between science and humanities and prevent over specialisation, and quotes T.H. Huxley's Rectorial Address at Aberdeen in 1874 approvingly:

> But the man who is all morality and intellect, . . . is after all, only half a man . . . there is also a beauty which is neither moral nor intellectual – the beauty of the world of Art . . . in the mass of mankind, the aesthetic faculty needs to be roused, directed and cultivated; and I know not why the development of this side of his nature . . . should be omitted from any comprehensive scheme of university education (UGC, 1925, 10–11).

Even the ambiguities within the traditional liberal view of university education are faithfully replicated as Pattison and Jowett are duly evoked in a debate, pronounced irresolvable by the UGC, as to whether 'the primary purpose of the University is to turn out exact scholars, or educated men of the world' (ibid., 24). The same ambiguity is present in the attitude towards the research and teaching balance of the lecturer role. While advocating the practice of granting sabbatical leave the Committee makes it plain that it regards it as unfortunate if research into an abstruse aspect of learning 'were to be rewarded in preference to work which bears fruit, not in an accumulation of publications, but in the inspiration of teaching' (ibid., 43).

The centrality of institutional autonomy to the traditional university ideal placed the UGC in an interesting position. As a convinced believer in the ideal as the appropriate academic orthodoxy the Committee naturally wished to propagate it, but at the same time the extent to which it could do so was limited by the central value that universities should be free to organise their activities as they chose. So in its 1925 *Report* the UGC unreservedly states that 'we must say at once that even if we thought we could propound, as we are sure we cannot, an ideal common policy for all universities, we should not feel the slightest wish to press its adoption' (ibid., 12). On the other hand, the Committee could not escape the inevitable administrative implications of its role as, effectively, a resource-allocating body of the state. However reluctantly, it was obliged to make choices which, no matter how obliquely stated, constituted policy formation. In fact it did not find that part of the exercise particularly difficult since it had, as we have seen, a set of principles derived from the traditional ideal which were readily used to guide such choices. Where the real difficulty arose was with policy implementation. Having made the choices how could these be conveyed to universities in a way which would produce the desired response but would not contravene their sacred autonomy?

The UGC was well aware of the pressures upon it to take positive action and there can be no doubting the sophistication of its analysis of the issues. Its discussion in the 1936 quinquennial report of the relationship between birth rates, secondary and higher education numbers and graduate employment is impressive in its detail. In the same report it deals also with possible salary and career structures for academic staff (at that time no national agreements existed) and makes a number of suggestions on how universities can best deal with the uncertain employment of junior staff (UGC, 1936, 15–39). Earlier reports deal with the balance between arts and science, with applied science in particular, with the unnecessary duplication of departments, with libraries and with the government of universities. In each case recommendations for action are never made directly. Instead a whole glossary of terms such as 'suggestions', 'considerations', 'issues for closer examination' are employed to avoid giving offence to the sensitivities of universities.

The UGC's language style at this time is thus a reflection of the inhibitions placed upon it by its own ideology. Given its position between the state and the universities the UGC was forced to certain inescapable conclusions about what needed to be done. Yet it had to operate within a consensus which denied its authority to manage. An example of the linguistic contortions to which this gave rise was its belief in 1936 that existing teaching facilities should be consolidated at the expense of new subjects. It expressed its view thus:

> It is clear that the final decision must rest with each individual University. Nevertheless, looking at the matter from the outside, we cannot but think that at the present time the first of the policies indicated would, as a general rule, be the sounder. We do not mean that new developments should be ruled out, for some of these may be urgently called for. It might indeed be better to regard the two policies, not as clear-cut alternatives, but rather as being different directions in which it was desirable to move at different rates of speed. But when new developments have to be considered, no university ought to shut its eyes to unnecessary duplication (ibid., 40).

The Committee's use of constructive equivocation as a management art form depended for its success upon the goodwill of the universities. It was assumed that the universities would read between the lines, heed the implied messages and respond accordingly; that they would spontaneously arrive at the conclusions which the UGC implied they should do.

Some voluntary coordination among the universities was attempted; notably through the annual Conferences of the Universities of Great Britain and Ireland organised by the Universities Bureau and the meetings of the Committee of Vice-Chancellors and Principals. However, their effect was clearly limited. For example, throughout the 1920s the Committee consistently advised universities to remedy particular deficiencies in the salaries of teaching staffs and in libraries. Increases in the block grants were obtained from the Treasury and given to the universities on the understanding that this would happen. Yet in its 1930 *Report* the Committee is clearly embarrassed by the Chancellor of the Exchequer's criticism that this advice has not been heeded and gives the dire warning that if improvements do not occur by the end of the next quinquennium it would be 'profoundly disappointed' (UGC, 1930, 51). By 1930 it is obvious that someone has to be responsible for the sums allocated to the universities and that so far as the state is concerned the UGC is it. Although the university-dominated consensus held firm, rumblings there undoubtedly were.

The UGC's acceptance of the principle of university autonomy meant that in its relationship with existing universities it had responsibility without power. However it was much less hesitant in its treatment of the university colleges already on the grant list which aspired to full university status. As the adviser to the Privy Council on which institutions should be granted a Royal Charter, the UGC had to develop the criteria on which judgements could be based. At this particular point in the legal process it therefore controlled both the identity of, and access to, university education.

Reading, Southampton and Nottingham served an extremely rigorous apprenticeship as they struggled to fulfil the criteria set by the UGC, derived as these criteria were from the traditional university model and not from the civic universities. In its reports the Committee makes it clear that as the custodian of traditional values it bears a heavy responsibility to ensure that the appropriate candidates are selected. It is in its monitoring of those beyond the boundaries of the university fold and the cultural consensus that the management potential of the UGC is most clear. In the case of Nottingham, for example, the Committee insisted, using financial sanctions, on a revision of its constitution. It was particularly concerned that academics should be represented on the college's executive body, the Council, in sufficient numbers to safeguard academic autonomy and to ensure that as a university it should not become the 'tied house' of any special interest or calling (Shinn, 1986, Chapters 2 and 3).

In the inter-war years the UGC acted as the vehicle of the Oxbridge definition of academic orthodoxy and dispensed state monies to the universities with very few real strings attached. That it was able to do so unchallenged by the state is a reflection of the cultural consensus which united academics, civil servants and politicians alike. Indeed, as Carswell points out,

> The universities of 50 years ago were very closely integrated with the state as it then was, but in a quite different way [from today]; and they formed just as indispensable a part of the framework of national institutions as they do now. The links however were personal and social, not bureaucratic or formal. The universities and the machinery of Government in both its political and official aspects formed a kind of continuum, in which only the sketchiest of formality was either expected or required to maintain necessary relationships (Carswell, 1985, 159).

During this period the middle ground between the universities and the state was also common ground where shared values ensured an amicable intercourse. Although up to 1939 private finance was seen by universities as the essential guarantor of academic freedom, the initial suspicion of state money had been largely replaced by the belief that there was little risk of state intervention and that, in any case, the UGC would ensure that the universities' view prevailed. The Second World War was to change all that.

WAR AND THE NATION STATE, 1939–52

The total, and willing, subjugation of the universities to the war effort created the habits, procedures and legitimations of massive state intervention in their day to day lives. University autonomy is not an issue when the survival of the nation is at stake. The movement and coordination of departments, the requisitioning of buildings, the wholescale evacuation of universities, including London University, from vulnerable areas, the stimulation and control of university activities and in particular scientific research 'directly related to the various and developing needs of the war machine' took place on a much larger scale than in the First World War (UGC, 1948, 6). When the war then ended, such an administrative and ideological impetus had been built up that it took some years before the old academic orthodoxy was able to re-establish itself. By the 1950s it had done so, but so many aspects of the universities–state relationship had altered in the meantime that significant amendments had to be made to the old orthodoxy to enable it to cope with the new situation.

Even before the war ended, economic and occupational pressures upon the universities to produce larger numbers of specific types of manpower for the post-war Britain provided additional justification for a continuing state hand in university affairs. Numerous UGC and inter-departmental reports were produced in the mid-1940s dealing with the university educational needs of various professions: for example the Goodenough Report (medical education), the Teviot Report (dentistry), the Loveday Report (agriculture) and, probably most significant, the Barlow Report which asked for a substantial increase in the number of science and technology students (Barlow Report, 1946). Barlow was equally forthright on the change of role that was required of the UGC in order to help attain that increase, commenting that 'the State has perhaps been over-concerned lest there should be even a suggestion of interference with the independence of the universities' and that 'we think that circumstances demand that it [the UGC] should increasingly concern itself with positive University policy'. Barlow concluded 'It may be desirable for this purpose to revise its terms of reference and strengthen its machinery' (ibid., 33).

The amount of state support required to finance the expansion recommended by these and other committees, to begin to repair the structural ravages of the war and to counter the effects on university income of wartime inflation was quite massive when compared with pre-war state investment in the universities (see Appendix 3, Table 1). In 1945 the annual recurrent grant to the universities was double its pre-war level and for the first time the state took on the burden of financing capital building projects. As the UGC observed, this dramatic change of scale was 'rightly interpreted by universities as initiating a new era in their financial relations with the state' (UGC, 1948, 11). The pre-war ideal that the state should be a minority shareholder supplying one third of the universities' income was abruptly and, it would seem, permanently destroyed.

As the reality of the funding relationship between universities and state changed, so did the administrative arrangements supporting that relationship. Formal recognition of the change came with the modification of the UGC's terms of reference in July 1946. To the function of enquiring into the universities' financial needs and advising the government accordingly was added the clause:

> and to assist, in consultation with the universities and other bodies concerned, the preparation and execution of such plans for the development of the universities as may from time to time be required in order that they are fully adequate to national needs (as quoted in Owen, 1980, 263).

If the Committee was to carry out its new planning and executive function properly, additional administrative machinery was required. The situation was particularly urgent in the case of non-recurrent grants where the demands from the universities for capital expenditure on buildings and equipment far exceeded the amounts the government was able to supply in the light of its overall post-war building programme. Detailed procedures had to be developed to enable the UGC to make the appropriate choices both between and within university submissions. Thus its works and buildings sub-committee, which included representatives of the Ministry of Works, examined the plans and estimates of cost of buildings proposed by universities and made decisions between competing tenders, using both financial and architectural criteria, which the universities had then to accept.

To deal with the recommendations of the numerous reports on specialised manpower the UGC introduced earmarked grants as a selective mechanism for use within the recurrent grant, stating that these are 'almost inevitable when it is desired, for reasons of national policy, either to introduce new subjects of study or to secure rapid large-scale developments in departments already established' (UGC, 1948, 78). During this period the principle of the block grant, whereby universities were given a sum of money which they then allocated as they wished, was dramatically eroded as earmarked grants were extensively used to foster specific developments deemed by the UGC to be in the national interest. Earmarked grants constituted 27 per cent of the recurrent grant in 1947–48 and 31 per cent in 1951–52.

Before the war the UGC was only really busy when it was assessing the quinquennial financial needs of the universities and it once passed two years without any meetings (Dodds *el al.*, 1952, 83). Now the administrative pressures were constant as its role and activities expanded rapidly. The numbers of UGC staff increased from five in 1939 to 22 in 1945. A network of specialist sub-committees was set up, nine by 1945, to deal with the implications for universities of the manpower reports and the implementation of the earmarked grants. The Committee was evolving into a quite different animal to cope with the 'new and intricate relationship between the State and the universities' and its central planning function (UGC, 1948, 81).

The ideological context had also shifted dramatically. In the immediate post-war Britain central planning was an accustomed part of life. Throughout the war the CVCP had taken on the major planning role for the universities with the UGC concentrating on the negotiation of the appropriate grants from the government. So it was not unexpected that the CVCP should issue *A Note on University Policy and Finance in the Decennium 1947–56* in July 1946, at the same time as the UGC's terms of reference were altered, which stated that

> ... the universities entirely accepted the view that the Government has not only the right, but also the duty, of satisfying itself that every field of study which in the national interest ought to be cultivated in Great Britain is, in fact, being adequately cultivated in the university system, and that the resources which are placed at the disposal of the universities are being used with full regard both to efficiency and economy ... The universities may be properly expected not only individually to make proper use of

the resources entrusted to them, but also collectively to advise and execute policies calculated to serve the national interest, and in that task, will be glad to have a greater measure of guidance from the Government than until quite recent days they have been accustomed to receive.

Although this enthusiastic view of the state's involvement with the universities was to be tempered as wartime memories dimmed, the inescapable fact of majority state funding had none the less to be squared with the traditional emphasis on university autonomy. If private money was no longer the final guarantor of university independence, what was? The answer, which swiftly and conveniently assumed the status of ideological myth, had three parts. First, pre-war scepticism about the intentions of the state was replaced by the belief that, so far as the universities were concerned, the state was benign. Second, the view developed that the state needed the universities – to produce qualified manpower and scientific research – as much as the universities needed the state. An equal 'partnership' based on mutual respect was therefore seen as emerging quite naturally. Third, just in case, the UGC itself took on the newly vacant role of guarantor of university autonomy and was henceforth presented as the 'buffer' between universities and state. As the trusted servant of university interests the Committee became a necessary part of the new academic orthodoxy and thus completed the remarkable journey between 1919 and 1945 from administrative device to ideological symbol.

As public money suddenly and understandably assumed a new respectability so far as the universities were concerned, so private money found itself quietly downgraded. The roles were reversed and we find the UGC saying in a 1944 'Memorandum on questions of principle affecting post-war grants to the universities' that the 'acceptance of Exchequer money through the University Grants Committee tends to be less injurious to academic independence than reliance on municipal contributions or private benefactions' (quoted by Shinn, 1986, 277). Not everyone was convinced that the new values would promote healthy universities. Margaret Fry, longest-serving member of the UGC between the wars, recalled the Committee's commitment to the formula that a university should receive one third of income from fees and other earnings, one third from endowments, and one third from public money, local and central, and commented on the increase in state contributions:

There is here a real danger lest some institutions should fall into a mood of overdependence, losing the habit of initiative for a spirit of 'we send in the bill, you draw the cheque'. It is for this reason that it is to be hoped that they will make strenuous efforts to maintain as large a percentage as possible of non-Governmental income (Fry, 1948, 230).

However, writing in 1948, she was clearly swimming against the ideological tide.

Although the principle of university autonomy was amended to incorporate the fact that universities were increasingly becoming publicly funded institutions and that central guidance of some kind was inevitable, in other respects the traditional university ideal held firm and maintained its grip on UGC thinking. Despite the pressures upon the Committee and the universities, the changes in the Committee's role and the dramatic expansion in student numbers, the Committee never appears to have questioned in any fundamental fashion the traditional purposes of university education and, in this respect, remained committed to the pre-war ideology. It was never able to develop a set of values which resolved the tension between liberal and vocational education. Instead it preferred to try and manage the resulting ambivalence.

At the beginning of its 1935–47 *Report* where it is dealing with all the changes which have taken place the UGC states that 'any conception that may have existed of the universities as places of cultural luxury catering for a small and privileged class has passed away and will not return' (UGC, 1948, 6). Yet everything else that the UGC says in this and the 1947–52 quinquennial report about the nature of university education indicates that it simply intended extending the experience of elitist education to a larger number of students without changing the aims, methods or context of the experience. Given that the aim was still to educate the whole man and not simply to engage in vocational training, all the facilities which contributed to the quality of university life had to expand at the same rate as the increase in the number of students. Thus the reports are concerned with maintaining the high staff–student ratio and providing proportionally more libraries, student union rooms, refectories and private rooms for staff. Residential accommodation was considered particularly important because without it there was the 'grave risk of impairing, not only the academic standards which can be measured directly by examination results but also by those imponderable elements which form so valuable a part of university life' (ibid., 38). The scheme of the University College of North Staffordshire, later Keele

University, supported by the UGC included provision for all staff and students to be accommodated on campus.

The UGC felt strongly that the provision of all these supports for the 'wider educational experience', that is, cultural socialisation, was particularly necessary with the sudden increase of state-assisted students from 41 per cent in 1939 to 68 per cent in 1947. Such students were not subject to the 'pecuniary test'. This test, the Committee argued, had had 'the indirect effect that a considerable proportion of such students came from homes with some tradition of culture and some interest in art, literature and music' and so had acted as a cultural selection mechanism (ibid., 34). However, the new type of student therefore arrived with a cultural deficit which it was the responsibility of the universities to make up.

The UGC had taken state finance and state demands for expansion and incorporated both within a revised administrative and ideological framework. The net effect was to give itself identity, legitimacy and a key role in the university–state relationship. The traditional liberal ideal still dominated the middle ground but was now clearly reliant upon the UGC to maintain the stability of the situation through the Committee's sponsorship of the idea of 'partnership':

> ... the dependence of the universities on the state is balanced by a dependence of the state on the universities. Without the state, the universities cannot obtain sufficient funds to enable them to do their work; without the universities there would be no way of meeting the need for men and women adequately trained to advance knowledge and to hold positions of responsibility in government, industry and the professions. This mutual dependence is, we believe, fully realised on both sides, and has led to a sense of partnership which is full of promise for the future (UGC, 1953, 76).

The question which was to develop in the next phase of the relationship was how far the UGC could hold the middle ground on behalf of the universities in the face of mounting pressure from the state.

CHALLENGE AND RESPONSE, 1952–74

By the end of the 1947–52 quinquennium the adapted traditional university ideal was fully ensconced in the UGC. The universities had compromised but were once again in control of the middle ground following the peacetime retreat of the state from their hallowed territory. Traditional university values held sway, earmarked grants were discontinued and the cultural consensus between universities and state seemed to have successfully manufactured the way forward. The situation seemed secure.

Three pressures combined to shatter the consensus and bring an end both to this privileged treatment and, eventually, to the UGC itself. First, the state developed an educational ideology which was, and is, fundamentally incompatible with the traditional ideal. Second, the inherent contradiction between the elitism of the liberal ideal as a guiding set of principles and the realities of mass higher education produced continuing and irresolvable political tensions. In the end something had to give. Third, in managing these tensions, the UGC evolved into an administrative entity with an identity, logic and preferences of its own. In this section we trace the interaction of these pressures up to the abolition of the quinquennial system, the UGC's major organising principle, in 1974.

In Chapter 1 and in previous work we have characterised the ideological challenge to the traditional academic orthodoxy as the 'economic ideology of education' (Tapper and Salter, 1978, Ch. 7). Its major tenet is that education is an economic resource which should be managed by the state to maximise its contribution to the British economy through the production of appropriate knowledge and manpower. It values applied rather than pure knowledge and, in particular, emphasises the importance of science and technology, views the teacher and student roles as primarily concerned with vocational training rather than character education, and believes the educational institution should be responsive and accountable to the economy and the state. It thus conflicts with the traditional ideal at every point.

Although the economic ideology of education first emerged as a coherent set of state-sponsored values in the post-war years, it was not until 1964 when the UGC was transferred to the newly created DES that it came into direct conflict with the traditional ideal. Up to that point, while the new ideology was sponsored by the Ministry of Education, the universities were administratively linked to the Treasury via the UGC. The two sets of values therefore developed in parallel, kept apart by two separate arms of the state.

During the 1950s the conflict between the two ideologies of higher education remained latent with the universities and the UGC protected by the Treasury from the main force of the rising ideology.

None the less, as the body responsible for the universities and the main link in the partnership between universities and state, the UGC had to confront a growing number of administrative issues as the expansion gathered pace. Procedures had to be developed, information gathered, choices made and money allocated. The 1957–62 *Report* notes how the Committee is obliged to

> fit individual universities' plans into a national context, bearing in mind such factors as available resources of academic manpower, potential student numbers in various fields, existing gaps in teaching or research, national needs and so on. Moreover the total cost of all the universities' desirable projects is likely to exceed any financial provision that any government would be able to make. It is our responsibility, therefore, to achieve some balance in the total of new developments, between fields of development, and between universities (UGC, 1963, 190).

As the responsibilities and functions of the UGC grew so, necessarily, did its size and complexity. Between 1953 and 1958 only a small staff increase occurred, from 22 to 25, but in the next five years the numbers doubled to 50. Extra staff were needed to cope with the expanding work load of the various committees: by 1963 there were ten sub-committees and panels (for example medicine, new universities, building procedures), six independent ad hoc committees (for example methods of university expenditure, halls of residence, teaching methods), and several joint committees (for example libraries, superannuation) (ibid., 17).

The procedures governing the allocation of non-recurrent grants were progressively refined, partly in response to pressure from the Parliamentary Accounts Committee (PAC) (see pp. 38–42). In the case of capital grants for buildings, the detailed UGC monitoring of applications from universities proved beyond the skills of the works and buildings sub-committee and a small department of architects and quantity surveyors was set up, thus professionalising the function, and became a permanent feature of the UGC's administration. Further controls in this area were introduced following the report of the Gater Committee in 1956 on universities' methods of contracting, recording and controlling expenditure from non-recurrent grants. A UGC circular was issued to universities urging compliance with the Gater Committee's recommendations on improvements in the handling of non-recurrent grants (Gater Report, 1956). A subsequent review by

Sir Arthur Rucker of universities' application of the procedures confirmed that the Gater recommendations had been implemented (Rucker Report, 1960).

The flexibility of the administrative web linking universities and state enabled the UGC to cope with the immediate pressures of expansion. When a fresh administrative need was identified an extra part was bolted on to the existing structure. For example, when it was decided in 1959 that seven new universities were required, a sub-committee was set up to establish selection criteria and vet applications. Uniform procedures were evolved to plan their development. By this kind of ad hoc adjustment the Committee steadily accrued both decision-making and resource allocating power.

On 1 April 1964 the UGC became the responsibility of the newly created DES. Thereafter, its ability to define the ideological and administrative nature of the middle ground between universities and state was never to be the same again. The Treasury had always been an amiable friend and protector of the Committee and the universities, acting as a first line of defence against demands from Parliament for greater accountability. Taking the Committee on trust, it had never had the expertise or the desire to question either the policies of the UGC or the values on which these were based. The DES was quite clearly different. It did have higher education policies and it did have values which conflicted with those of the UGC.

Transfer from the Treasury, the senior Department of State in Whitehall, to the DES also led to a considerable fall for the UGC in the Whitehall pecking order. Its status was less and it was at a greater distance from the centres of Whitehall power and financial decision-making. It found itself having to bid first with the DES and then, within this, to the Public Expenditure Survey Committee (PESC) cycle – an exposed position at the end of a long chain of government decision-making (Shattock and Berdahl, 1984, 483–4). Although it took the UGC some time to come to terms with the fact, its days of special privilege were numbered.

The privileged treatment previously accorded the universities was founded on a consensus between themselves and the state regarding both the nature of a university education and the manner in which university–state relations should be managed. Requests from the universities for policy guidance from the state, such as that by the CVCP in 1946, were based on the assumption of shared values. As Niblett points out, 'unless there had been fundamental trust that any British government would have a close understanding of what university ideals were, no such request for guidance could or would have been made' (Niblett, 1952, 168). Transfer of the UGC to the DES brought exposure to the hostile economic ideology of education and the end of the consensus.

If the requirements of the economy are to be directly and effectively translated into precise educational policies, forecasts have to be made about the types and amounts of manpower which education should be producing. We have already seen how a plethora of committees enjoined in this task in the immediate post-war period when belief in the state's ability and right so to do was high. This activity then declined, particularly so far as the universities were concerned, during the 1950s but then re-emerged with added force in the 1960s. For the UGC it represented both a general ideological pressure for responsiveness to national needs and a question as to whether the Committee had the right or the ability to give universities specific student targets.

An important vehicle for the resurgent interest in manpower planning was the Committee on Manpower Resources for Science and Technology, chaired by Sir Willis Jackson and appointed by the Secretary of State for Education and Science and the Minister of Technology in 1965. This produced a series of reports which promoted the idea that one of the major weaknesses of the British education system is its failure to train and keep the quantities of scientists and technologists necessary for an expanding economy. First, the Dainton Report demonstrated the 'drift from science' in the schools and urged universities to reconsider their entry requirements in order to increase the flow of candidates into the sciences (Dainton Report, 1968). Second, the Jones Report showed there was a net 'brain drain' of engineers, scientists and technologists from our shores and argued that 'if scientists were brought up to believe (and trained by curricula which recognised) that manufacturing industry was an honourable occupation on which depended the economic strength and prosperity of the community, more would choose it as a career' (Jones Report, 1967, 37). Third, the Swann Report showed that postgraduate courses tended to produce individuals geared more towards further academic study than work in industry (Swann Report, 1968). Pressure for the reform of university teaching and research in other subjects came from the Bosanquet Committee on agriculture (1964), the Northumberland Committee on veterinary medicine (1964) and the Royal Commission on medical education (1968).

In the face of such continuing public pressure the UGC had no choice but to respond, though its conversion to the new order was ever less than wholehearted. Throughout the period up to 1974 there is a duality in UGC reports which suggests a probable division between its academic membership and its full-time officers. Thus, on the one hand, the 1962-67 *Report* evinces considerable scepticism about manpower forecasting indicating that

> In the Committee's experience, the precise nature of the qualifications of the university graduate is seldom, except in the specifically vocational field of university training, directly related to the category of employment which he pursues as his life career ... Their versatility is in itself a national asset (UGC, 1968, 95),

and that the 'whole field is, therefore, one of particular difficulty and sensitivity from the Committee's standpoint' (ibid.). In addition, notes the UGC worriedly, there is the problem of relating student demand to manpower requirements since the size and balance of the flow of candidates for university admission are not related to any significant extent to the size and balance of the national needs for graduate manpower (ibid., 97).

On the other hand, the same report contained a detailed discussion of the Dainton, Jones and Swann Reports and others and their implications for the universities. The reports had been referred to the relevant sub-committee which in some instances had then come back with recommendations for selective action. In the case of agriculture several university departments had closed on the UGC's recommendation and in the case of area studies earmarked grants had been used to speed developments. However, in the largest and most important fields of science and technology the Committee relied on blanket exhortation of the universities to gear a larger part of their 'output' to the economic and industrial needs of the nation, arguing that 'few things could be more vital to the national economy at the present time than the proper deployment of highly qualified scientific manpower and the application of research to the solution of current technological and economic problems' (ibid., 107).

Coupled with these pressures was the fact of continuing rapid expansion. Between 1962 and 1967 the full-time student population rose from 113,000 to 197,000 and the number of institutions on the UGC's Grant List from 26 to 42. This was what Carswell has called the universities' Augustan Age, a rather brief one as it happens. To deal with it the UGC's staff more than doubled from 50 in 1962 to 112 in 1968 and the number of sub-committees increased from 10 to 14.

As the size and complexity of the UGC grew, rather like Topsy, so the strength of its internal administrative dynamic began to assert itself in the form of demands for better management tools and information. Whether it liked it or not, the UGC was seen by the DES as responsible for the universities just as the local authorities were responsible for the polytechnics. Yet it had no established means of executive management and relied instead on implied threats and informal arm-twisting. A prior condition of a move towards rational management is a reliable and uniform information base. In 1965 a working party was set up under the chairmanship of Sir Harold Sanders 'to review the content and layout of the financial and other returns submitted to the University Grants Committee by universities with a view to improving them as instruments of comparative analysis of university past and projected expenditure' (ibid., 141). Armed with this information the UGC intended to improve its own decision making and to promote greater cost consciousness among universities by publishing annual statistics of subject group expenditure and student load.

At this point, the duality in the Committee's thinking, or double-think, becomes very obvious since its recurrent funding of the universities is founded on the block grant principle which, as the Committee reiterated in its 1962–67 *Report*, 'has long been regarded as necessary to ensure a reasonable measure of academic freedom and to avoid the "management" of the universities by the Government or by the Committee. We regard the maintenance of this principle as one of our cardinal duties' (ibid., 137). If funding cannot be directed because universities can spend their block grant as they wish then management information becomes irrelevant. In fact the contradiction is more apparent than real because by 1967 the block grant principle had become no more than a useful political myth. In order to receive a block grant universities were obliged to submit detailed development plans and the UGC made it perfectly clear that once the grant had been allocated 'no major departures from the lines of development that have been discussed should be made without reference to the Committee' (ibid., 138).

For the 1967–72 quinquennium the UGC took the logic of this position a step further and, in addition to sending a private letter to each vice-chancellor, issued a public Memorandum of General Guidance which covered in detail the UGC's judgements about the general policies and particular problems common to most of the universities for the quinquennium. In the private letter each university was informed of an individual target of student numbers, divided into four categories by postgraduates and undergraduates and by science and arts-based subjects.

The traditional ideal assumes that universities are autonomous institutions free to determine their own curricula and research activities. In the post-war years the concept of partnership between the universities and state had been evolved in order to retain the idea of autonomy and to include the reality of state funding. The UGC played a necessary part in this arrangement. Summarising the position in its 1962–67 *Report*, the Committee stated that provided universities were duly responsive to national needs and operationally efficient 'their proper freedom would be respected and safeguarded by the interposition between them and the Government of an independent University Grants Committee in a buffer role' (ibid., 82). However, the reality of central direction by the UGC in the 1960s contradicts this passive interpretation of the Committee's role and so in the same report it observes 'we are now inescapably involved in making positive judgements, an activity *which goes far beyond the capacity of a buffer or shock-absorber'* (ibid., 179, our stress). As the Committee becomes more 'dirigiste', as it puts it, so its language changes to include words like 'cost consciousness', 'plant utilisation' and 'unit cost'; words which resonate uneasily with the style of the traditional ideal but which are perfectly compatible with the economic ideology of education.

During this period, the increase in the UGC's power over the universities is matched by a decrease in its power *vis-à-vis* the central bureaucratic state. Its declining influence in Whitehall and Westminster was made abundantly obvious in 1968 with Parliament's decision that the accounts of the universities and the UGC should be open to scrutiny by the Comptroller and Auditor General. The decision was reached in the face of outright UGC opposition based on the argument that this would be an infringement of university autonomy. As well as introducing greater accountability, the state also took two important areas under its direct control. After the war there had been a well-established practice whereby the universities raised their scales of student fees in a uniform manner in accordance with the proposal of the CVCP and with the UGC's approval at the beginning of each quinquennium. In 1966 it was decided that in future the DES would determine the level of fees instead. Second, in 1970 new machinery for salary negotiations was established which included the AUT, CVCP and DES but excluded the UGC.

As the prestige and influence of the UGC diminished so, inevitably, it became increasingly unable to determine the nature of the middle ground between universities and state. The fading power of the traditional ideal in this arena is matched by the irresistible rise of the economic ideology of education, producing a UGC with a totally split personality. With the transfer of the UGC from the Treasury to the DES the protective cloak of the cultural consensus is stripped away and the UGC exposed to the normal exigencies of government. Clear and final recognition of this came with the abrupt ending of the quinquennial system in 1975, half way through the 1972–77 quinquennium, when inflation reached 20 per cent and the government abandoned the universities' building programme.

MANAGEMENT OR MARTYRDOM, 1975–88

By 1975 the UGC was in a state of simmering uncertainty as it strove to reconcile two irreconcilable ideological positions. The Committee was not helped by the attitude of the DES, which, because it had not worked out how to get more control over the education system as a whole, was unable to give the Committee clear signals on what should be done. Then came the economic crisis of 1974–75 which to the DES was an opportunity very much to be seized and used to demolish its historical role as a department with 'responsibility but without power'. Having waged and won an ideological struggle which, by the end of the 1970s, had left itself centre stage, the Department could then turn back to the problem of the universities in the 1980s. In between, the UGC was left treading water.

Traditionally the DES had shared power in primary, secondary and further education with the teacher unions and the LEAs. In a decentralised education system the Department was obliged to persuade and cajole in order to get things done since it had no direct control over curriculum, examinations or finance. The economic crisis gave the DES the opportunity to wage an ideological campaign which argued that if education was to act as the servant of the economy and help save the country from bankruptcy then it had to be efficiently managed: the country could not afford to leave educational change to the vagaries of the present system of decentralised control. Educational power must be centralised to ensure the efficient use of education as an economic resource.

In *Education, Politics and the State* we showed how the Department deliberately and effectively stage-managed the Great Debate on education to promote these ideas, beginning with Prime Minister James Callaghan's speech at Ruskin College, Oxford in October 1976 (Salter and Tapper, 1981, Ch.9). With the able support of Her Majesty's Inspectorate (HMI), the DES produced a series of publications in 1977 and 1978 which seized and held the ideological initiative to such effect that the teacher unions were swept to one side and the LEAs forced to concede that change must come. Ironically, the position has since been consolidated with the help of the New Right which, through its demands for better quality and higher standards, could be used to justify greater accountability to the state (see pp. 29–35). Having thus legitimised the principle of central control in education, it has been put into practice through successive Education Acts which have given the Department progressively greater controls in all sectors of education, including the universities.

During the mid- and late 1970s and with rather more important matters in mind, the DES chose to leave the UGC and the universities on ice. If the UGC had any lingering belief that it still enjoyed a special relationship with the central state bureaucracy this was soon dispelled as the effects of the economic crisis came home. At the end of 1973 the Committee was told that there would be a 10 per cent cut in the rest of the quinquennial grant. Then in 1974–75 the incoming government reduced university building starts from £30.6 million to £11.5 million. Thereon the quinquennial system was dead and the universities spent the rest of the decade crisis planning on a year to year basis and wondering what was going to happen next.

The bureaucratic pressure within the DES for the rationalisation of higher education as a whole increased with the merger in 1980 of Higher and Further Education Branch 1 (HFE1) which was responsible for non-university higher and further education, with HFE3, which handled university policy, to form a new 'super-branch', FHE1. The clear intention was to develop the means to manage higher education as a single entity. With non-university higher education well in hand it was time to deal with the universities themselves.

It is an interesting coincidence that in July 1981, at the same time as the Green Paper *Higher Education in England Outside the Universities* proposing the setting up of NAB was published, major cuts were announced in the recurrent grant to universities. Over the next three years the cuts were to amount to 17 per cent for the university system as a whole. As a catalyst for jolting the UGC into a more active management stance the cuts produced considerable effect as the Committee suddenly found itself in the business of the allocation of even scarcer resources. There was no time for the considered discussion of the ideological soundness of the task before it. Selection criteria had to be rapidly developed and judgements made using an information base which had not been designed for the task because intervention on such a scale had historically been regarded as unnecessary and undesirable. Precisely what these criteria were is unknown but they produced reductions in the recurrent grants of individual universities ranging from 44 per cent to 6 per cent.

Once the UGC was moving, the DES gradually accelerated the administrative momentum, steering in a particular direction. In July 1982 Sir Keith Joseph, Secretary of State for Education and Science, wrote to the UGC requesting the development of a strategy for higher education into the 1990s. The following year a further letter from the Secretary of State set out what was wanted in the familiar terminology of the economic ideology of education: more efficient use of resources, a shift towards technological, scientific and engineering courses and other vocationally relevant forms of study. The letter also stressed the importance of cooperation across the binary divide (UGC, 1984, 41).

The ensuing ideological battle was short and not particularly sharp, with the result a foregone conclusion once the state had demonstrated it was prepared to use its financial muscle. In 1964 Robbins had noted that 'there is no absolute safeguard against interference with the distribution of grants to universities. It is a convention that Government abstains. But it cannot bind its successors: nor is its agreement likely to imply abstention in the face of major difficulties' (Robbins Report, 1963, 237). As the system of values of which that convention was a part withered, so did the power of the convention. A blur of official documents followed Sir Keith's requests culminating in the Green Paper on Higher Education in May 1985 in which the DES, unequivocally and symbolically, asserted its ideological victory.

There is little confidence shown in these documents in the ability of the traditional ideal to resist the march of the new values. Instead there is an awareness that the universities would have been better advised to put their own house in order in the late 1970s – though whether this would have made any difference to the state's ultimate intentions is open to doubt. The amount of movement towards the state management of universities varies, with the UGC's *A Strategy for Higher Education into the 1990s* (1984) accepting it with reservations and the CVCP's Jarratt Report (1985) on efficiency in universities embracing it wholeheartedly. Indeed, the Jarratt Report may well prove to be a seminal document in that it sets out the administrative apparatus the universities require in order to be able to deal effectively with the pressures from the state. In so doing, it makes no genuflection to the traditional academic orthodoxy but instead asserts a system of administrative values based on the principle that 'universities are first and foremost corporate enterprises to which subsidiary units and academics are responsible and accountable' (CVCP, 1985, 22). Significantly, the Report also saw itself as the vehicle for change and recommended both the monitoring of universities' responses to its proposals and an inquiry into the role, structure and staffing of the UGC which it viewed as not interventionist enough. Less categorical, but basically moving in the same direction, were a procession of reports from the Advisory Board for the Research Councils (ABRC) and the Advisory Committee for Applied Research and Development (ACARD) examining the funding and organisation of university research and ways in which research resources can be more selectively allocated (ABRC, 1983 and 1983a; ABRC/ACARD, 1983; ABRC/ACARD/DES, 1982; see pp. 175–7).

The political significance of the Green Paper *The Development of Higher Education into the 1990s* is that it is a statement of the economic ideology of education as it applies to higher education in particular, with the recently added dimension of the efficient management of educational change by the central state very much in evidence. Not surprisingly, it constantly echoes the Ministry of Education's reports of the 1950s with its emphasis on economic performance, international competition, and the need for qualified manpower (particularly scientists, engineers and technologists). New Right themes are blended in in terms of an over-dependence on public funding contributing to higher education's insensitivity to economic needs and reluctance to change. Better institutional management is advocated as the means for overcoming these problems.

Having obtained ideological supremacy, the DES needed to translate this advantage into tangible gains. The Green Paper therefore announced the Department's acceptance of the Jarratt Report's recommendation that a review of the UGC be conducted. This review by Lord Croham, and the likely flavour of its conclusions, was given added weight by the subsequent announcement in the Secretary of

State's letter that the review would form part of the government's policy for applying to non-departmental public bodies the methods and lessons of its Financial Management Initiative with the objective of improving performance. The review was thereby explicitly locked into part of the state's administrative dynamic.

In the meantime the UGC's own administrative dynamic had begun to respond to the financial and ideological pressures from the central state for the more direct management of resources. This internal administrative response of the UGC has to be seen quite separately from its external ideological response since it was driven by separate forces. The cathartic experience of the 1981–84 cuts had brought home the absence of the administrative techniques and information needed to make the decisions required. It was imperative that new techniques be devised which would stand up to both private and public scrutiny. In November 1985 the Committee sent out Circular Letter 22/85 'Planning for the Late 1980s: The Resource Allocation Process'. This was the first step in what the UGC saw as the development and progressive refinement of funding according to a known formula based on planned student numbers and teaching and research based criteria. In the subsequent and supporting Circular 4/86 'Planning for the Late 1980s: Recurrent Grant for 1986/87' it states:

> The Committee's approach to the distribution of grant represents a radical break with tradition. In the past grants have been settled by adjustments to figures rooted in the concept of deficiency funding and representing the accumulation of earlier decisions which, because they were taken at different times and for diverse reasons may have produced inequities. Universities have rightly complained that the process is obscure and have encouraged the UGC to develop a more rational and systematic approach.

For the new system to work efficiently the UGC had to have a suitable information base as a necessary aid to its decision making. However, for obvious historical reasons universities have quite different systems for recording and storing data about their own organisation and finance. Following a recommendation from Jarratt, a joint CVCP–UGC working party was set up on management statistics and performance indicators in order to help establish a uniform information base, producing its report in autumn 1987.

The Croham *Review of the University Grants Committee* (1987), in the short period that it was relevant before it was overtaken by the speed of events, supported the direction in which the Committee was heading. It welcomed the new resource-allocating methodology and made recommendations designed to improve the UGC's financial management of the universities and render it more accountable and responsive to both the government and employers. However, for the DES, Croham was simply a holding operation while it prepared for the formal and statutory recognition of its ideological victory. With its hegemony over the traditional liberal ideal now assured, the Department was no longer interested in yet more amendments to the creaking, seventy-year-old administrative device called the UGC and once it had prepared the necessary legislation Croham became irrelevant. To the victor goes the spoils and with the implementation of the 1988 *Education Reform Act* and the creation of the UFC the division by the state of the spoils of higher education began.

CONCLUSIONS

The resilience of the traditional university ideal is considerable. It is undoubtedly alive and well in universities. However, it is now equally certain that the struggle for the middle ground between universities and state is over and that the state has won. Ideologically and politically, the state has reclaimed the territory which it leased to the universities when it created the UGC by a Treasury Minute in 1919. Given the strength of the economic ideology of education, there is little possibility that academic values will again dominate the universities–state relationship. After years of managing, or more accurately not managing, educational change through a laborious process of prodding and nudging, the central state created a new organisation, the UFC, with the express intention of making its power felt.

The shift in the balance of power between universities and state since 1919 has not been a steady and predictable process of educational change. Between the wars, the universities' initial suspicion of routinised state contributions to their resources was soon replaced by a confidence in their own ability to determine the form that relationship should take. This confidence was reinforced by the reality of their financial independence whereby only a third of their funding came direct from the UGC. In a surprisingly short period of time, given its non-statutory basis, the UGC acquired a self-confidence in its own role as propagator of traditional university values. The reports of the 1920s and 1930s resonate with its self-belief in its mission. Those colleges which aspired to university status were required to serve a long and arduous apprenticeship to ensure that they adequately fulfilled the criteria laid down by the UGC.

During this first phase of the UGC's development the state had no alternative view of university education with which to challenge the Committee's traditional values. Nor did it wish to do so. The common cultural background of the Committee members and the Treasury officials to whom they related ensured a sympathetic hearing for their requests for funding and Parliament did not consider it appropriate to monitor the monies allocated to them. At this stage, the middle ground between universities and state was very much common ground.

The subordination of the universities to the national war effort during the Second World War produced an unprecedented acceptance of state intervention in their affairs which continued for some years after the war had ended. At the same time, numerous reports were published demonstrating the contribution universities should make to the production of professional manpower. Given the ravages wrought upon themselves by the war, the universities were only too willing to accept state money to help rebuild both the nation's qualified manpower and their own infrastructure. The effect upon the proportion of universities' income received from the UGC was marked, rising from 36 per cent in 1938–39 to 60 per cent in 1947–48.

With the reality of financial dependence upon the state came a significant amendment to the traditional liberal ideal of the university. Whereas previously it had been the universities' ultimate financial independence which had been seen as the guarantor of their autonomy, now the UGC was accorded that honour and duty. Within this revised system of values, the Committee was the 'buffer' between universities and state and the relationship between universities and state was characterised as a 'partnership' based on mutual dependence.

Faith and trust in the UGC on the part of the universities was clearly necessary in the post-war era given its expanded activities and influence. Earmarked grants were extensively used, constituting 31 per cent of the recurrent grant in 1951–52, to promote particular subject areas, and a detailed administrative machinery was developed by the UGC to vet and control university building projects. Its permanent staff increased from five in 1939 to 22 in 1945 and nine specialist sub-committees were set up to deal with the additional administrative demands.

Although the Committee's administrative form evolved rapidly in the post-war years its relationship with the state, that is the Treasury, remained much the same. It remained protected from wider political pressures and, in particular, from the emergence in the 1950s of the hostile economic ideology of education in the Ministry of Education. Then, with the transfer of the UGC to the newly created DES in 1964, its unique access to a major centre of political power was ended. Its status in Whitehall declined and it became part of the embryonic system of higher education.

The demands of the economic ideology of education that the universities be responsive to industry's needs for scientific and technological manpower coupled with the massive expansion in student numbers of the 1960s led to further growth in the administrative web linking the Committee and the universities. The UGC was in the unenviable position of being held responsible by the state for a university system which it did not have the power to manage effectively. In addition, its adherence to the traditional university values and the importance of university autonomy meant that at periodic intervals it had to assert that it did not have the right to intervene in university affairs while at other times it would claim that it was becoming more *dirigiste*. The effect of this 'Janus-like posture' (UGC, 1968, 180) upon the personality of the Committee was to split it completely.

With the economic crisis of 1974–75 and the effective end of the quinquennial system the UGC was placed in a position of limbo from which it was only rescued by the 1981 cuts. Previously the DES had concentrated its efforts to expand its ideological and managerial power on the primary and secondary sectors of education and had largely left the universities alone. But with the cuts the pace of change quickened as the UGC, in company with the ABRC and the research councils, was forced to devise new methods of allocating resources which were too scarce even to be spread thinly. As a result the mid-1980s saw the publication of a plethora of reports from the UGC, DES, ABRC and CVCP where the final decline and fall of the traditional liberal ideal of the university and the rise of the new managerialism was duly recorded. In the event, the ability of the UGC to resist state pressure once its ideological base had been eroded proved to be very limited. The task now was to recast the relationship between the state and the universities in a new form: one that recognised the vastly increased role of the Minister and the Department but rejected the administrative straitjacket that increasingly had been the hallmark of the UGC.

7

The National Advisory Body and the Polytechnics and Colleges Funding Council

The histories of the National Advisory Body for Higher Education (NAB) and the Polytechnics and Colleges Funding Council (PCFC), although sequential, constitute quite different stages in the expansion of DES power and in its ability to manage change in what became known as the Public Sector of Higher Education (PSHE). In many ways the NAB was simply a neutral arena in which the plurality of interests then extant in PSHE could apply their lobbying skills in the hope of influencing the outcome of its deliberations. The territory of the NAB was poorly defined, its sovereignty questionable, the rules of engagement vague and the alliances both within and across its borders many and varied. By contrast, the PCFC was clearly a colony of the DES, statutorily dependent on the Department for its membership, exclusive in its decision making and unrepentently executive in its style.

In charting this sea-change in the satellite organisations of the central state, we are basically tracing the last ten years of a war of attrition on the local authorities waged by the DES over two decades. Although a prime example of bureaucratic in-fighting at its best, it is also a demonstration of the importance of the overlap between the bureaucratic and political dynamics at key points in the change process. Without that overlap, and the extra impetus it generated, much of the Department's guile would have gone unrewarded.

RESPONSIBILITY WITHOUT POWER, 1972–82

The 1972 White Paper *Education: A Framework for Expansion* set out a ten-year strategy for education in terms of 'the objectives at which the Government are aiming, the lines on which they intend that each programme should develop and the resources they are planning to devote to their attainment' (DES, 1972, 1). In the case of higher education this meant that by 1981 there would be significant change: an increase of full-time students from 463,000 to 750,000 (the new total to be split evenly between the university and non-university sectors), a decrease in the number of initial teacher training places from 114,000 to between 60,000 and 70,000, and a real increase in public expenditure from the 1971–72 budget of £687 million to £1,120 million. So far so good. As a planning exercise pure and simple the document is clear and convincing. The only problem was that the Department did not have the direct power to implement its proposed policies. It had instead to work through a plethora of indirect and cooperative mechanisms in order to achieve its ends.

Hence *Education: A Framework for Expansion* is noticeably light on the organisational details of how its targets are to be achieved. The Department's dependence on the goodwill of the local authorities is manifest and reflected in its ritual, and obligatory, genuflections to the importance of the consultative way forward:

> Last year, after long and helpful discussions between the Secretary of State and the local authority associations, it was agreed in principle that improved arrangements were needed for the co-ordination and provision of higher education in the non-university sector if the anticipated programme of expansion was to be planned to the best advantage (ibid., 46).

And it welcomed the recent decision of the associations to set up the Local Authorities' Higher Education Committee whose function was 'to consider and advise on the provision, coordination and future development of higher education in the local authority sector' (ibid.). At the same time it noted that the colleges of education, the majority of which were voluntary colleges outside the local authority sector, would have somehow to be included in a reformed system but that the nature of the organisational solution remained 'unresolved'.

In order to understand the complexities of the situation faced by the DES in 1972, and the distance it had to travel if it was to become a state agency with real clout, it is necessary to unravel the threads of the limited powers which it was able to exercise in the public sector of higher education, both formal and informal, as it strove to nudge its policies forward. An overarching complication was that these powers were separately, and differently, exercised in the local authority and voluntary colleges sectors.

While recurrent funding for the voluntary colleges was controlled and allocated directly by the DES, that for local authority colleges was very emphatically not. From 1959, finance for Advanced Further Education (AFE) in the 105 LEAs had been allocated through a national 'pool' which, from 1968, was managed by the LEA Pooling Committee with a DES chairman and secretariat. The Committee had no expenditure control powers; it was purely concerned with what LEA expenditures were 'poolable' and could be included in the global needs element sum of the Rate Support Grant (RSG) to local authorities. However, LEA contributions to the pool were not related to their AFE constituencies but were made in proportion to their school population (69 per cent) and non-domestic rateable value (31 per cent) (Matterson, 1981, 122). From the Department's point of view the problems inherent in this system were twofold. First, the responsibility for authorising the expenditure was separate from the responsibility for raising the money and hence the possibility of establishing a central-local accountability line was remote. Second, it was essentially a demand-led system largely insensitive to central direction and so incompatible with any national planning ambitions the Department might have.

However, what the Department did control was capital funding and, within the considerable constraints of frequent oscillations in public expenditure targets, used it as a rather blunt instrument of policy. In the further education system, LEAs initiated building projects subject to the approval of the DES for any capital expenditure over £40,000; for teacher training colleges in the maintained sector, the threshold was £20,000. Voluntary college capital projects were funded 80 per cent by the DES and 20 per cent by the voluntary body (Locke, Pratt and Burgess, 1985, 81).

It can be argued that this control was primarily a negative one dependent upon a flow of requests for approval on which the Department could impose a reactive, and *post hoc*, pattern. This was certainly the case in the area of course approval where the 1944 Education Act gave the Secretary of State the power and the duty to decide whether a proposed new course in further education or teacher training should be set up. The criterion used in both sectors was the administrative viability of the course: the demand for it and the geographical proximity of similar courses. Effectively this decision was made on the advice of the Regional Advisory Councils (RACs) and Regional Staff Inspectors (RSIs) in further education and the Area Training Organisations (ATOs) and the university-based Institutes of Education in teacher training. So in practice the power of the Secretary of State was diluted by the functions of the infra-structure on which he was dependent. As a means of influencing the national pattern of advanced further education it was also heavily circumscribed by the fact that the power of accreditation and valida-tion of courses rested in other hands. Once approved by the DES, a course would then enter a quite separate cycle of assessment by an accrediting body, generally the Council for National Academic Awards (CNAA), the Technical Education Council (TEC), the Busi-ness Education Council (BEC), or, in the case of some teacher training courses, a university, where the criteria used would be the academic viability of the course. It was therefore quite possible for the DES to approve a course only to find it subsequently rejected by an accrediting body!

Armed with a ten-year strategy for public sector higher education but lacking the means to ensure its ready implementation, the Depart-ment had to employ and evolve a network of indirect mechanisms which blocked some courses of action and encouraged others. It was a network made up of the legal powers of the Secretary of State, statutory instruments, guidance issued by the DES through circulars and administrative memoranda, and the conventions of the 'national system locally administered' through the DES–LEA partnership. For several reasons, the primary vehicle for this ambitious undertaking was teacher training.

It is noticeable that seven out of the 1972 White Paper's nineteen chapters are devoted to teacher training. In part this was because of the pressures for change generated by demographic shifts, the frag-mented organisation of teacher training itself, and the recommenda-tions of the James Report (James Report, 1972). But in part also, one suspects, it was because teacher training was what might be called a suitable case for treatment. It was already vulnerable enough to be used as an instrument for prising loose the local authority grip on advanced further education and establishing the precedent that it is the central state which decides education policy. With higher educa-tion as a whole set to expand, but initial teacher training numbers to contract, it was clear that the colleges of education were an organisa-tional stress point which needed to be rationalised, either through closures or through other measures. The White Paper gave some guidance to what this might mean when it stated that

> The Government intend that ... some colleges either singly or jointly should develop over the period into major institutions of

higher education concentrating on the arts and human sciences, with particular reference to their application in teaching and other professions. Others will be encouraged to combine forces with neighbouring polytechnics or other colleges of further education to fill a somewhat similar role (DES, 1972, 44).

The advantage of teacher training as a vehicle for the expansion of DES power was that it allowed the optimum and focused use of the powers already possessed by the Department. It was, and is, the statutory duty of the Secretary of State to determine the number of teacher training places and, in a situation where the policy was one of contraction, this became a 'capping' power which could be used to force the pace of organisational change. Detailed guidelines and criteria for the implementation of these changes were then set out in Circular 7/73 and LEAs and voluntary bodies invited to prepare plans on the future of their individual colleges. This left the DES in the position of being able to make its selection of the plans it approved depending on how well they fitted its designs. Course approval was rationalised by the Further Education Regulations of 1975, which brought together the arrangements for controlling courses in further education and teacher training under the single umbrella of the RACs and Secretary of State; and the level of teacher training accreditation was standardised by Circular 9/78 which abolished the Certificate in Education to make teaching an all-graduate profession. Finally, from 1974–75 the previously separate further education and teacher training local authority pools were merged into a single AFE pool.

The effect of this carrot-and-stick approach to the central management of educational change was dramatic. By 1981 change had been initiated in 200 institutions of further and higher education: 25 colleges of education had been closed, 12 integrated with universities, 37 amalgamated with polytechnics, and from 78 colleges of education and 34 colleges of further education had emerged 59 colleges of higher education – a new creature on the educational landscape (Locke, Pratt and Burgess, 1985, 35). But for an increasingly ambitious Department it was a tedious and long-winded way in which to implement policy. A week may be a long time in politics, but a decade of shepherding reluctant institutions is even longer. New mechanisms of central control had to be found which drove policies forward and forged enduring linkages between planning, financial and decision-making procedures.

By the mid-1970s sufficient progress had been made in the Department's drive to propagate the economic ideology of education and its legitimation of central educational control to justify the setting up of an inquiry on the maintained sector (Salter and Tapper, 1981, Ch. 9). In terms of concepts and style, the resulting Oakes Report is a clear affirmation of new economic and organisational values. It defined its objective as 'the creation of a management system which would make most effective use of the available resources to meet the demand from students who qualify for higher education and, in so far as they can be assessed, future needs for qualified manpower' (Oakes Report, 1978, 10). This, it maintained, would be a rational system with the functions of, first, intelligence – that is the collection of information on the demand for, and supply of, higher education; second, the planning of changes to meet the demand; third, within limits set by the government, determining necessary provision and where it should be made and allocating resources; and accordingly, fourth, overseeing the cost-effectiveness of the system as a whole (ibid.). As a statement of a DES planning utopia the report undoubtedly had much to recommend it. But when its recommendations are assessed using the crude political criterion of their likely impact on the centre–local balance of power, the conclusions reached are much more equivocal.

Although Oakes recommended the setting up of a national body, the inquiry's terms of reference set clear limits on its possible functions by stating that 'local education authorities will be major providers of higher education, and this has ruled out of consideration the wholesale transfer of institutions to other management' (ibid., 8); in other words independent polytechnics directly funded by central government were not on the agenda. Furthermore, the recommended membership of what was to be a purely advisory body reveals a rough balance between local authority and DES interests: it was to consist of an independent chairman, eight to ten local authority members, three National Association of Teachers in Further Education members (NATFE), two Committee of Directors of Polytechnics (CDP) members, three representing the Secretary of State and eight to ten others nominated by the Secretary of State. Crucially, if the local authority members were united on an issue but in a minority, the matter was to be referred to the Secretary of State; in other words the local authorities had a veto. Funds for the national body were to be provided by local authorities collectively through a pool.

Given the dominating position of the local authorities in the Oakes proposals, it is reasonable to suppose that the Department's enthusiasm for them was at best lukewarm and that it was not unduly dismayed by the opportunity presented by the Conservative victory in 1979 to return to the drawing-board. Oakes had taught the DES a number of important lessons about the unbridled pluralistic politics of public sector higher education which it turned to useful effect in the period between the arrival of the new government and the announcement of the setting up of the NAB in December 1981. In particular it had learnt that covert control of the bureaucratic agenda is at least as important as overt political dominance of the structure. This is reflected in its handling of the competitive game play leading up to the creation of the NAB.

The Department's first step was to cap the AFE pool using its new powers under the 1980 Education Act. As well as forming a natural part of the Conservative government's drive to control public expenditure this measure created an unprecedented situation in maintained higher education and an objective need for an entirely new set of bureaucratic procedures with which to deal with it. At a stroke the system had been shifted from one which was demand-led by the local authorities to one where the rationing of scarce resources was the overriding issue. The political opportunity, which the DES immediately seized, was the definition of the new resource-allocating procedure. From mid-1980 a working group led by Stephen Jones, assistant secretary at the DES with responsibility for the local authority sector of higher education within Further and Higher Education Branch 1, worked at developing a mathematical formula based on average unit costs which would resolve the technical problems of allocating a cash limited pool (*The Times Higher Education Supplement*, 1981; David, 1981). The clear implication of its proposals was that the local authorities were to be marginalised by a DES defined and administered formula funding system. Once the formula was in place the traditional duty and right of LEAs to define educational and resource needs would be rendered redundant by the formula's 'objective' decision-making.

It is doubtful whether the local authorities were fully aware of the significance of these developments or, if they were, whether they had the united political will to generate an alternative approach. Their energies were concentrated instead on two issues: ensuring that they would dominate any national body for public sector higher education and opposing the ambitions of their larger polytechnics for independence and national status. On both issues they were inevitably in continuing conflict with the polytechnic directors and chairmen (see for example Flather, 1980 and 1980a).

In January 1981 the Stephen Jones proposals on formula funding were leaked to *The Times Higher Education Supplement* in concert with proposals to establish a national body with minority local authority membership for a new higher education sector of 98 institutions made up of 29 polytechnics, 38 local authority colleges and 31 voluntary colleges – a constituency remarkably similar to that of the PCFC eight years later (*The Times Higher Education Supplement*, 1981; David and O'Leary, 1981). In an internal memorandum the Secretary of State, Carlisle, argued that the projected contraction of higher education in the 1980s required central control and management and added, in the familiar language of the economic ideology of education, that this was 'to safeguard excellence while also achieving a more cost-effective system of higher education offering courses relevant to the nation's economic needs' (ibid., 1981, 2). Not surprisingly, the reaction of the local authorities was swift and hostile. More importantly, they succeeded in creating an alliance with the Conservative Party's National Advisory Committee on Education which effectively fragmented the political party dynamic and ended the DES's chances of getting its radical new scheme adopted in the immediate future. Following Cabinet level discussions, in July the Green Paper *Higher Education in England Outside the Universities* was published containing two possible models of the projected national advisory body. Model A was a revamped version of one canvassed by the Committee of Local Education Authorities (CLEA) with an all-inclusive sector of colleges and polytechnics and Model B was the DES's preference for a central body with substantial controls over a sector of about 90 institutions. When the structure of the National Advisory Body was announced in December 1981 the political compromise was obvious, with the weight of the formal advantage going to the local authorities. Their skilful manoeuvring within the Conservative Party had produced the desired result. As Sharp sums it up: 'In many ways the need to preserve Conservative Party unity had prevailed over a scheme which, albeit in different guises, senior DES civil servants had been pushing for over a decade' (Sharp, 1987, 163).

THE NATIONAL ADVISORY BODY: 1982–88

The new body had a three-tier structure: (i) a Committee composed of the Under Secretary of State, the independent chairman of the Board and three representatives each from the Association of County Councils (ACC) and the Association of Metropolitan Authorities

(AMA); (ii) a Board with an independent chairman, six representatives from the DES, three each from the ACC and AMA, two each from the CDP and NATFE, one each from the Association of Principals of Colleges, the Standing Conference of Principals and Directors of Colleges and Institutes of Higher Education, the Council for National Academic Awards (CNAA), the Business and Technical Education Council (BTEC), and the Trades Union Congress (TUC) and one observer each from the UGC, the Confederation of British Industry (CBI) and the Welsh Joint Committee; and (iii) ad hoc groups of appropriate interests to examine particular academic areas and subjects and report to the Board. It was, indeed, a pluralistic paradise with a built-in capacity for endless manoeuvres, shifting alliances and repetitive debates; a single national forum for the game play previously conducted in a variety of political arenas.

Although at the public level the Department had lost on points to the local authorities and although the NAB was a far cry from the DES dream world of central planning and management, at a more subtle level the new body could be seen to have certain advantages. Initially the Department's view was that the NAB in its existing form was very much a temporary solution, a pause between the necessary and the desirable: Waldegrave, then the minister responsible for higher education, described its emergence as 'a fire brigade exercise' and the DES formally referred to it as the *Interim* National Advisory Body (O'Leary, 1981, 9). Wary of the substantial local authority presence on the new body, in the short term the Department retained its direct control over the voluntary colleges of higher education rather than including them under the umbrella of the NAB: hence its inaugural full title was the National Advisory Body for *Local Authority Higher Education*. But beyond this scepticism lay the recognition that the NAB might be used as a mechanism for legitimising a more focused and enhanced deployment of the Department's existing powers.

The NAB was not a statutory body and so whatever it did had to make use of the current legislative framework. Its purpose was

> to advise the Secretary of State on the academic provision to be made in institutions in selected fields and, in respect of those fields, on the appropriate use of his powers with regard to the apportionment of the advanced further education pool and to the approval of advanced courses (DES, 1981, 24).

The extent to which the power to decide on 'the apportionment of the advanced further education pool' could be enhanced was dependent upon the formula funding methodology developed by the Stephen Jones working group. What were the implications of the methodology for the maintained higher education sector and how forceful would the NAB be in introducing it? The hope of the Department was that it had constructed a procedural mechanism which, under the pressure of known cash limits, would begin to introduce rational allocative criteria to a sector which had traditionally relied on historical ante-cedents as the basis for the distribution of the AFE pool. As the DES observed in its 1981 *Annual Report*:

> For the previous methods, which had relied heavily on local authorities' forecasts of AFE expenditure, the new method substituted a central calculation of requirements by relating a set of common unit costs to the student numbers in each authority. *The effect was to put the greatest pressure to reduce expenditure on those authorities and institutions with the highest unit costs* (ibid., our stress).

The technical simplicity of this statement is perfectly balanced by the complexity of the political repercussions which reverberated through the PSHE, over the next seven years as the NAB struggled to impose a succession of different funding formulae on a diverse and resistant sector of what, by 1988, was over 400 institutions. A survey of unit costs conducted in 1982 revealed that the gap between the highest and lowest institutional unit costs was £3,000, more than the average unit cost for all institutions, and that the largest colleges were more expensive than the average polytechnic (O'Leary, 1982). Given such variation, any redistribution of funding based on average unit costs, however weighted, was bound to be painful for some institu-tions. Theoretically, the pain could be ameliorated by local authority 'topping up' of the pool allocation to its colleges or polytechnics to its previous level. However, the extent to which this occurred varied depending on the local relationships, not always convivial in the case of polytechnics, and the separate downward pressure on local authority finance from the mid-1980s onwards. It was therefore inevitable that there would be pain and that the NAB and its formula would come under attack from the most disadvantaged institutions in a particular year.

What of the second DES power, 'the approval of advanced courses'? In practice this had been delegated to the RACs and their decisions had, through an incremental effect, produced a national distribution of courses which had never been reviewed as a single system. This the NAB swiftly proceeded to do in its 1982–83 planning exercise using a number of different scenarios ranging from level funding to a 25 per cent cut. Underpinning the exercise was the assumption that in future individual course approvals would be superseded by a new pattern of scrutiny by broad subject groups or programmes and whole institutional reviews (*The Times Higher Education Supplement*, 1982). Like the funding formula, this was an attempt to rationalise a sector where national criteria had never been applied before. The only difference was that courses, rather than money, would be redistributed. Over the next six years, the combined effect of these twin central pressures for a reallocation of funding and courses was to put the NAB centre-stage in a fluctuating interplay of organisational relationships.

Throughout this period of political game play the objective of the DES, in what was essentially a holding operation, was the accumulation of bureaucratic advantage through the manipulation of the NAB's relationships with the other players; not an easy task given the as yet unsophisticated and highly visible nature of its powers, the influential position of the local authorities, and the volatile nature of the relationships themselves. Despite the fact that a single body, the NAB, was dealing with both funding and course approval lines of control over the sector, the actual decision-making procedures, and the information-collection functions on which those decisions were based, remained separate areas of activity. The enduring question in the rationalisation of any area of education is how to link issues of cost with issues of quality in order to be able to control the relationship between the two and ensure that lower cost does not equal lower quality. In the case of the NAB this issue dominated its relationship with two independent sources of information on course quality: the CNAA and HMI.

As the major accrediting body for the sector, the CNAA automatically collected information on the academic quality of courses which, from the NAB point of view, would be extremely useful in its planning exercises. Unlike the UGC, the NAB did not have an infrastructure of subject committees regularly visiting and monitoring institutions. It was therefore inevitable that the NAB would press the CNAA to release this information and, as the NAB sought to improve its management of the cost–quality equation, to release it on a regular basis. The CNAA was in a difficult position. To retain its legitimacy as an accrediting body it had to retain its independence, and be seen to do so, but given the insecurity of its own position (the Lindop inquiry into its future was appointed in June 1984), it was anxious to be seen to be useful. As an uneasy compromise, it contributed information to the NAB's first planning exercise, including a ranking of town and country planning courses to the much publicised chagrin of the polytechnics, and argued that it had an 'independent contribution' to make to the long-term planning process (Gold, 1984).

A further difficulty was that the closer the CNAA got to the NAB, the more sensitive became its relationship with the freedom-loving CDP. Its periodic attempts to devolve some accrediting and validating powers to some institutions through different permutations of its 'partnership in validation' scheme failed to satisfy most, and alienated many, of the senior institutions in the sector as they looked increasingly towards the university model of self-validation and accreditation (see for example Gold, 1985). Conversely, the more independence the CNAA gave to public sector institutions, the less useful it would be to the NAB and, by inference, its progenitor, the DES. The last thing the Department wanted to see at this stage was a group of institutions in the public sector of higher education, with degree-awarding powers, drifting out of its control into quasi-university status. When the Lindop review of the CNAA recommended that a top tier of such institutions be set entirely free it received short shrift indeed from the Secretary of State, Sir Keith Joseph (Gold, 1986).

As a source of information on course quality, HMI was in a much less ambiguous position than the CNAA, could freely offer its services to the NAB, and was no doubt encouraged, or told, to do so by the DES. Its established membership of the RAC course approval committees meant that its role as a quality monitoring agent was already accepted and could be developed without much hindrance. We have argued elsewhere that the logic of HMI's position in the early 1980s meant that whatever independence it enjoyed from the DES would be eroded by pressures for it to service the Department's policy needs more directly (Salter and Tapper, 1981, 109–11). It is certainly true that by 1984 its role in PSHE was being described by the DES as less advisory and more 'inquisitorial' as it built up a database of quality judgements (Gold, 1984a).

However, it would be wrong to assume that HMI's information-gathering function could be neatly slotted into the NAB's operation. In fact quite the reverse could happen and there were examples of both the CNAA and HMI opposing NAB policy in order to protect course quality: in 1983 the CNAA criticised the NAB's first plan for not being selective enough to protect high quality courses and in 1984 HMI wanted the pool allocation formula changed to increase funding for initial teacher training (O'Leary and Gold, 1983; O'Leary, 1984). The organisational identities of both the CNAA and HMI were too firmly established to allow them to become a ready instrument of the NAB's quality control needs in the way that the NAB, as a newly created, politically sensitive and rapidly evolving animal, required. Ideally it would have created that function in-house but did not have the resources or political support so to do.

Nowhere were the ambiguities in the relationships between the NAB and the other game players more clearly evidenced than in the field of teacher training where the DES continued to maintain its particular interest. Teacher training was conducted by both the local authority and the voluntary colleges. Overall numbers were set by the DES on the advice of the Advisory Committee on the Supply and Education of Teachers (ACSET) so the planning exercises of the NAB had to take account of these targets. Accreditation and quality issues were separately addressed by the CNAA, the education sub-committee of the NAB, HMI and the DES-sponsored Council for the Accreditation of Teacher Education (CATE). How these various bodies were to relate, and whether the NAB should in some way orchestrate their activities, always remained unclear. Not unnaturally there was pressure from the NAB for the voluntary colleges to be included in its brief in order that it could plan for them as well as for local authority teacher training colleges. In February 1985 the Department, probably with some trepidation, duly extended the remit of the NAB from its existing *Local Authority Higher Education* to include the voluntary colleges and the responsibility for teacher training, and so become the NAB for *Public Sector Higher Education*. The following year it took the responsibility for teacher training back again (*The Times Higher Education Supplement*, 1986, 36)!

The basic problem faced by the DES was that the highly visible politics of the NAB sector made stable alliances difficult to establish and even more difficult to sustain. Since the pluralistic make-up of the NAB required such alliances if serious rationalisation of the sector was to take place, stalemate became the order of the day and, partly through the blocking power of the local authorities and partly through this inertia, the DES came to see the NAB as the protector of the status quo. Repeated calls by the Department for the closure of courses and colleges almost invariably produced an NAB response which recommended inaction or delay. Hence the 1986 planning exercise was completed without a single closure or merger in a sector of 400 institutions (O'Leary, 1986).

Nor did the new approach of formula funding escape the attentions of the adversaries. If it had been the hope of the DES that this approach would allow resource allocation decisions to rise above the common political fray to a plateau of rational-technical debate, then it was not long before it was sorely disabused. The diversity of the sector meant that any attempt to impose a funding method based on a common unit of resource would help some institutions and harm others. As a result, the formula itself was politicised and, whenever allocations were about to be announced, became the focus for strenuous bouts of special pleading. The polytechnics regularly, and usually successfully, insisted that the higher quality of their courses should be recognised through a special weighting to take them above the average unit cost more appropriate to the colleges.

By the mid-1980s it was clear to any disinterested observer that the NAB's role as a national planning and funding agency was severely constrained by the anarchic politics inherent in its constitution. As a holding operation for the central–local tensions in PSHE it had, from the DES perspective, outlived its usefulness and a new way forward had to be found. Two documents prepared the ground, in different ways. The first, in 1985, the Green Paper *The Development of Higher Education into the 1990s*, was an emphatic statement of the economic ideology of education as applied to the higher education sector and dealt with how that sector could contribute to improved economic performance through the production of qualified manpower, particularly scientists, engineers and technologists, more applied research, better links with industry, more efficiently managed institutions, and so on – the customary litany (DES, 1985). As such, it conducted the ideological exercise which, we have argued, is a necessary precursor of structural educational change (Salter and Tapper, 1981, Ch. 3). The second, in 1987, the White Paper *Higher Education: Meeting the Challenge*, then set out the organisational details of the proposed new arrangements (DES, 1987).

By this time the central state was in a much stronger position to force through the changes it required. Five years of arduous compromise with the multiplicity of interests in PSHE had convinced successive Secretaries of State that there must be an easier way of dealing with this sector. With the ministerial support it required now in place, the Department was able to put forward its original 1981 proposals in the knowledge that it had at last reached the point where the final victory over the local authorities was in sight. Its confidence was reflected in the unequivocal style of the White Paper which stated baldly that the 'existing national planning arrangements are unsatisfactory', that 'more progress needs to be made in rationalising scattered provision and concentrating effort on strong institutions and departments' and that 'a more effective lead from the centre' is called for (ibid., 29). And in a calculated, probably long-nursed, side-swipe at the disruptive habits of local authorities, the Department quotes the Good Management Practice Study of the NAB as showing that

> the good management of polytechnics and colleges is inhibited by the excessive engagement in their affairs of local authorities exploiting their role as the formal employer of staff and the overseer of budgeting and purchasing matters (ibid., 23).

THE POLYTECHNICS AND COLLEGES FUNDING COUNCIL, 1988–92

In accordance with the provisions of the 1988 Education Reform Act, the Polytechnics and Colleges Funding Council (PCFC) was incorporated on 1 November 1988. Unlike the unwieldy NAB, its membership was restricted to fifteen: between six and nine of these were to have had experience in higher education and the remainder in industry, commerce and finance (ERA, Chapter II, Section 132). All were to be appointed by the Secretary of State for Education and Science. There was no representation for the local authorities, trade unions or special interest groups such as the CDP. The break with the pluralistic past was complete.

It was considerably more, or perhaps more accurately less, than the simple transfer of a group of institutions from one pair of political hands to another. The NAB advised on the funding of 405 institutions: 29 polytechnics and 346 other colleges under local authority control, plus 30 voluntary and other colleges directly funded by the DES (DES, 1987, 25). The PCFC administered funds to 83 independent institutions: 33 polytechnics, 23 general colleges and 27 specialist colleges (PCFC, 1991, 27). The difference is explicable in terms of the Department's ambition to create a unified system of higher education which included both the universities and the maintained sector. Had it merely transferred the motley collection of 405 NAB institutions to the PCFC lock, stock and barrel, the administrative difficulties of subsequently integrating this with the university sector would have been insurmountable given the predominantly further education character of many of the colleges.

The NAB system therefore had to be unscrambled using a clear set of numerical criteria which selected local authority entrants to the PCFC elite on the basis of: (a) 'substantial size' (350 or more full-time equivalent home and European Community higher education students) and (b) 'engaged predominantly in higher education' (more than 55 per cent of their activity in higher education) (DES, 1987, 29-30; ERA, Chapter II, Section 121). The obvious consequence was that the smaller, predominantly further education colleges were filtered out and remained under local authority control, albeit only until the 1992 *Further and Higher Education Act* and the creation of the Further Education Funding Council liberated them as well. Such radical realignments in higher education naturally required suitable linguistic recognition and so we find that for a brief four years in British educational history there appears the 'polytechnics and colleges sector' – the transition phase between the 'public sector of higher education' and the ultimate goal of a single 'higher education sector'.

With a slimmed-down and more homogeneous sector now in place, run by a PCFC devoid of the institutionalised acrimony which had characterised the NAB, the Department could look to the future with an unprecedented confidence and optimism. Not that it was taking any chances. Just in case it had forgotten anything it included this legal catch-all in the 1988 Act: 'The Secretary of State may by order confer or impose on either of the funding councils such supplementary functions as he thinks fit' (ERA, 1988, Section 134). And the Secretary of State's guidance to the PCFC leaves no doubt as to its preferred style of operation:

> I shall ... expect to see two key features. The first is a means of specifying clearly what polytechnics and colleges are expected to provide in return for public funds. The second is a systematic method of monitoring institutional performance. I attach particular importance to the latter since, without measures of performance, the Council will have the means neither of satisfying itself that institutions are providing what has been promised at acceptable quality, nor of making comparative assessments of institutions as a basis for future allocations of grant (PCFC, 1990, 13).

It was clearly intended that the PCFC should resolve the old conundrum of the cost–quality relationship in education, once and for all.

However, the difficulty embedded in the new situation was, as always, what the appropriate balance should be between institutional independence and central control. The DES might have had one expectation of the PCFC but the newly liberated polytechnics, having shaken off the shackles of local authority imperialism, had quite another. Furthermore, they were encouraged in their belief both by the emphasis in the White Paper *Higher Education: Meeting the Challenge* on the importance of entrepreneurial skills, attracting private money and competition and by the stress in the letter of guidance to the PCFC on institutional flexibility within a non-bureaucratic funding methodology. Now that central control had become a realistic possibility, the tension within the state between the values of bureaucratic management and market mechanisms was unavoidably highlighted. Over the forthcoming years these values were to fuel the many debates about accountability, funding methodology, and strategic planning.

At the initial meeting between the PCFC and the heads of institutions in December 1988, the PCFC told them that its job was to fund, not plan, and that the polytechnics and colleges must contrive their own best balance between the cost of their courses, their academic quality and student demand for them (*The Times Higher Education Supplement*, 1988). After this rather rash statement of a 'hands off' policy, the PCFC spent the remainder of its four-year tenure constructing, and experimenting with, various financial and administrative systems of accountability. Its fundamental imperative was that it was accountable to the DES and Parliament for the monies which it dispensed, that this accountability had an unyielding statutory basis, and that it therefore had to possess the means to assess and, if necessary, correct, errant institutions. For its part the DES, after its experience with the poor or non-existent accountability systems of the NAB and UGC, was determined that state money should not be allocated without a fair return. It is worth noting that the Education Reform Act gave the Funding Councils explicit powers when making grants to include conditions 'enabling the Council to require the repayment, in whole or in part, of the sums paid by the Council if any other condition subject to which sums were paid is not complied with' (Section 134). Another Cardiff was not an option, or so it seemed.

In this spirit, the PCFC rapidly constructed an infrastructure of financial accountability and audit embodied in a Financial Memorandum to which all institutions were required to adhere. It made it a condition of funding that institutions appoint both an audit committee and an internal audit service using the Council's 'Audit Code of

Practice' which it duly evaluated (National Audit Ofice, 1991, 16). However, no matter how comprehensive may be the web of audit and control, when situated within a system of devolved decision-making it will always face the risk that managerial incompetence will find a way to overspend. Then follows, under the pressure of parliamentary scrutiny, a further attempt to produce a watertight system of financial accountability while simultaneously recognising the importance of institutional independence. PCFC experience of this continuing dilemma was stimulated by the financial problems faced by Dartington College of Arts in 1990 and highlighted in the National Audit Office report on the PCFC. It responded by issuing a circular to all its polytechnics and colleges which stressed 'the importance of not undermining the position and responsibilities of senior managers at institutions while at the same time securing satisfactory oversight of the financial health of institutions so as to meet the requirements of parliamentary accountability'. As an added safeguard, the PCFC required that it be automatically notified of a specified list of major types of change in an institution, though what it would do with the information was unclear (PCFC, 1991a, 2). But at least it could be seen to have taken action!

Given the continuing pressure from the New Right for the introduction of market mechanisms into the relationship between state and higher education, it was to be expected that one of the Council's key priorities would be the development of a new methodology for the distribution of funds between institutions which introduced an element of competitiveness into the situation (National Audit Office, 1991, 10). As this methodology began to emerge, so it became clear that there was a conflict between the logic of competition, on the one hand, and that of public accountability, on the other. If competition between institutions is to be effective as a means of improving the quality of the higher education service, two criteria have to be met: first, institutions must be independent to act as they see fit and, second, the system must reward some and penalise others (there will be risk and there will be winners and losers). However, if public accountability is to be effective two different criteria have to be met: first, institutions must be monitored, and where necessary corrective steps taken, to ensure that public funds are used efficiently (their independence is restricted) and, second, the risk element in the competition must be controlled to prevent institutional collapse since this is both politically unacceptable and a clear sign of accountability failure (there can be no outright winners or losers).

The key political question was whether a compromise could be found which simultaneously satisfied all four criteria. In its consultative document *Funding Choices* the Council recognised that the use by the NAB and UGC of a centrally determined unit of resource as the mainspring for the funding of teaching 'does not encourage institutions with average or below average costs to seek further improvements in efficiency or to seek radically different and more cost-effective ways of providing teaching' (PCFC, 1989, 19). To achieve those goals competition on the basis of institutionally determined price is required instead, it argued, and set out a number of funding options. The favoured option was what has become known as the 'core plus margin' approach which was duly employed in 1990–91. In that year institutions received 95 per cent of their 1989–90 core funding to enrol 95 per cent of their 1989–90 student numbers – each institution bidding for the remaining margin of unallocated funds, proposing price as well as number of students, for nine academic programme areas. In this way, it was hoped, limited competition could be introduced while protecting institutions through core funding from excessive and destabilising change.

Where did this leave the requirement for public accountability: the need to ensure that the state received an appropriate return for its funding? *Funding Choices* had suggested that the quality of the education provided could be monitored using HMI and performance indicators and subsequent adjustments made to institutions' allocations, though there was no indication of how this funding-quality relationship would be managed in practice. In taking this issue forward, the Council's Committee of Enquiry into Performance Indicators significantly shifted the ground of the argument when it maintained that 'the evaluation of an institution's performance *must be rooted in a planning process* through which the institution has set out its mission and objectives in terms which allow actual and planned performance to be compared' (PCFC, 1990, 33, our stress). Given that such a planning process would need an information format common to all institutions to facilitate inter-institutional comparisons, a timetable and central coordination, one can see immediately that it would severely constrain the operation of any market mechanisms, and no doubt please the DES immensely.

The translation of discussions about funding into discussions about planning continued in the PCFC's consultative document *Recurrent Funding Methodology: Developments to the Basic Approach for 1991–92* where one of the key areas identified for improvement was the role of strategic plans in the bidding process. Detailed guidance then followed in the consultative document *Strategic Planning, 1992–93* on the components and five-year cycle of strategic planning and the function within this of an institution's Annual Operating Statement as a means for the review of performance. Each institution would develop its own plan which would simultaneously provide information for both itself and Council use, 'facilitate comparisons of performance against the plan, make the planning process live and pro-active and facilitate future developments in performance indicators and teaching quality' (PCFC, 1991b, 4). Having said all this, the document was refreshingly honest about the DES bureaucratic dynamic driving the Council's advocacy of strategic planning:

> The Council's main need for strategic information is to inform the DES cycle in securing funds for the sector – and subsequently in being sure that those funds have been used effectively (ibid., 6).

Without the information, the DES's ability to compete successfully in the inter-departmental competition for funds would be reduced.

As strategic planning began to spin its bureaucratic web around the funding methodology, so the operation of the embryonic market in higher education was further restricted. In reacting to the tensions generated by this process, institutions found themselves in a double bind. On the one hand, the uncertainties of the new bidding arrangements left the polytechnics, in particular, arguing that quality, and not just price, should inform the bidding assessment decision – which would require a centrally led infrastructure to make such judgements. On the other, their instinct was to oppose any central moves to limit their independence and, in the first few months of the Council's existence, they had objected strongly to requests that they submit corporate plans for Council examination (Yarde, 1989). But with the disappearance of the NAB and the consequent truncation of their lobbying lines of access, institutions found themselves simply reacting to a PCFC-led agenda of events.

CONCLUSIONS

With the publication in 1972 of *Education: A Framework for Expansion*, the DES embarked on what was to prove a twenty-year programme to bring both maintained and non-maintained sectors of higher education under a single system for the central management of educational change. In the case of the PSHE, this programme had three stages: ten years of nudging and pushing using a variety of informal methods, six years of pluralistic politics within the unstructured orbit of the NAB and four years developing the tools of central management under the aegis of the PCFC. Each stage provided the DES with useful political lessons and a guide to its handling of the subsequent stage.

In 1972 the Department had only limited direct control over the funding and administration of public sector higher education. It directly funded the fifty-plus voluntary colleges, administered the RACs and the course approval system, and approved capital schemes above a certain level. Beyond that, recurrent funding was allocated by the demand-led AFE Pool, colleges were largely the responsibility of the local authorities, and accreditation and validation power rested with independent bodies, notably the CNAA. In this situation, the management of change was a circumspect affair requiring the manipulation of regulations and guidelines, the judicious use of the negative power of approval for courses and capital schemes, and lengthy negotiations with the local authorities. It says much for the Department's tenacity that between 1972 and 1982 it used such cumbersome methods to restructure teacher training, for which it had direct responsibility; but to apply such inefficient methods to the whole of the devolved PSHE would have achieved very little for a great expenditure of time and effort.

Although by the early 1980s the Department was clear that what it wanted was a maintained sector of higher education concentrated in fewer than a hundred institutions, centrally funded and managed, it lacked the support of the political party dynamic: the local authorities were strong enough to ensure that there would be a high cost to be paid by any minister supporting a policy which seriously undermined their role in PSHE. Thus the NAB was born: a tangible tribute to the need for a national system of maintained higher education in the context of a devolved system of provision and power. It is almost as though its constitution was designed to provoke irreconcilable disputes, rather than constructive advice on the rationalisation of the sector, given the range of interests represented. The Machiavellians might argue that that is what the DES wanted in order to demonstrate the unworkability of the arrangement and the appeal of its own favoured option, but not – surely? – for six years.

Some advances were made by the Department during the NAB period 1982–88. The AFE Pool was capped using new powers incorporated in the 1980 *Education Act* rendering the allocation of scarce resources an unavoidable management issue, the principle and practice of the central formula funding of PSHE became an accepted canon, and the idea that the rationalisation of PSHE could be achieved through agreement by its constituent interests was effectively disproved – at least to the satisfaction of successive Secretaries of State under pressure to impose public expenditure limits on such a diversive and unresponsive area. So although the NAB was a holding operation by the DES, it was none the less effective in getting the political party dynamic into line and ensuring that the legislative support for the NAB's successor was strong and unequivocal.

With the 1988 *Education Reform Act* the building blocks for the unification of higher education were put into place in the form of the common statutory definition of the PCFC and UFC. During its brief period in office, the PCFC embarked on the difficult but necessary task of reconciling in administrative terms the implications of a dual emphasis in higher education on market mechanisms and publicly accountable central management. By the end of its life in 1992, a balance was being struck between the limited competition embodied in the 'core plus margin' funding mechanism and the controlling potential of the Council's strategic planning approach. How the HEFCs are likely to use this inheritance is discussed in the final chapter.

8

The Research Councils and Science Policy

In modern society economic advance is dependent upon the production and application of scientific knowledge. As the twentieth century has progressed the state has become increasingly involved in the financing and management of science as its importance to the economy has grown. As producers of knowledge the universities naturally form part of the state's concern. However, they are not the only part nor, by any means, are they the dominant part. Today the universities sit within a network of industrial, charitable and public institutions which the state pays to produce scientific knowledge.

The evolution of the state's relationship with the universities in the field of science policy has to be set within this wider context if the forces structuring this relationship, and the consequent pressures for change upon the universities, are to be properly understood. A complicating factor is the range of agencies involved in the funding of higher education's research function. The main funding bodies have been the UGC (followed, of course, by the UFC and now the HEFCs), the research councils and government departments, complemented by an assortment of coordinating and monitoring bodies.

There is also a definitional problem. Historically 'science policy' has meant different things at different times and has been expanded and contracted depending on the interests of those using it. In its most truncated form it simply means policy about 'the production of scientific knowledge' or 'scientific research'. In its expanded form 'the production of scientific knowledge' is seen as merely the first step in a continuing process of industrial innovation. Within this expanded definition science policy is also concerned with the application and development of knowledge for commercial purposes and with the maintenance of a pool of qualified manpower to support this process.

Each variation on the definition of science policy is ideologically loaded in the sense that it constitutes part of a value position held by one or more groups in this particular political arena and we view them in this sense. We neither assume nor believe that there is an objective definition of science policy. The analysis will trace successive attempts by the central state to gain control of its funding of science and of the satellite agencies it has used to allocate research resources to higher education, often in the face of trenchant opposition from the scientific community.

Given that our chapters have a particular institutional focus, our primary concern is with the research councils and their associated advisory bodies. We have concentrated upon the funding of research in science, as opposed to in the arts and social studies, because it has absorbed most of the state's research budget. Moreover, not only is scientific research very expensive but it also makes more institutional demands than research in other knowledge areas.

The analysis falls into four phases:

Phase One: First Principles, 1900–39
Phase Two: Expansion Through Confusion, 1939–65
Phase Three: Halcyon Days, 1965–75
Phase Four: A Management Challenge, 1975–the present.

FIRST PRINCIPLES, 1900–39

In the early days the state's involvement with scientific development was invariably a response to the needs of particular government departments. Thus in 1909 the Post Office Research Section was established, and in the same year the Development Commission was set up to aid in the scientific development of agriculture and fisheries. Eventually, in 1931, the Commission was to become the Agricultural Research Council (ARC). Similarly, in the field of medicine the *National Health Insurance Act* of 1911 provided for some medical research and in 1913 the Medical Research Committee was created, duly becoming the Medical Research Council (MRC) in 1920. Probably most significant of all was the creation in 1916 of the Department of Scientific and Industrial Research (DSIR) in direct response to the demands of the war effort.

It was the activities of the DSIR during the First World War which kindled government awareness of the importance and use of scientific research both in stimulating industrial advance and in assisting in the formulation of policy. The question then arose of how best to integrate this new function into the normal machinery of government.

While the scientific research was conducted and paid for by a particular department there was no difficulty; the problem arose when the research was of general use or overlapped the concerns of more than one department. In addressing this issue in 1918, the Report of the Machinery of Government Committee (the Haldane Report) decided that the organisation of the DSIR, which gave ministerial responsibility to a non-departmental minister, the Lord President of the Council, provided a suitable model. The Report's chief justification for this was that

> It places responsibility to Parliament in the hands of a Minister who is in normal times free from any serious pressure of administrative duties and is immune from any suspicion of being biased by administrative considerations against the application of the results of the research (Haldane Report, 1918, 34).

What became known as 'the Haldane principle' was that the control of research should be separated from the executive functions of government. However, what has become lost in the mists of time is that Haldane's justification for advocating this separation was that it would result in a more efficient machinery of government. There is no suggestion in his Report that the principle should be adhered to for its own sake. Indeed, it is clear that he saw the DSIR type of organisation as a temporary measure which would in due course have to be superseded by a different structure once government research expanded further. In the light of the way in which the Haldane principle has subsequently been evoked to justify the continued autonomy of research, it is interesting to note that his expectation, as yet unfulfilled, was that a structure would emerge with

> A Minister specifically appointed on the grounds of his suitability to preside over a separate Department of Intelligence and Research, which would no longer act under a Committee of the Privy Council, and would take its place among the most important Departments of Government (ibid., 35).

In the event, the DSIR was used as the model for the MRC (1920), the ARC (1931) and the Nature Conservancy (NC, 1949). This model was characterised by independence over scientific decisions, a council membership consisting of independent individuals (both scientists and laymen), full-time scientifically qualified secretaries and direct negotiation of funding from the Treasury.

The transition of the research council model from, as Haldane saw it, an administrative compromise with a limited life expectancy, to an ideological symbol of the necessary autonomy of research to be protected as a sacrosanct principle of a civilised society, was accomplished with remarkable ease in the same way as the pre-war UGC had gained its mossy respectability. Part of the reason why the state did not oppose the establishing of a principle which, in its reverse form, legitimised the non-accountability of the research councils and the absence of state controls was that relatively small amounts of money were involved (Appendix 3, Table 6). Consequently before 1939 there was no pressure on the state to develop a view of how its support of science in general, and the research councils in particular, should be managed. In 1939, expenditure on the research councils was £1,328,000 – one third of the total civilian science budget (ACSP, 1964). The fact that there was a dramatic fourfold increase in spending between 1939 and 1950, following the steady state years of the 1930s, is an indication of the impact of the Second World War on science policy. Equally important was the emergence of a set of values regarding the purpose of the state funding of scientific research. Where the problem arose was in translating these values into a new form of organisation which would be an effective vehicle for the implementation of a science policy.

EXPANSION THROUGH CONFUSION, 1939–63

In the period following the end of the Second World War, opinion was unanimous that 'the war had shown that victory could not be achieved without the mobilisation of all our scientific resources; and that it was plain that the same would be true if we were to succeed in the task of national reconstruction' (ibid., 1). The very exigencies of war had provided valuable lessons of the ways in which 'science can at all times be more rapidly and effectively applied to the solution of urgent problems' (ACSP, 1950, 15). In the formal statements of the time, no one was in any doubt as to the task that faced the nation now 'impoverished by costly war' and with 'diminishing natural resources' (ibid.). Science was seen as the country's saviour. The country was now dependent on 'our ability to meet competition by applying scientific knowledge more successfully than our rivals to the industrial processes by which raw materials are transformed into manufactured goods' (ibid., 16). Science was unequivocally seen as an economic resource to be managed by the state in order to maximise its contribution to the British economy through the production of the appropriate knowledge and manpower.

Given the purposes thus ascribed to science, the question which faced the decision-makers in 1945 was what structure would be appropriate for its organisation and how relevant was the research council model to such a structure. The answer they came up with was an organisational compromise which effectively institutionalised confusion and ambiguity in the science policy field, and allowed the universities to gain ideological and political control of a hefty slice of the science policy budget.

In 1947 the Scientific Advisory Committee to the wartime Cabinet was replaced by two bodies: the Defence Research Policy Committee, assisting the Ministry of Defence, and the Advisory Council on Scientific Policy (ACSP), advising the Lord President to the Council on the general formulation of civil science policy. The Lord President was responsible to Parliament for the research councils and their establishments which reported to him through four Privy Council committees, one each for the MRC, ARC, NC and Advisory Council for Science and Industrial Research (ACSIR, which oversaw the work of the DSIR). However, although in formal constitutional terms a line of accountability to Parliament was thus established, it left the Lord President in the position of responsibility with no executive power. The accountability relationship between the research councils and Parliament was further weakened by the way in which they were funded. Only the DSIR received its finance through a separate parliamentary vote which MPs could debate and challenge, the other three being supported by grants-in-aid which do not allow any opportunity for parliamentary discussion.

Under the new structure the Haldane principle was used to legitimise the idea that, so far as the research councils were concerned, scientists should manage their own affairs. The councils were allowed to determine for themselves what funding they thought they should have, using their own internal criteria. Annual submissions for funding were simply channelled from the research councils to the Treasury via the ACSP and the Lord President of the Council. However, it has to be remembered that civil science expenditure by the state is composed of departmental spending, which is accountable to Parliament, as well research council spending. How significant a part of the total civil science budget was the non-accountable funding of the councils? The table below provides some idea. (It is clear that the limited statistical information available on the science policy field during this period is an indication that the state did not see science as an area which it should be managing.)

CIVIL SCIENCE AND RESEARCH COUNCIL EXPENDITURE BY
SELECTED YEARS 1939–63 (£000s)

	1939	1956	1959	1962	1963
Civil Science	3,993	32,700	64,200	110,100	154,086
Research Councils	1,328	12,000	17,600	31,610	36,096
Research Councils as percentage of Civil Science	33	37	27	29	23

Source: ACSP *Annual Reports*, 1947-63; *Trend Report*, 1963.

Throughout this period between one quarter and one third of a rapidly expanding civil science budget was allocated through the research councils.

The Advisory Council for Science Policy was therefore in the interesting position of advising the Lord President on the formation of policy for (a) departments for which he was not responsible, and (b) research councils for which he was responsible but over which he had no executive authority. In the circumstances, it is remarkable that throughout the 1950s the ACSP felt so able to issue such stentorian advice as it did to all and sundry. Its analysis of what was needed in the science policy field was consistent, lengthy and, given its structural position, almost totally meaningless. It is the first example of the state's ability to form an ideology of why science should be managed at the same time as completely failing to develop an administrative framework to show how it should be managed. There were to be other examples later.

The terms of reference of the ACSP contained the broad definition of science policy which views scientific research as the vehicle for meeting industrial need. When created in 1947 it was asked to advise on how scientific and technical help could be used in the reconstitution of the national economy, to review the nature and performance of existing scientific organisations, to launch a series of investigations which would provide the kind of information required for the formulation of long-term policy, and to identify new areas of scientific research 'where it is felt the national effort is inadequate either from the standpoint of the advancement of pure science or the application of scientific research to industrial need' (ACSP, 1951, 8; ACSP, 1964, 1).

Throughout the ACSP's seventeen-year life, until its demise in 1964, its constant preoccupation was with how science could be employed to produce the maximum impact on economic productivity.

Reviews were held of how state-funded scientific organisations could better perform their appointed task of serving the economy. In its reports the targeting and allocation of resources to achieve this goal were accepted without question. Thus Sir Ben Lockspeiser's review of the DSIR emphasised the role of the DSIR in the exploitation of research results and 'the need for the critical examination of programmes with a view to the selection, for special attention, of items most likely to lead to important practical advances' (ACSP, 1950, 9). And the ACSP's *Sixth Annual Report* in 1953 was devoted entirely to the issue of 'The Exploitation of Science By Industry' and dealt with the provision of properly trained scientists and technologists, scientists and management, new and old production, the volume of investment, and narrowing the gap between scientific discovery and industrial output. The Council's Committee on Scientific Manpower worked assiduously to produce statistics on the supply of, and demand for, skilled scientists, and 1954 began monitoring the number of graduate science teachers in schools and technical colleges as a guide to the nation's capacity to produce scientists.

Given the ACSP's apparently unswerving allegiance to the idea of science as the handmaiden of industrial innovation, it is interesting to ask how it squared this idea with the orthodox university view that scientific research should be concerned with pure rather than applied knowledge, and should not be swayed by, or accountable to, external pressures such as those emanating from the economy. The question is important not only because a proportion of research council monies went to the universities in the form of project grants but also because the research council committees were dominated by academic scientists. For some time the Council chose to ignore the issue. When, in the mid-1950s, it did address the issue it simply reaffirmed the legitimacy of the universities' values, and thus exempted them from many of its statements and recommendations. In its 1956–57 *Annual Report* the Council recognised that most of the country's pure research was and should be carried out in the universities and that too much contract research, which was necessarily applied research, was undesirable:

> Although one must recognise that some contract work is almost inevitable in view of the specialised knowledge to be found only in universities, it is essential that this should not be allowed to grow to proportions which would hamper the universities *in the free and untrammelled pursuit of knowledge, which is their primary function* (ACSP, 1957, 8, our stress).

Apparently universities should not have 'to resort to contract work' (ibid.).

In its review of the financing of scientific research in British universities in its 1957–58 *Annual Report* the ACSP decided that the existing system of dual funding by research councils and UGC was satisfactory, and that the reviews carried out by the research councils identified gaps in the research effort. It suggested, as a refinement, that there should be a transfer of funding responsibility from research councils to universities (and hence to the UGC) when branches of knowledge which had begun as experimental projects became 'established activities'. However, although the ACSP could make recommendations about what should happen in universities it was in a decidely weak position to insist on anything since the majority of funding for university research came from the Treasury on the advice of the UGC. Effectively the Chancellor of the Exchequer was the minister for the universities and there was no formal relationship between him and the Lord President of the Council whom the ACSP advised. The two major sources of funding for university research (research councils and UGC) were therefore linked to the state by two quite separate lines of responsibility.

The logic of the ACSP's position as overseer of civil science policy none the less meant that from the mid-1950s onwards it felt obliged to include the UGC within its brief. It was, after all, monitoring scientific effort in general as well as the flow of scientific manpower into and out of the universities. From 1955 it began to include the UGC in its civil science statistics, and its working assumption was that half of a university lecturer's time could be considered as devoted to research. However, even if the ACSP had had either the power or the inclination to unravel the tangled lines of funding between the state and the universities, other matters were far more pressing in the mid-1950s. A massive and unplanned expansion took place in the fields of nuclear physics and space research. To begin with, the reaction of the Council was that of the astonished diarist, meticulously noting events but uncertain of how to react. Between 1955–56 and 1959–60 the total government Research and Development budget rose by 40 per cent in constant value terms: from 1.7 per cent of GNP to 2.3 per cent (ACSP, 1960, 4). By 1961–62 it had risen to 2.7 per cent of GNP. By far the largest part of this increase was taken up by spending on nuclear science which in 1961–62 amounted to £54,130,000, half of the total civil science budget (ACSP, 1962, Appendix F). With equipment costs soaring and international projects such as the CERN accelerator creating open-ended commitments to unknown future expenditure, the ACSP was like a man at the wheel of a juggernaut over which he had no control.

As the body responsible for a state-funded activity which, following the Haldane principle, was supposed to be self-regulating but now clearly was not, the ACSP was obliged to begin to ask some elementary management questions even if it was not in a position to do anything with the answers. What should be the balance of expenditure between different areas of science? What criteria should be used to determine the balance? Assuming priorities can be established, what forms of organisation should be used to implement them? Even the universities did not escape the Council's worried musings:

> Our resources are limited and more concentration of our effort is required; attempts to pursue certain types of scientific activity in many different universities can result in a dispersal and dilution of effort such that in the end we achieve much less than could reasonably be expected from the total expenditure involved (ACSP, 1960, 13).

It was driven to accept that 'this implies some sacrifice of the freedom of universities to make their own arrangements' but could 'see no alternative if a country of our size is to participate effectively in these expensive fields of research' (ibid.).

The ACSP was not the only body concerned about the rapid expansion in the science budget. In 1961 the Office of the Minister for Science (a role which Lord Hailsham combined with that of Lord President of the Council) produced a report from the Committee on the Management and Control of Research and Development (the Zuckerman Report). This report asked whether state-funded R and D institutions could

> ... work more effectively than they now do; whether Government can get better value for the large sums of money which it makes available for research and development carried out on behalf of the armed services; and whether better management can increase the effectiveness of the scarce scientific and technical manpower engaged in the civil field (Zuckerman Report, 1961, 3–4).

The Committee was not at all satisfied with what it found and made a number of detailed recommendations designed to increase the

effectiveness of scientific organisations. These included the amalgamation of the smaller research establishments by both research
councils and government departments, better liaison between government establishments and universities, improved contacts with industry and, probably most importantly, the creation of suitable
machinery by the 'user' of the research to formulate requirements
according to known and appropriate criteria. Zuckerman further
recommended that these criteria should include a project's cost-
effectiveness, applicability, and marketability.

The ability of state-sponsored committees to analyse what needed
to be done in the science policy field was undeniable. Following
Zuckerman, in 1963 the Committee of Enquiry into the Organisation
of Civil Science (the Trend Report) identified the same problems of
escalating cost, duplication of effort, lack of coordination, the need
to foster and encourage new 'growing points', and even went so far as
to question the traditional distinction between pure and applied
knowledge:

> The time lag between the discovery of new scientific knowledge
> and its application to practical needs has steadily diminished in
> recent years, with the result that it is no longer realistic to seek to
> maintain a sharp distinction between research and development,
> which are tending to interact more rapidly and more directly
> (Trend Report, 1963, 19).

Organisationally, argued Trend, the science policy field was a mess.
New developments which did not fit within the existing framework
were dealt with by the expedient of creating new agencies such as the
Atomic Energy Authority (AEA, 1954) and the National Institute for
Research in Nuclear Science (NIRNS, 1958) which failed to conform
to a uniform pattern. Lines of responsibility were frequently confused
as in the case of the European Organisation for Nuclear Research
(CERN) which fell between several departments in terms of responsibility for policy and finance. And the division of functions as
between the various autonomous agencies and the interested government departments was, said Trend, 'obscure' (ibid., 24).

Trend was in no doubt that the way to achieve the more efficient
management of science was through central coordination. His Committee recommended that the Minister for Science be given 'additional substantive responsibilities' and considerably strengthened
staff support. While the responsibilities had a familiar ring about
them, and included such chestnuts as identifying national scientific

needs and allocating resources among the research councils, it was none the less clear that Trend intended to move beyond the tradition of management by exhortation which had characterised the work of the ACSP. He wanted a structure of responsibility whereby the Minister for Science became the minister responsible to Parliament for financial allocations to all non-departmental agencies. If his recommendations had been implemented, the Haldane vision of a government department of first rank responsible for research would have come a step nearer. However, this was not to be.

Because another Committee, that of Lord Robbins on higher education, was simultaneously at work, the Trend Committee made no recommendations about ministerial responsibilities for the universities; but it did suggest that there would be advantages in placing this under the Minister for Science. In the event, none of these centralising moves came to fruition. Science policy in the post-war period up to 1965 is characterised by a tenfold increase in real terms in the state funding of scientific research, a rhetorical commitment to the broad definition of science policy as servant of the economy, a growing awareness of the need to inject organisation and coherence into a fragmented and frequently non-accountable area of government expenditure, and a total inability to transcend the ambiguities of its organisational starting point. In the face of such flaccidity, the way was open for the universities to launch a counterattack.

HALCYON DAYS, 1965–75

By 1965, the funding of university research through an ad hoc administrative arrangement had been graced with the term 'dual funding system'. Historical accident had, in the absence of challenge, assumed the status of accepted policy and been nicely blended with the traditional university ideal with its emphasis on pure, rather than applied knowledge, and institutional autonomy. But for the fact that the Haldane principle had been concerned with governmental efficiency and seen the research council model solely as a temporary administrative convenience, one might be forgiven for viewing the dual funding system as consciously designed to protect university independence.

None the less, regardless of its origins, there is no doubt that up to 1965 it *did* protect university independence. Despite the unremitting barrage of support for the economic interpretation of science policy, the research council enclave remained unscathed and, using the orthodox view of academic research, well able to maintain its ideological defences against intruders. Then in 1965 came the Science and Technology Act which changed both the organisation and funding of the research councils. What effect did the Act have on the independence of university research?

The Act created three new research councils: the Science Research Council (SRC), the Natural Environment Research Council (NERC) and the Social Science Research Council (SSRC). The first two of these followed the Trend recommendations, and the SSRC owed its existence to the recommendations of the 1965 Heyworth Committee. The DSIR was disbanded and its work split between the SRC, which took on the pure research, and the Ministry of Technology which assumed responsibility for the research establishments oriented primarily towards technology and its application to industry. All five research councils (ARC, MRC, NERC, SRC and SSRC) were brought under the Secretary of State for Education and Science whose own post had been created in 1964 by the merger of the Ministry of Education and the Office of the Minister for Science.

At the same time as assuming responsibility for the research councils the DES also gained control of their finances. Annual budgets to the research councils were henceforth to be allocated by the DES through the Science Vote rather than primarily through grants-in-aid from the Treasury. Financial accountability to Parliament and political responsibility were therefore integrated for the first time. Since in the previous year the UGC, the other arm of the dual funding system, had also become the political and financial responsibility of the DES the initial impression is that the state is finally bringing together the disparate lines of accountability and gaining effective control over university research. Such an impression can in fact be shown to be largely illusory once the administrative structures involved are analysed in more detail.

From 1965, the forum for the annual arbitration of research council budgets was a newly created body called the Council for Scientific Policy (CSP). Although similar in title to the now disbanded ACSP, the CSP's brief was much narrower since it carried responsibility solely for the research councils rather than for the whole of civil science as the ACSP had done. (At this time research council expenditure constituted between a quarter and one third of all government expenditure on civil science.) As a result of the 1965 Act there was now no body with overall, supra-departmental responsibility for civil science. The effect was to create more, rather than less, fragmentation in the science policy field. No one was less concerned about this than the universities. At a stroke the previous body to which the research councils had been accountable, the ACSP, had been removed along with its continual rumblings about centralisation, applied research, value for money, and the needs of the economy. In its place as the national source for authoritative pronouncements on science policy was the university-dominated CSP.

In its first report the CSP made no bones about where it stood and the strength of its statement is an indication of the intensity of the discussion at that time:

> It is necessary at the outset to deal with the misconception that the advance of scientific knowledge itself can be directed from the centre. This would be to misunderstand the original and spontaneous nature of science. The advance of scientific knowledge cannot solely be achieved *by the arbitrary selection of national scientific goals and by committing resources to them* (CSP, 1966, 2, our stress).

The contrast between this 'spontaneous' concept of science and the 'directed' view advanced in the last ACSP report of 1964 could not be more vivid. In its dying moments the ACSP insisted that 'the problem of priorities in science and technology lies at the heart of national science policy, and therefore of our national destiny'. 'This', it said, 'is the most important issue we pass on to our successors' (ACSP, 1964, 4). Furthermore, by this stage it had decided that scientists could not make the key decisions but that 'it will be up to the Government itself to decide, on the best advice that can be tendered, what our national priorities should be' (ibid.).

However, the CSP, insofar as it can be seen as the ACSP's successor, was clearly determined to show no respect whatsoever for the wishes of the dead:

> We believe that Research Councils must be free to determine, in relation to scientific priorities, their own programmes within their own terms of reference. If this principle is damaged the system, which has stood the test of time since its enunciation in the Haldane Report of 1918, is certain to decay (CSP, 1966, 10).

The CSP was convinced that the nature of scientific activity made it a quite unique area of government policy requiring 'special techniques of management to develop and succeed' since it is 'a field where scientific considerations and standards are overriding and where judgments upon these must be made by scientists' (CSP, 1967a, 1).

In transmitting the orthodox academic view of science as a necessarily spontaneous and self-regulating activity, the Council naturally assumed a narrow definition of science policy, and a correspondingly limited conception of its own role in the formation of such policy. Whereas the ACSP had seen scientific research as part of the process of industrial innovation and science policy as the way of achieving a more efficient integration of science and industry, the CSP saw science as an endeavour, justifiable in its own right. For the CSP science policy then became defined as planning in order to create the 'environment for scientific vitality' and 'to maintain morale in science' (ibid.), thus maintaining scientists in the manner to which they had become accustomed.

Although the initial position of the CSP was that its function was to promote the health of the scientific community, which might or might not be the same thing as the economic health of the country, it faced the reality that when it succeeded the ACSP in 1965 the 'science budget' (by which it meant the DES Science Vote, not the total government spending on R and D) was expanding at a rate of 13 per cent per annum, so doubling every six years. This growth rate subsequently slowed and went into reverse, but in the mid-1960s was quite large enough to make the Science Vote a visible part of the political agenda and to raise the obvious question of why it should receive such large amounts of funds.

Even the CSP could not believe that the state would give scientific research unlimited credit in perpetuity. But there appeared no prospect of a natural slowing down in the exploding areas of nuclear physics and space research. Not only were the existing commitments such as CERN continuing to expand but also new ones were coming on stream such as the 300 GeV High Energy Machine which alone would take up 7 per cent of the entire nuclear physics budget (ibid., 15). Arguments were going to be needed, the CSP realised, to justify continued spending at current levels. But would reiteration of the traditional value of 'knowledge for knowledge's sake' be sufficient? Some obviously thought so. In the case of the 300 GeV accelerator a CSP working group decided that 'the essential justification for the project is *the intrinsic scientific interest of the results*, which are likely slowly to permeate the whole of physics and indeed the whole of science over the next generation' (ibid., 28). Others at the CSP were less sanguine about the political usefulness of such arguments and concluded:

> Inevitably these trends will impose an increasing need for careful selection in planning research programmes and if resources of the right magnitude are to be deployed there will have to be further progress towards specialisation at selected centres together with concentration of resources in some fields of science (ibid., 16).

It was in pursuance of this approach that the Working Group on the Support of Scientific Research in the Universities was set up in 1967.

From fairly early on in its life the Council therefore began to display the same qualities of schizophrenia as we have already diagnosed in the UGC. Caught between, on the one hand, the demands of a role which, in the absence of infinite governmental largesse, inevitably entailed the selective allocation of finite resources and, on the other, the claims of traditional university values which were opposed to the central direction of research, the CSP entered a perpetual circle of equivocation.

When the Working Group on the Support of Scientific Research in the Universities eventually reported four years later in 1971, the length of its deliberations indicating probable disagreements, its work contained the normal hallmarks of an attempt to strike an impossible compromise. While it noted the 'obvious economic advantage of avoiding duplication of effort' through the concentration of research resources and the increased efficiency of researchers working in proximity with others of like interest, it also made the standard case for not separating teaching and research, and for maintaining an evenly spread 'floor' of research:

> Those who are good at research may not always be the best instructors, but they give an extra dimension to teaching, while those who are good both at research and at teaching add something to their subject and department which the teacher cannot hope to rival. In turn, research benefits from being associated with teaching because the exercise of teaching under-graduates, particularly in their first years, demands simplicity, clarity and a fundamental approach to the subject (CSP, 1971b, 49).

Not all the research councils could afford the luxury of unquestioning adherence to the traditional values. As a result of the rapid expansion of nuclear physics and space research the SRC was under more pressure than the other research councils to make judgements about how its resources should be allocated. In an interesting appendix to the report called 'SRC Policy on Selectivity and Concentration in the Support of Research' it explicitly adopted such a policy and accepted that this 'will mean that the SRC will inevitably exercise more influence over university research' (ibid., 54). In the early 1970s the shift of resources away from the 'big sciences' duly took place as the SRC carried its policy forward.

The ability of the CSP to act as vehicle for the direction of state funded research in universities was limited not only by its ambivalence about its role but also by the administrative procedures it adopted and the support it received. The secretariat of the CSP was provided by the Science Branch of the DES. In preparing the draft annual budgets of the research councils for consideration by the Council, Science Branch continued the ACSP's practice of projecting a research council's expenditure forward on the basis of existing commitments and any new ones it might be considering. These 'Forward Looks' were constructed in consultation with the research councils, and in the period up to 1975 rarely resulted in anything other than marginal shifts in the distribution of a council's resources; a major exception to this being the SRC's reallocation of monies away from big science. Anything other than this 'planning by projection' was in any case beyond both the skills and the resources of Science Branch. In the mid-1960s the technicalities of how it might be possible to establish specific criteria for national science priorities, let alone implement them, had not been discussed in anything other than the most general terms. Moreover, the CSP simply did not have the resources to engage in anything other than a superficial planning exercise even had it wanted to.

Given the nature of the dual funding system whereby the UGC supplied the capital equipment and ancillary support staff and the research councils funded the projects and personnel, it was, and is, inevitable that the systematic planning of scientific research in universities would require coordinated action by the two state agencies. However, although the DES provided the funds for both UGC and research councils, administratively they related to quite different parts of the Department's structure; a fact which meant that there was no internal administrative pressure for the coordinated planning of university science.

With the demise of the ACSP, and in the absence of a government view on scientific priorities, the 1960s proved halcyon days for the universities. They received a steadily expanding flow of money from the state with few or no strings attached and benefited from the research councils' increased share of the total government R and D budget (see Appendix III, Table 7). Traditional university ideas about the autonomous nature of the scientific activity either dominated the CSP or created an inhibiting confusion about its role. Then in 1971 came the rude shock of the Cabinet report by Lord Rothschild on government research and development.

Rothschild insisted that applied research and development should be governed by what he called the 'customer-contractor principle' where 'The customer says what he wants; the contractor does it (if he can); and the customer pays' (Rothschild, 1971, 3). Although Rothschild explicitly excluded basic, fundamental or pure research from the application of this principle he also maintained that an appreciable part of the work of the ARC, MRC and NERC was applied. The report went on:

> But this work had and has no customer to commission and approve it. This is wrong. However distinguished, intelligent and practical scientists may be, they cannot be so well qualified to decide what the needs of the nation are, and their priorities, as those responsible for ensuring that those needs are met (ibid., 4).

Rothschild made short work of the Haldane principle and concluded: 'The concepts of scientific independence used in the Haldane Report are not relevant to contemporary discussion of government research' (ibid., 10).

In the face of such an outright ideological attack, proposals for the redistribution of research council resources and for greater accountability, the CSP felt obliged to defend its position. In a straightforward restatement of traditional values the Council maintained the utmost importance of what it rather grandly called 'this symbiotic relationship between the universities and the research councils' (CSP, 1971c, 12). For this relationship to survive and prosper scientists must remain in control of their own territory, asserted the Council unequivocally: 'It is a characteristic of basic and strategic science that neither the devising of programmes of work nor the assignment of relative scientific priorities to each programme can be carried out by non-scientists' (ibid., 13). For good measure, and recognising the need to consolidate its own power and to buttress what suddenly appeared rather weak defences, the CSP proposed the setting up of a statutory body with a charter which would protect the independence of government-supported basic and strategic science. Subject to the Secretary of State's power of direction, this body would determine broad problems of science policy and allocations to the research councils.

The CSP continued to assert its belief that 'in a civilised and affluent society science is worthy of support for its own sake, as a cultural pursuit aimed at extending the boundaries of knowledge', though with regal generosity it did concede that 'those who provide resources have every right to be satisfied that their investment is justified in terms of social and economic return *as well*' (CSP, 1972, 4, our stress). It even went so far as to discuss the findings of the Working Group on the Determination of Scientific Priorities, though these were of such generality as to be meaningless in any practical policy sense.

In the event, the government came down on Rothschild's side in the 1972 White Paper *Framework for Government Research and Development* and strengthened the power of the departments at the expense of the research councils. In future, departments would have members, rather than assessors, on the research councils in whose work they had an interest and a proportion of the budgets of the ARC, MRC and NERC was to be transferred from the DES's Science Vote to the relevant executive departments (Agriculture, Health, Environment and Trade and Industry) with the expectation that these funds would be used to commission applied research from the research councils. All government departments were to have a Chief Scientist and these were to be full members of a new body, the Advisory Board for the Research Councils (ABRC), which was to replace the CSP. Although the ABRC was to have responsibility for advising the Secretary of State for Education and Science on the allocation of the Science Budget among the research councils, the government made it clear that it saw the Board as a means both for developing greater partnership and cooperation between research councils and departments, and for promoting close liaison between councils and the users of their research (ABRC, 1974, 4–6).

For a period of just under ten years the CSP had institutionalised the orthodox academic view of how the state should dispense funds for university research. Despite frequent misgivings about a system which encouraged scientists to determine their own research priorities with little or no reference to national economic or social needs, the CSP had presided over a steadily expanding budget which relied on self-regulation as a management technique. Although at times the logic of its budgetary responsibility had forced it to make genuflections in the direction of selectivity and priority setting, these had always had a ritual quality about them given the Council's ambivalence about its role and the limited administrative support available to it.

While Rothschild and the reforms which followed made it plain that the universities' traditional values would not necessarily serve as protection against state intervention, the economic crisis and subsequent cuts of December 1973 made it plainer. The effect of the cuts was to reduce the 1974–75 Science Budget by £6.5 million, 2.1 per cent in real terms compared with the previous year and 4 per cent compared with the expected total (ABRC, 1976, 13). For the first time in the post-war era university science had received a reduction in its budget. The effect was as much psychological as economic: no longer could the universities assume they were a privileged sector of state expenditure. They were as vulnerable as the rest.

A MANAGEMENT CHALLENGE, 1975 – THE PRESENT

Despite the Rothschild reforms, it was clear that any government would continue to face two very basic problems in the general field of science policy: first, how to formulate policy and, second, how to implement it. In the debate surrounding the Rothschild Report it was patently obvious that no government consensus had been reached on the answer to either of these questions. The reports on research and development by the Select Committee on Science and Technology in 1971–72 reveal inter-departmental differences and rivalry in research funding, Committee scepticism regarding the general applicability of the customer–contractor principle and a proposed Minister for Science to overcome what the Committee regarded as the parochial, short-sighted and occasionally non-existent nature of the departments' science planning. An exasperated Committee commented: 'It still remains the fact that no machinery for assessing priorities and expenditure on a national as distinct from a departmental basis exists. We believe such machinery is badly needed' (Select Committee on Science and Technology, 1972, vii). Post-Rothschild, science policy remained a fragmented field.

A number of changes introduced in 1976 were designed to strengthen the machinery for coordinating scientific advice to the government but these in no way interfered with either departmental

173

or research council autonomy. They included the establishment of the Committee of Chief Scientists and Permanent Secretaries under the chairmanship of the Lord Privy Seal; the creation of the post of Chief Scientist in the Central Policy Review Staff; and the amalgamation in the Cabinet Office of the Secretariat functions of the Science and Technology Group with the Economic and Industrial Secretariat. A rather intricate game of committee-room musical chairs was being created where overlapping membership came to be used as an informal means of limited policy coordination. At this stage, although Rothschild and the 1975 cuts had demonstrated that university science was neither sacrosanct nor inviolable, the incompetence of the state in the general field of science policy ensured the universities a temporary protection. In any case, following the 1975 cuts the Science Vote recovered and, throughout the remainder of the 1970s, remained stable in real terms and maintained its command over 15 per cent of the total R and D budget (see Appendix 3, Table 7).

The period up to July 1981 when the government announced drastic cuts in the UGC's budget can be seen as a 'phoney war' between the DES and the universities during which the Department was primarily concerned with extending its power over secondary education before turning its attention to the higher education sector. There is certainly nothing in the ABRC's reports of the 1970s to indicate that it felt obliged to assume a more directive stance towards science in the universities. Its *Second Report* describes the strengthening of that 'long-standing feature of science planning', the 'Forward Look' method of estimating future research council expenditure – a method responsive to the scientific community's definition of research priorities (ABRC, 1976, 18). Admittedly mention is made of selectivity, and the research council committees are 'invited' to use a suggested list of ABRC criteria, but the rhetoric is unconvincing.

By 1979 the Board had obviously decided it should act as a lobby for more money to be given to science, rather than as a mechanism for husbanding existing resources. Thus its *Third Report* is devoted to listing the harm being done to 'the country's scientific capability' and the reasons why there should be a real growth of 4 per cent per annum in the research councils' budget. The arguments advanced are an uneasy amalgam of the traditional and economic views of university research with the sections titled: 'the importance of fundamental research', 'intellectual and cultural activity', 'research as an ingredient of material and social progress', 'highly trained and versatile manpower' and, in conclusion, 'why the country should spend more

174

on basic scientific research'. In that the arguments were largely ideological, were not statistically based, had no managerial or planning content, and hence contained no justification of why the rate of growth should be 4 per cent rather than, say, 10 per cent, they can be seen as the swan-song of an old style relationship between university research and the state. Thereafter, the language, style and reality were to change considerably.

Up to 1981, developments in the broad area of science policy were not guaranteed to exert much pressure on the ABRC. The *Review of the Framework for Government Research and Development* published in 1979 was a fairly anodyne document which, on the one hand, recognised that 'Government does not have a single science policy: it has a whole range of policies' as a result of departmental autonomy and, on the other, came up with very few suggestions as to what should be done about it (Cabinet Office, 1979, 1). So far as the research councils were concerned, the *Review* concluded that increased departmental representation on the SRC coupled with the establishment of the ABRC had 'proved adequate to ensure that the SRC's programmes are adequately related to the longer-term objectives of Departments and has doubtless contributed to effective and beneficial collaboration between the SRC and the Departments in the support of their industrial policies' (ibid., 16). And the ABRC was given a clean bill of health and described as having helped the research councils to adjust their priorities in accordance with national needs (ibid., 17).

But regardless of what the *Review* said, by 1981 that part of the state to which the research councils directly related, the DES, had decided to act. That it was able to act was in part a result of political factors, but act it did. The period following the July 1981 cuts in the UGC grant is a period of accelerating state control over university science. The state was aided in its task by the sudden realisation by the ABRC and the UGC that the historic dual funding system was already on the point of collapse. Reporting in 1982, the joint ABRC/UGC Working Party on the Support of University Scientific Research, chaired by Sir Alec Merrison, conducted the first statistically based analysis of the dual funding system and showed that expenditure on equipment, laboratories, libraries and technicians had been declining steadily over the past decade relative to the size of the system. The whole infrastructure of university science had been eroded by universities taking the soft option of cutting those costs which could be cut most easily and quickly, which were generally those related to research. Given that the system of research support had already been severely undermined

175

the Merrison Report concluded that 'we can see no way in which the rapid reductions ahead can be absorbed without widespread and substantial short-term damage to a number of institutions, including some given a measure of protection' (Merrison Report, 1982, 25).

In a situation where the dual funding system was already under severe stress, and where support from the UGC was now going to be reduced still further, it was obvious that choices were going to have to be made and scientific resources selectively allocated. The problem the Merrison Report faced was how to say so without offending traditional university values. Since this was in fact impossible the Report compromised by giving half the answer. It recommended that universities should develop procedures for concentrating their research resources into selected areas, the suggested mechanism was 'Research Committees', and inform the UGC of the result of this exercise. The UGC would then be in a position to identify nationally those areas not adequately covered. The Report continued:

> While it would be wrong therefore for the totality of UGC research support to be determined in relation to the level of external grants, it would be right to recognise that external grant income is an important factor which should be taken into account, alongside a range of others (ibid., 30).

What Merrison completely omitted to deal with was the role of the ABRC and research councils in a selectively operated dual funding system and how the two arms of the system would relate under such a new arrangement.

None the less, what it did do was to open the debate on the future organisation of university science which others then carried forward. In his book, *The Politics of British Science*, Martin Ince argues that coordination of science policy in Britain tends to mean cross-membership of committees (Ince, 1986, 28). While one may dispute whether much coordination yet exists in practice, it is clear that this cross-membership at the national level facilitates flows of ideas and establishes dominant patterns of thought about how science should be organised. One particularly influential group was the Advisory Council on Applied Research and Development (ACARD).

Having originally been set up in 1976, ACARD languished until 1982 when, in the government's response to yet another request for more central coordination of science policy, this time from the House of Lords Select Committee on Science and Technology, its remit was extended to include such duties as providing advice on applied research, design and development in the UK, the application of research and technology in accordance with national economic needs, and the coordination, in collaboration with the ABRC, of these activities with research supported through the DES. Although based in the Cabinet Office it was to share its secretariat with, and have overlapping membership with, the ABRC (Cabinet Office, 1982). Up to this point ACARD had dutifully produced reports on subjects such as biotechnology and information technology, but lacked the political access to achieve any real impact. Its first joint report with the ABRC in 1983 conjures up a feeling of *déjà vu* in that it replicates many of the themes concerning the relationship between science and industrial innovation contained in the last report of the Advisory Council for Scientific Policy in 1963 (ACARD/ABRC, 1983). Twenty years have passed and the state is once again insisting that university science accepts its economic responsibilities and thereby the broad definition of science policy. The interlude is over and this time there will be no Council for Scientific Policy to protect the university enclave.

The joint ACARD/ABRC report recognises that a key question is how priorities for scientific research can be established. It is all very well to talk of the selective funding of science as an aid to industrial productivity but if criteria cannot be developed to guide selective judgements then the talk is clearly bogus. Two further reports from ACARD developed the science and industry argument further. The Muir-Wood report *Improving Research Links between Higher Education and Industry* (1983) discussed actual mechanisms for bringing the two together and, more importantly in the long term, *Exploitable Areas of Science* (1986) explored the methodology and management necessary for the deliberate exploitation of science. The latter report maintained that 'the support of exploitable areas of science can properly be viewed as an investment decision, in which current outlays are incurred in anticipation of future returns' (ACARD, 1986, 25). It recommended the creation of a small management group to steer the process of identifying exploitable scientific areas, supported by an appropriate information system.

It took time for the ABRC to digest the implications of this ideological shift for its own role and work out how it should proceed. Meanwhile, the individual research councils varied in the extent to which they took on board the resurgent economic view of science. Following a significant reduction in its budget as a result of a redistribution of the Science Vote in favour of the Science and Engineering Research Council (SERC – the renamed SRC), the

Agriculture and Food Research Council (AFRC – the renamed ARC) had no choice but to engage in a restructuring designed to create 'efficient management structures' (AFRC, 1987, 2). Similarly, the NERC accepted that it would have to live with a reduced income and, in the language of the new values, stated:

> At the same time that criteria and mechanisms for the selection of priorities, where appropriate, are developed in NERC, criteria and mechanisms for measurement of research output, in both scientific and utilitarian terms, will also need to be developed (NERC, 1985, 2–3).

Ince has shown how SERC's strategy since 1984 has also been guided by the potential industrial relevance of research as well as scientific merit (Ince, 1986, 46).

Others were less eager to embrace the new order with its implication that the level of funding received by a research council should be capable of being justified in terms of external criteria (economic and social) rather than in terms of criteria internal to the scientific community itself (intrinsic scientific merit). In its 1986–87 *Annual Report* the MRC accepts the need for judging research in terms of its economic and social returns, for quality and for the efficient use of resources but laments that it 'must make it clear that if strenuous efforts to make better use of resources do no more than allow the Council to accommodate a declining budget then the wealth of scientific opportunities presented by medical research will not be fully exploited' (MRC, 1988, 1). Precisely what is meant by 'wealth of scientific opportunities' is not explained and the presumption is that it is the right of the research council and the scientist to define such a concept and, by implication, the level of resources required.

While the debates within the research councils were continuing the pressure for the more effective management of the university system were being stepped up. The improved management of research formed an important part of the UGC's response. Following Merrison, in *A Strategy for Higher Education into the 1990s* (1984) the UGC announced that 'to ensure that resources for research are allocated and managed to their best advantage' the following principles should apply:

> (i) The UGC should be more selective in its allocation of research support among universities.
> (ii) Each university should know what resources it is devoting to

research and the distribution of these resources should be a matter of careful planning.
(iii) Allocation by the UGC and planning by the university should be interactive processes (UGC, 1984a, 17).

Having laid down the principles, the UGC then had to develop the appropriate managerial techniques to put them into action.

The use of research-based criteria to inform the allocation of resources to a university was a key part of the UGC's shift to formula funding. The Committee outlined the new method in Circular Letter 22/85 'Planning for the Late 1980s: The Resource Allocation Process' and Circular Letter 4/86 'Planning for the Later 1980s: Recurrent Grant for 1986/87'. The significance of this change for the universities was considerable. Universities would have to compete for scarce resources according to publicly known criteria which, in the area of research, would relate particularly to their performance. Those which conducted more and better research would get more UGC money. To all intents and purposes the universities were given an incentive scheme to establish research management structures.

However, given the fact that state funding of university science was channelled through research councils as well as the UGC, change in the management mechanisms of one arm of the dual funding system had to be coordinated with change in the other if either were to be effective. Although the ABRC related to the Secretary of State for Education in the same way as the UGC, that is, it acted in an advisory capacity, it related to the universities differently in that it was the autonomous research councils which actually allocated the money to the universities. In addition, the formulation of the Board's advice to the Secretary of State has historically been dependent upon the 'Forward Looks' produced by the research councils. Not surprisingly, therefore, it has taken the ABRC a little longer to adjust to the new managerial ethos but with the publication of *A Strategy for the Science Base* in 1987 it laid its cards on the table. The report presents strategic advice on the development of the science base and deals with its organisation and management, strategic priorities and exploitation and the adequacy of the funding of the science base. It suggests a future pattern of higher education provision where institutions would be categorised into three types according to the amount and type of research conducted. A move strongly reinforced in the 1980s by the various UGC subject reviews in, for example, physics, chemistry and the earth sciences.

CONCLUSIONS

Although the differentiation of higher education institutions into primarily research or teaching bodies is a logical consequence of the selective allocation of research resources, it is a logic which challenges the orthodox view on the unity of teaching and research. It is scarcely surprising, therefore, that the universities' reaction to the ABRC's report was almost wholly hostile, damning it out of hand and refusing to recognise that its recommendations were part of a wider and inexorable push by the state to bring university research into a public, accountable arena. In terms of science policy formation, the report represented a move from ideology and rhetoric to the practicalities of policy implementation. In the past the leap from argument to policy had always been blocked by a combination of ideological and institutional barricades. With *A Strategy for the Science Base* the process of shunting those barricades to one side had begun.

The shift has been aided by the research evaluation exercises and by the successive refinements to the formula used to fund universities from 1985 onwards. The changes to the formula have placed increasing emphasis on the separation of teaching and research, regardless of the resistance within the universities to this shift. The formula has had two main components; T (Teaching) and R (Research), with the R component made up of four elements: CR (contract research), DR (research grants), JR (results of the research assessment exercise), and SR (student load of department). The trend has been to alter the weighting in the formula in favour of the JR component, and to weaken the link between a department's teaching and research functions. The UFC's Circular 6/91 confirmed 'the phased move of the JR: SR ratio from the average of 1:1 to an average of 2:1 by 1994/95'. Given that the R component constitutes about a third of the universities' total income, this is a significant redistribution of resources which will intensify the move towards an elite group of institutions specialising in research. The mechanism suggests that 'to those that hath research shall be given', making it difficult for predominantly teaching institutions to break into the elite research circle. In addition, it can be expected that major research council investments will go overwhelmingly to those institutions with an established track record of obtaining grants and a known ability to deliver.

Over the past few years there have been numerous calls for the abolition of individual research councils and the creation of a super research council as a means of further rationalising the organisation of science. Although these calls have been resisted, they have none the less had their effect. The ABRC has been reconstituted so that under its new terms of reference it will, as its chairman Sir David Phillips put it, 'act as a single unit throughout, to produce a corporate view of the overall interests of the research council system' (*The Times Higher Education Supplement*, 30 March 1990, 7). How far this will allow the research councils to preserve their traditional independence from the central state will not be known until the impending White Paper on science is published, but the omens are not encouraging.

In 1989 the continuing demands from Parliament for more coordination in the science policy field met with a sympathetic response from the Cabinet Office report, *Civil Research and Development*, which accepted that there should be 'a strengthened central structure' through, first, collective ministerial consideration – under the Prime Minister's leadership – of priorities in science and technology, and, second, an expanded role for ACARD, renamed the Advisory Council on Science and Technology (ACOST). These sentiments were not new, and one could be forgiven for viewing them sceptically, but after a long political gestation they were followed up in 1992 with the transfer of the staff of the science branch of the former DES, along with the ABRC and the science staff of the Cabinet Office to the newly created Office of Science and Technology (OST), itself part of the Office of Public Service and Science (OPSS). The fundamental review of British science promised by the impending White Paper promises was awaited with keen interest.

9

The State, the Market and the Managed Institution

This concluding chapter has five goals. First, we will outline what we consider to be the main characteristics of the contemporary model of higher education in Britain. This will build on a much earlier attempt of ours to create models that encapsulated the changing character of the British university system (Tapper and Salter, 1978, 142–78). Second, we present our understanding of how this model relates to the state. The purpose of state action has been to create a new system of higher education; how it is to be sustained depends on the state's maintenance of a controlling framework. In other words, an integral part of the new system is how the institutions of higher education are to relate to the state. The key actors in the process of change have been neither those institutions themselves nor societal pressures, but rather the state itself. If there is anything different about our analysis, it is the role we have accorded the state in the change process. While recognising the inevitability of policy differences and oscillations within the state, not to mention the constant redefinition of its institutional character, our understanding of the process of educational change stands or falls on our judgement of the state's role. Our third concern in this chapter, therefore, must be to return to our theory of educational change.

In the process of discussing the above three topics, we need to consider, as our fourth task, those important changes in the government of higher education which have not been analysed previously. These are the winding up of the PCFC and the UFC with the amalgamation of their functions in the Higher Education Funding Councils (HEFCs), and the removal of responsibility for the research councils from the Department of Education and Science (DES), thus to become the Department for Education (DFE), to the Office of Science and Technology (OST) which is located in the Office of Public Service and Science (OPSS). Fifth, and finally, we intend to make our usual prognosis. It is an especially appropriate task in the context of this book because it is our contention that, while there may be further tinkering with both structures and procedures, the framework for the future government of higher education has now been put in place. It is a framework which has broad political support, and thus is likely to be modified only at the margins should there be a government of a different political colouring, and it is now accepted – although certainly not embraced – by the most important interested parties in British higher education. We realise, however, as must all of those rash enough to engage in prediction, that our assessment may be made to look foolish in the light of future developments.

THE CHANGING MODELS OF HIGHER EDUCATION IN BRITAIN

The two traditions of higher education in Britain have been formed by the universities and the public sector of higher education, which was most visibly symbolised by the polytechnics. Formerly the distinction between the two sectors was dependent upon the authority the universities possessed to grant their own degrees, whereas the public sector institutions offered courses that led either to external university degrees (the University of London was the main validating university) or, in recent years, to degrees validated by the CNAA. However, the formal distinction was enhanced by a range of more significant social, cultural and pedagogical variables. Before enumerating their most important characteristics, it is necessary to issue the usual health warning with respect to model building. Within each of the two traditions there were critical internal differences, and inevitably there has been a measure of shared culture as well as contrasting values. Furthermore, as we have discussed, some have argued that the polytechnics underwent an 'academic drift' which drew them closer to the university model. Indeed, the Colleges of Advanced Technology, which grew out of the tradition of public sector higher education, were reconstituted as universities on the recommendation of the Robbins Report. What, therefore, we are constructing is ideal types, formed from our distillation of the real world, rather than creating models that are actually to be found in the real world. Finally, it is a distilled reality that reflects twentieth-century experience, especially the years since 1919.

The University Model

a. *Student Recruitment*   Universities were elite institutions recruiting a small percentage of the university age-group (18–21). While there may have been local biases in the pool of potential undergraduates, the universities saw themselves as institutions with a national, even international, appeal. University education was geared to the interests of an academically gifted minority, and entry was controlled by the individual universities and not dependent simply upon performance in public examinations. The Oxbridge colleges, with their own examinations and elaborate interviews, represented the most extreme form of internally controlled selection procedures.

b. *The University Experience* Undergraduates underwent three years of full-time study at the same university. It was a form of education which, although not necessarily anti-vocational in its purpose, tended to emphasise the importance of acquiring a broad-based educational experience. Thus the stress was upon teaching undergraduates to think critically rather than their acquisition of specific job-related skills (it is a question of what was given priority, for obviously the two tasks are not mutually exclusive). Even in the vocationally oriented disciplines the focus was upon learning general principles. The teaching of specific job-related skills could be left to the initial years of post-university training which were a form of apprenticeship undertaken in, for example, hospitals (medical training), solicitors' offices (legal training) or in industry (training in engineering and technology).

The university experience was as much about the acquisition of social and cultural values as it was about acquiring a formal education. Although not all universities could create the intimate environments associated with the ancient institutions, some did establish both colleges and halls of residence. For many middle-class families a university education was integral to their children's *rites de passage* as they moved from adolescence to adulthood.

c. *Teaching and Research* Historically the British, especially the English, universities concentrated their energies upon teaching, that is the transmission of established knowledge. However, within their confines were always to be found those devoted to scholarship, the individual pursuit of new knowledge. In the twentieth century the university don was reconstructed as a person who both taught and undertook research. Teaching and research were perceived as having a symbiotic relationship, that is they supposedly enhanced one another. Although the dividing line between the two is not always easily discernible, the research tradition has strongly emphasised the importance of basic, as opposed to applied, research. The individual academic supposedly fulfilled a dual role, and the university came to be regarded as a centre for both the transmission of established knowledge and the creation of new knowledge. To undertake one without the other was to risk losing the accolade of don in the case of the individual, and of university in the case of the institution. Research was supported by a dual funding system. A significant element of the universities' recurrent grants was intended to support the research activities of their academic faculty (there was an assumption that academics spent somewhere in the region of 40 per cent of their time on research), and much of the research infrastructure in universities was paid for by the UGC in the form of earmarked grants. In addition to the UGC's across-the-board input, individual scholars (increasingly teams of scholars applying for long-term grants for research in designated areas, or for resources to underwrite institutes devoted to favoured areas of research) could apply for funding for their own projects from the research councils.

d. *Autonomous Institutions Controlled by the Dons*   It is this particular aspect of university life which brings us closest to the concerns of this book, that is the relationship between the state and higher education. Throughout much of the twentieth century there was an informal bargain that in return for increasing financial support from the state, the universities would respond to national needs. The state made its resources available in a form which respected the autonomy of the universities; there was a consensus that the universities could be relied upon to fulfil their part of the bargain without experiencing state pressure in a direct and pressing manner. The universities were independent corporate bodies in charge of their own affairs. While this much is generally agreed, what institutional authority should be exercised by the dons is in dispute. If pedagogical issues were the concern of the academic faculty, it does not follow that such matters as planning, finances and administration should also be under faculty control. And yet academic policy could not be formulated without these critical supportive props. On this issue it makes most sense to draw a broad distinction between the Oxbridge tradition of donnish domination, and the civic legacy of strong councils in which the donnish input is more restricted. Historically the respective inputs have fluctuated in importance, with a strong reassertion of the civic legacy in recent years.

It follows logically from what we have said so far that just as there was a tradition of university independence from the state (in spite of ever greater dependence upon the state's financial input), so the universities were not expected to rush lemming-like to fulfil specific societal demands. For example, while the state would expect a positive response to increased demand for higher education, or pleas for the expansion of research and manpower training that allegedly would benefit the economy, the universities most decidedly were not service stations as in Clark Kerr's multiversity model (Kerr, 1963). The possible changes in the character of the university in response to such demands were matters for negotiation in which the universities could rely upon respect for their autonomy, as well as the potential status that they had to confer, as significant bargaining counters.

In spite of our earlier recognition that the British university system was composed of categories of individual institutions that differed from one another in important respects, it is vital to recall that a great deal of discussion of British universities has centred on *the idea of the university*. Thus for all their unique qualities, British universities have been seen as belonging to a common intellectual and socio-cultural tradition that created a shared identity, It is, therefore, part of the traditional model of the British university that there is the idea of a university which encompasses the individual institutions.

The PSHE Model

a. *Student Recruitment* While British higher education as a whole has been widely described as elitist in character, this is a tag that is far less applicable to the PSHE sector. Its institutions catered mainly for people in the local community and their courses frequently led to non-degree qualifications. Although entry may have been restricted to those with the required prerequisite qualifications, potential students did not have to jump over the entry barriers that the universities customarily erected. It may have been a wild exaggeration to label the polytechnics 'the people's universities' (Robinson, 1970), but it would be an even greater misnomer to portray them as elitist institutions.

b. *The Experience of Formal Education in PSHE Institutions* This would vary widely as they offered courses of contrasting lengths that made different demands of their students. Courses could cater for both full-time and part-time students, as well as others who coupled periods of full-time education with full-time employment. The general stress was upon a vocational education that offered students job-related skills, and many courses led to professional qualifications.

All learning situations involve the inculcation of socio-cultural values as well as the transmission of a formal body of knowledge. Indeed, it may prove difficult to appreciate the formal messages without prior acquisition of the supportive socio-cultural props. Notwithstanding this truism, the PSHE institutions were not – with some important exceptions like the teacher training colleges – designed with broad socialising goals in mind. They rarely offered residential facilities, and many of their students, who may have been attending on a part-time basis, continued to live at home, commuting as their course requirements demanded. In these terms the Oxbridge undergraduate college, which conveyed the sense of a closed community with a tightly controlled value system, was at the other end of the spectrum.

c. *Teaching and Research* Over time some of the public sector institutions, most notably the polytechnics, established a research tradition, but they were first and foremost teaching institutions. Their core funding did not assume that their academic faculty was engaged in research. Not surprisingly the comparatively small research tradition that was established strongly reflected the vocational orientation of the institutions; they were in the business of undertaking what is commonly referred to as applied research. Given the historical commitment of the research councils to fund basic research, the state's support for research in the PSHE institutions was inevitably parsimonious.

d. *Public Sector Institutions Founded Locally and by Voluntary Associations, and Restructured by the Central State* These were not institutions, like the universities, with charters granted by the Privy Council and recognised as having independent corporate identities. While many universities were products of state action, and all have been remodelled by the state over time, the ancient universities have a history which predates the emergence of the modern state. In effect most PSHE institutions were created, funded and managed by the local state, and consequently the town hall and the local education authority have been decisive voices in the governing of most public sector institutions for much of their histories. As we have documented, it was the intervention of central government which set some of the public sector institutions (in particular the polytechnics and colleges of education) on the road to institutional self-government, and increased in the 1960s the voice of academic faculty in the government of their affairs. None the less, we are looking at institutions which were always more responsive to direct state pressure, whether it be the local or the central state, and which lacked a tradition of academic involvement in their internal government.

Like many of the civic universities, the public sector institutions were invariably created to cater for local needs and interests, and – unlike the civic universities – this remained the essence of their purpose. As a consequence they were very responsive to immediate social and economic presssures. This was a powerful attraction to Harold Wilson's first Labour government as it sought to regenerate the economy through what was grandly referred to as 'the white heat of the technological revolution'. If the universities could not be relied upon to respond rapidly to the nation's pressing needs (note, for example, the strong sentiment in certain quarters of Attlee's post-war reconstruction administration that the universities had equivocated in the face of demands for expansion, and that they had failed to deliver the necessary manpower to rebuild the shattered economy) then what better option was there than to turn to institutions which could be relied upon to deliver the goods?

The key differences in the two models can be conveniently summarised in the following simple diagrammatical form:

IDEAL TYPES ONE AND TWO:
THE UNIVERSITY AND PSHE MODELS OF HIGHER EDUCATION

The University Model	The PSHE Model
Entry	
Pre-selected and controlled	Pre-selected
Formal Experience of Higher Education	
Degree programmes	Varying qualifications
Full-time study	Full-time, part-time and sandwich courses
Liberal education bias	Vocational bias
A socio-cultural socialisation process	Little socio-cultural socialisation
Teaching and Research	
To transmit and expand knowledge	Teaching institutions
A dual role for each academic	Academics as teachers
Basic research tradition	Some applied research

Relations to State/Society and Tradition of Internal Government

Institutional autonomy	Controlled by the local state and voluntary associations. Increasing central state input
Negotiated response to societal demands	Ready incorporation of societal demands
Donnish domination	External political and bureaucratic influence replaced by internal managerial control

The recent history of higher education in Britain is centred upon the fusion of these two contrasting traditions. The first question that needs to be answered, is what model has emerged from the fusion? Second, and more importantly given the concerns of this book, how will the new model relate to the state? In particular, what mechanisms will the state employ in order to sustain and to develop this model?

To claim that the two established traditions have been fused in recent years, or are in the process of being fused given the contemporary endeavours to add flesh to the HEFC skeletons, may be to misinterpret the nature of what is happening. Fusion suggests the coming together of contrasting elements to create a new whole. It could be argued that the new model of higher education in Britain has simply brought together the two traditions under the common university label (at least as far as the former polytechnics and the old universities are concerned), and that these will continue to flourish within the framework of the new mechanisms of control. The new model purposely negates the idea that universities have a common identity and shared purposes; they are intended to be different kinds of institutions pursuing different kinds of goals. In fact this was a process set in motion long before the passage of the *Further and Higher Education Act*, 1992, and owes much to the *dirigiste* impulse of the UGC in its final years as it pushed for the rationalisation of degree programmes, offered earmarked resources for favoured academic subjects, and differentiated more clearly support for the funding of teaching and of research. It was a *dirigisme* that led to greater institutional differentiation within the old university model. However, it would be an exceedingly shallow analysis that saw the change process as no more than bringing different traditions under the umbrella of a common funding council, without also understanding

189

that the character of the system has been pushed in directions which will make it difficult for most institutions to continue to conform easily to either of the two old models. In other words the amalgamation process has generated important changes in the general character of the system of higher education, and thus to cling to the past is not a risk-free strategy. In very broad terms the system of higher education in Britain has moved towards the PSHE model in all respects except for its relationship to the state.

Higher education in Britain has frequently been described as elitist and compared – usually unfavourably in this regard – with its American counterpart, apparently a mass system of higher education. It is difficult to draw a clear dividing line between so-called elite and mass systems of higher education, and there appears to be little analysis which attempts to do so (it is crucial to compare like with like, and note, for example, that British and American comparisons would need to consider graduation rates as well as the range of institutions that could be said to offer courses that count as higher education), but the sheer size of the expansion in recent years of undergraduate numbers in British universities would suggest that we are moving decisively closer to the American mass model. Much of this expansion may reflect merely a widening of opportunities for middle-class citizens, but there is no doubt that the student base has become more socially heterogeneous and more closely representative of the population at large as increasing numbers of women and mature students have taken up higher education courses.

The expansion of numbers is of secondary importance to ideological change. Universities are no longer perceived as offering an educational experience from which only a comparatively small minority of the most gifted 18-year-olds can benefit. They exist to cater for a broader, and more diverse segment of society at large. More may not mean worse, but undoubtedly it means different. While some of the old universities may retain entry procedures that remind one of obstacle races, many are now prepared to make standard offers without interviews, and see their candidates only at open days. The universities of Oxford and Cambridge are making an increasing number of conditional offers, and Cambridge has abandoned college examinations.

Clearly universities across the board are no longer the all-embracing institutions they once aspired to be. Even Oxbridge colleges, sometimes stimulated by the lure of fee income and consequently full to the seams, will entrust their undergraduates to the tender mercies of landladies. And halls of residence at the redbrick universities degenerate into little more than sleeping quarters and, at Sussex, only on weekdays as the London magnet draws many students away for the week-ends. The marginalisation of any one institution's attractions will inevitably increase with the growth in home residence, the pressure of the commuting grind, the spread of modularity (and thus the possibility of easy institutional transfers), and the spread of semesterisation (with the prospect of summer schools and two-year degrees). As the idea of the university evaporates, so inevitably the idea of what it means to be a student must also change.

And if dons ever have imagined that they could remain cloistered in the groves of academe throughout, and often beyond, their working lives, then they are indeed in for a rude awakening. The most significant change has been the erosion of tenure, speeded up – but not instigated – by the *Education Reform Act*, 1988. The expansion of scientific research brought about the growth of an academic lumpen-proletariat, certainly not well-paid and with precarious job prospects in view of short-term project funding. This development was substantially reinforced by successive cuts in the universities' recurrent UGC income in the decade from approximately the mid-1970s to the mid-1980s. In the context of an apparently never-ending cycle of decline in core funding, it was dangerous to make too many full-time tenured appointments; the much safer option was to fill short-term posts, invariably at the lower end of the salary scale. Then came the 1988 *Education Reform Act* with its restriction of tenure to those already in place, and who were fortunate enough never to be promoted or successful in finding a job in another university! Now the Law Lords have reaffirmed the jurisdiction of university visitors and, depending on university statutes, no academic – regardless of date of appointment – may have tenure.

If it were not enough that a faculty member could remain in situ only as long as there was a demand for his/her mental labour, then the state – through its ever more pressing requirement that teaching and research should be treated as separate functions – was to demonstrate that it had the capacity to turn the screw tighter. While this represents a clear challenge to the prevailing idea of the university don, the attempted formal separation of roles reflects the fact that not all academics undertook research even if their universities were funded as if they did. Moreover, there were some alleged practical advantages from role separation: those who were teachers could possibly be made to teach more, whereas the concentration of research monies could lead to the output of more (and better?) research. It is difficult not to escape the conclusion that this is a change driven as much by finance as ideology, with the in-built supposition that role separation will result in greater value for money.

In terms of the developments we have observed so far, it could be expected that the new model university system will be directed more strongly towards applied, as opposed to basic, research. It will be interesting to see how in the long term the HEFCs distribute their research funding between the old and the new universities. The research councils have moved in the direction of devoting more earmarked resources for designated projects and programmes with a much stronger stress upon both the potential practical applicability of research, and the need for closer research cooperation between higher education institutions and industry. There is no guarantee, however, that the funding councils will follow a similar path. The potent basic research legacy of the old universities may prove difficult to break. Furthermore, if the research element in the funding councils' budgets is to be distributed selectively, following closely the rankings established by the three evaluative exercises to date of the UGC/UFC, then clearly the old universities, and their continuing commitment to basic research, will win out. Moreover, governments may feel, notwithstanding the pressure to relate higher education more closely to the needs of industry, that with the squeeze on the public sector borrowing requirement, their prime concern should be to underwrite the costs of basic research, albeit on a selective basis, and that universities – new and old – should seek funding for applied research in the market place. Of course one way around the dilemma, which to a limited extent has already been put in train, is to transfer the research resources of the funding councils to the research councils, and to leave the former, perhaps only for the time being, with the responsibility for funding teaching alone.

For quite some time now there has been considerable speculation as to the possible development of a three-tier university system structured around the simple balance of research and teaching commitments within the individual institutions: primarily research institutions, primarily teaching institutions, and those institutions with faculties/departments moving in different directions. This seems to be a realistic prognosis, with evidence to suggest that it is already emerging. It is possible that some institutions may be able to sustain both a high quality research output with first-rate teaching standards. In such circumstances, whether the same body of academics, or even the same institutions, will perform the dual functions would be a matter for research. It may be true, contrary to established wisdom, that good teachers are not necessarily in the forefront of their disciplines, and that in order to be in the vanguard of research it may help if one can avoid at least the demands of routine undergraduate teaching. Within Oxbridge it is possible to imagine a situation in which research is essentially a university-sponsored activity, while much of the teaching, even for scientists outside their critical laboratory work, remains the responsibility of the colleges. In due course, when some of the present moves towards the assessment of teaching quality start to bear fruit, we may be closer to answering such questions.

Significant as the changes in the pedagogical character of higher education have been, the changes in its relationship to the state and society have been as, if not more, dramatic. The former public sector institutions have moved decisively, thanks to long-term pressure from the central state, from being locally funded and controlled institutions to nationally funded institutions with the same mechanisms of control as those that govern the old universities. In a comparatively short space of time the polytechnics and colleges have been removed from local authority supervision to the NAB, from the NAB to the PCFC, and in the most recent move from the PCFC to one of the HEFCs. While the parliamentary battles may have focused most attention upon the old universities as their supporters strove to protect individual institutions from the direct attentions of the Secretary of State, to defend tenure, and to build into legislation guarantees of academic freedom, the public sector institutions were quietly undergoing a revolution in their relationship to the state. An evaluation of the significance of the changes for the old universities depends upon how one interprets the differences in the links between, on the one hand the Secretary of State, the UGC and the universities, and on the other hand the Secretary of State, the UFC/HEFCs and the universities. But, regardless of what judgement is reached, the changes have by no means been as drastic as those affecting the former polytechnics and colleges.

Interestingly, the old universities – given that the pedagogical changes affected them more intimately – have experienced a greater shift in their relationship to society than the former polytechnics and colleges. The expansion of student numbers, the admission of a wider ability range, the erosion of the full-time and continuous three-year degree programme pursued throughout at the same university, and the increasing introduction of more vocationally oriented courses has meant – at least on the teaching side – a greater awareness of and responsiveness to market pressures. Somewhat ironically, the state has used its power not to promote its own direct authority, but rather to sponsor institutional responsiveness to society. However, such a strategy may in fact enhance rather than diminish the ultimate authority of the state!

While the amalgamation of the PCFC and the UFC into the HEFCs is the most significant change in recent years in the state's institutional mechanisms for governing the system of higher education in Britain, the transfer of responsibility for the funding of research from the DES (to become the Department for Education, DFE) to the Office of Science and Technology (OST) in the Office of Public Service and Science (OPSS) is not far behind. The move is to be followed by the publication of a White Paper on science which will undoubtedly have much to say about the government's future intentions as to its funding commitments. In the meantime the transfer, which has received broad political support, has given greater visibility to the science lobby and, not surprisingly, has also been welcomed by organisations representing scientific interests. While its policy significance will not be fully revealed until the White Paper has been published, the separation of ministerial responsibility for the universities and the research councils could point to an increasing divergence of interests. The most obvious form this could take would be for the research councils to look with increasing favour upon applications for research grants that do not originate in the universities. In a context of scarce resources, and political pressure to demonstrate value for money, the universities could find themselves in a more competitive situation. Such a move would be likely to speed up the separation of research from teaching commitments in the universities, and to reinforce the research selectivity process. The more competition there is for research council grants, the less the universities are likely to feel that they can afford to spread their own support for research across the whole spectrum of their knowledge maps.

In view of the above developments, it is evident why we have argued that it is increasingly difficult to think in terms of one dominant idea of the university. The present drive is for a pluralist model in which different ideas of the university are pursued, and their relative success is dependent upon their ability to secure resources from both the state and in the market. While there may be good political reasons why no government could contemplate the collapse of a university (note how the financially insolvent University College of Cardiff was rescued by its amalgamation with the University of Wales Institute of Science and Technology (UWIST) and a large infusion of additional Exchequer funding), it does not follow that universities can afford to take their futures for granted. In spite of the ability of the universities to resist, at least to date, some of the more overtly competitive strategies that their paymasters have wanted to foist on them (note, for example, the absymal collapse of the UFC's bidding system, and their successful resistance to the charging of top-up fees), the university world has lost that aura of quiet contemplation and leisurely response to external pressure that not so very long ago was its hallmark. If institutional differentiation is the first characteristic of the new model, then flux is the second. Within such an environment it is not surprising that there has been a greatly increased emphasis upon the need for more administrative expertise. University government and administration have become more demanding over time, and it is now difficult for dons to combine their academic functions with participation in these further activities. The age of the donnish domination of the university is in terminal decline.

As before, these characteristics can be enumerated in simple diagrammatical form.

IDEAL TYPE THREE:
THE NEW UNIVERSITY MODEL OF HIGHER EDUCATION

Entry

A mass system of higher education; entry open to those with the prerequisite qualifications which are defined less restrictively over time.

Formal Experience of Higher Education

Reproduces the PSHE model, see Ideal Types One and Two

Teaching and Research

An increasingly clear-cut separation of these two primary functions of higher education, with differentiation between institutions, departments within institutions, and individual members of the same departments. An increased awareness of the need to support applied research.

Relations to State/Society and the Tradition of Internal Government

Increased responsiveness to societal demands.

Retention of the bulk of state funding through intermediate institutions – the HEFCs and research councils – rather than direct departmental funding. In a formal sense the universities remain autonomous institutions.

A shift in the power balance within universities: restriction in the influence of bodies controlled by the academic faculty with an increase in the influence of both officials and lay persons.

With the merging of the PCFC and the UFC, following the passage of the 1992 *Further and Higher Education Act*, and the transfer of responsibility for the research to the OST, it is our prediction that the seismic changes that have shaken the world of higher education in the past fifteen years or so are drawing to a close. Of course the HEFCs have to work out the all-important methodologies for funding research and teaching, and the forthcoming White Paper on science will have major ramifications for the research councils, but the basic framework is in place and its likely mode of operation is fairly predictable.

Because they have exercised state power for over a decade, the changes have been pushed through by Tory governments, often in the face of strong resistance, inside and outside Parliament, from the opposition parties – and indeed from within the Conservative Party itself. The political heat that has been generated may have created the impression that, were there to have been a government of a different political persuasion, the process of change would have been otherwise. While it would be foolish to deny the possibility that other governments would have acted differently in certain key respects, it is our contention that there is also a considerable measure of cross-party support for the most critical changes that have occurred. To some extent this is a consequence of the sheer longevity of the Conservative governments; in the circumstances pragmatic acceptance of change may be a more realistic response than protracted outright opposition. Moreover, it is also possible that the widely commented upon 'ratchet effect' has been at work; the ideological high ground has been held for so long by the political right that increasingly parties in the centre and to the left have been ideologically undermined. Even if the values of the political right have not contaminated the opposition, we have witnessed – especially in education – a growing acceptance of some of its main concerns, and a fascination with some of its proposed solutions.

It is also important not to forget that the Conservative governments have done many of the things which the opposition parties have been demanding for many years. It is very likely that NAB would have been created sooner if the Labour Party had won the 1979 General Election. The amalgamation of the PCFC and the UFC to form the

HEFCs, with the creation of a more diversified system of higher education, has wide political support. The setting-up of separate funding councils for England, Wales and Scotland (with the latter responsible to the Scottish Education Department in the Scottish Office) is also part of the political consensus. The Labour Party has long advocated the need for a mass system of higher education which is more responsive to the wider society, and in particular to the needs of the economy. The attempt to give science, and more especially scientific research, a higher profile by establishing an Office of Science and Technology also received broad political backing. So widespread was the consensus for the higher education clauses (but *not* further education clauses) of the 1992 *Further and Higher Education Bill* that they were enacted with virtual cross-party support. The parliamentary opposition came from the old university lobby in which Tory MPs and Lords were prominent.

Perhaps the best indication of the extent to which the opposition to the changes of the past decade has been eroded is to examine the changing policy position of the AUT. For many years the AUT, exhibiting at times a knee-jerk reaction, showed unmitigated hostility to all government proposals. Contemporarily a policy strategy, devised by the AUT's Executive, has been adopted which accepts the provision of mass higher education, recognises that this will be accompanied by some reduction in the unit of resource, stresses the importance of maintaining (even improving) the quality of learning, includes the retention of high quality research as 'central to the universities' function' (note, the universities as a collective whole rather than the function of any individual university), and urges the need to improve salaries and conditions of work for university staff (AUT, 1992, 2). There is nothing in the document with which a member of the current government would be likely to disagree. The AUT is one of those interests which, as its Executive recognises, has been forced to readjust its position in the light of changing realities. If, for example, it had continued to insist upon the definition of a university as an institution in which all the academic members undertook their teaching duties within departments devoted to research then 'AUT would find itself with many members in institutions which it did not consider to be "proper universities"' (ibid., 3) – an impossibly divisive situation for the union to countenance.

While the emerging model of higher education may receive widespread acquiescence, if not actual support, there are two areas of disagreement. The first, and most obvious, is what level of resources should be committed to higher education. The alleged parsimony of the government is an easy target for opposition parties, which are in general agreement that higher education should be more generously funded. But the charge of parsimony is all too easy for opposition parties to level at governments. Faced with the responsibilities of office – the need to respond to a range of equally pressing demands, to keep the public sector borrowing requirement under control, and to evaluate carefully the potential political cost of raising taxes – former opposition parties often realise that their erstwhile plans need to be soberly reassessed. The second, and more interesting, point of conflict, concerns the mechanisms that will enable the new model to function, and in this regard there is as much conflict within the Tory Party as between it and the other parties. It is one thing to create a system, quite another to sustain it.

MANAGING THE NEW UNIVERSITY SYSTEM: THE NEXUS OF STATE, SOCIETY AND THE UNIVERSITIES

In our chapter on the UGC we argued that the Committee, from the very beginning, had accepted overall responsibility for managing the university system on behalf of the state. For much of its history it exercised its responsibilities without experiencing either direct political interference from governments or bureaucratic pressures from other parts of the state apparatus. The Chancellor of the Exchequer and the Treasury were lenient, if not always especially generous, paymasters. Furthermore, the socio-cultural links between the Treasury and the UGC were close, their respective personnel appeared to be drawn from the same social backgrounds and they shared similar values. In much the same vein, it would be absurd to claim that the relationship between the UGC and the universities was anything other than harmonious. Formally the UGC may have been part of the state, and university development may have been directed by the UGC, but appearances were otherwise. Over time these appearances began to change: the DES assumed responsibility for the UGC and the research councils, the books of the UGC and the individual universities were opened for parliamentary scrutiny, and the guiding hand of the UGC became more publicly visible and apparently more assertive. From the 1960s onwards the UGC appeared to be subject to more explicit political direction, and more amenable to pressure from the state. In turn the notion that universities were autonomous institutions, in charge of their own destinies, became harder to sustain as the UGC's control over the development of the university system became more public.

It is difficult to pinpoint a precise date to mark the dividing line between these differing stages in the history of state–university relations, but it is ironic to note that the rate of change undoubtedly increased in the first half of the 1980s. While the government was generally committed to relaxing state controls, the UGC was assuming an ever more *dirigiste* posture. The most obvious explanation is that only the UGC was in a position to distribute with any semblance of rationality the severe cuts in the universities' recurrent income. That is, the UGC had to adopt a more visible hands-on role in order to mitigate the effects of government policy. This was acceptable to the government because at that time the only alternative strategies were either to impose a uniform cut across all the universities, or to have required the DES to exercise discrimination on its behalf. In either case it would have been open to the charge of direct government interference in university affairs, and it is dubious whether the DES would have had either the expertise or the will to have imposed selective cuts. At least in the short term, the government needed the UGC.

The cynics may argue that, once having exercised control beyond its wildest dreams, the UGC simply extended its tentacles. The context, however, was one of a continuing squeeze upon recurrent income, coupled with the initiation of special programmes. Again it can be claimed that, given these conditions, the UGC's higher profile served the best interests of the university system, and was not designed merely to enhance its own aggrandisement. Regardless of how the motives of the UGC are interpreted, its management of the university system had become by the mid-1980s both very explicit and very public. As a consequence there was strong pressure upon the universities: to rationalise their academic programmes (UGC enquiries invariably suggested that small departments should be closed with, in some cases, an expansion of larger departments), to distribute their research income more selectively (the UGC started to distinguish more explicitly between the teaching and research elements in its funding of the universities, and it initiated the research selectivity exercises), and to encourage particular areas of academic development (those that could expect earmarked resources). It was difficult not to form the impression that the UGC was now managing the system on behalf of the state, rather than making representations to government on behalf of the university system, while the individual universities continued to determine their own futures. This image was strongly reinforced by the UGC's move towards formula funding which seemed to suggest that the UGC was rapidly becoming a rational management body as opposed to a committee of eminent insiders who exercised their collective judgement. The impetus for such developments may have been political, instigated by the government of the day, but the UGC was devising the overall pattern of the universities' response to the tightening financial strait-jacket and the ever-recurring demand that the universities should be more responsive to the nation's economic needs.

There are varying interpretations of the demise of the UGC: apparent intense government malaise with the pattern of its selective cuts in recurrent university income which seemingly discriminated unfairly against those universities with a strong vocational and technological bias, its alleged failure to build positively upon the more *dirigiste* role that it had acquired in the early 1980s, or simply the need – so it was claimed – to place the UGC upon a statutory basis, rather than to permit its continued existence to remain sanctioned by a Treasury Minute. It is likely that if the Labour Party had won the 1979 General Election, the UGC would have survived, and that it would have been encouraged to develop an enhanced planning role – under closer political and departmental direction – *vis-à-vis* the universities. It is our contention, however, that sooner or later, a Conservative government, strongly infused with the ideology that the market knows best, would have reached the conclusion that the UGC needed to be replaced by a body apparently more in tune with its own thinking. The UGC was an organisation that represented traditional university values (even its decisions in response to the income cuts of the early 1980s could be interpreted in that light), and it was widely regarded as a lobby on behalf of the university estate. The Thatcher governments were inclined to see professional bodies as defenders of vested interests, and the UGC could be perceived in much the same way. Even if the government were satisfied with the UGC's actions in the early 1980s, it could scarcely tolerate indefinitely its assuming increasing responsibilities while remaining only on the fringes of the state apparatus, particularly in the light of the intensifying conflict between the government and the universities. In such circumstances an unreformed UGC was always a potential thorn in the side of government; it could annoy even if it could not wound.

The consequence was the replacement of the UGC by the UFC which, following its amalgamation with the PCFC, has been superseded by the HEFC, with separate councils for England, Scotland and Wales. Superficially, it would appear that the UGC has been replaced by an alternative bridge between the state and the universities, although the continuity in formal structure is far less important than how the varying institutions relate to one another in the actual conduct of their business. However, there are continuing pressures within the Conservative Party to dismantle this institutional structure, and for the state to encourage a much closer relationship between the universities and their clients. On the teaching front, this could mean giving students vouchers with which they would purchase directly their higher education. On the research front, the state's resources could be allocated entirely to the research councils which would then distribute them to deserving applicants – from the universities or elsewhere. Whereas research quality could be ensured by appropriate processes of evaluation, teaching quality could be measured by the changing pattern of student demand.

There have been some tentative moves to decrease the reliance of higher education upon the financial input of the funding councils, and much exhortation to encourage universities to increase their non-governmental income. Student fees have been increased sharply, although except for those who pay their own fees (mainly overseas students who are required to pay full-cost fees), the consequence is simply that this income reaches the institutions via alternative state channels. Whether this increases client pressure by making the universities more aware of the link between their income and their student numbers is a moot point. Certainly, given the pressure upon institutions to increase the intake of fees-only students, it could have some effect. The introduction of the loans scheme, with loans assuming an increasing profile in the pattern of student support, may also intensify client pressure upon the universities. Presumably the thinking is that, if students have to bear a greater proportion of the costs of pursuing higher education, then they will be more careful about where they decide to study and what they decide to study, and be keener to ensure that their chosen university delivers a high quality education. But until universities start to charge differential tuition fees (as occurs with overseas students, and already in other cost areas such as accommodation), to be paid for directly by the student (even if the student does not personally meet the cost), then the attempts to forge different client–institutional relationships through such mechanisms can at best be described as marginal.

There are two interrelated problems faced by those who want

universities to be more directly responsive to society. Historically, society, at least in England, has been largely indifferent to its universities which may reflect a deep-seated university antipathy towards the concerns of society at large. In the twentieth century the universities became the responsibility of the state, and ever more dependent upon it financially, so establishing a mould which is going to be extremely difficult to break. Although growing dependence upon the state has been a common development for university systems throughout the Western world, it has been taken further in Britain than almost anywhere else. At least, therefore, for the immediate future the British universities will continue to be overwhelmingly dependent upon state funding. Those, therefore, who believe that universities need to offer a more diverse range of services, competing vigorously with one another for students and research income, have to face the reality that their functions – that is, teaching and research – will be underwritten by the Exchequer. The infusion of public monies not only makes universities amenable to public accountability pressures but also means that inevitably they will face demands to accommodate themselves to public policy as determined by the government of the day. Even if a programme of student vouchers were to be instigated, not only would the service have to be administered bureaucratically, by the state or privately, but much more significantly it would reflect publicly defined policy goals. Although there would be a societal input into the shaping of those goals, their final form would be established in the various institutions of the state, and not in the market-place.

The current relations between the state and the universities can best be described as an attempt on the part of the government to create a managed market financed essentially by public money, the universities are given wide institutional control over their own affairs while operating within centrally defined and regulated parameters that are managed by the funding agencies. There are thus three levels to the current relationship between the state and the universities: the parameters which are under the control of the state, the management of those parameters (which includes translating them into precise operational procedures) as carried out by the funding bodies, and the autonomy of the individual universities which is exercised within the framework of the above two levels of control. Some have argued (Griffith, 1989; Millar, 1992) that to all intents and purposes the funding bodies (previously the UFC and the PCFC and now the HEFCs) are little more than creatures of the ministers and their departments, and that university autonomy – with the connivance of the CVCP – is a dead letter. Even if one feels that the evidence can be reasonably interpreted to support this conclusion, it is none the less necessary to appreciate the continuing subtlety in state–university relations, While universities may be under state control, we need to be aware of the form in which the state exercises that control, for without such analysis the temptation is to simplify what remains an interesting and delicate relationship.

There is a powerful tradition that ministers should not interfere directly in the affairs of individual universities, and certainly not in academic matters. Moreover, for the state apparatus to concern itself with the day-to-day management of university affairs would require it both to accept extra burdens and to expose itself to a great deal of hostility which almost certainly it would prefer to avoid. If there is control, therefore, it has to be couched in broad terms. On the financial front there is the obvious question of the government's commitment to university funding. In the early 1980s it was possible to legitimise cuts in funding on the grounds of a shrinking demand for higher education; in the late 1980s expansion finds political favour and there is a purposeful attempt to stimulate demand among previously under-represented groups. It is possible to use demographic trends to justify policy decisions, but it is politics and not demography that determines policy. Universities and polytechnics were encouraged to expand by accepting fees-only students, and subsequently this was made more attractive by sharply increasing the value of those fees, although this was *not* the policy intention behind this shift. Currently, and deeply influenced by the desire to contain the level of public sector borrowing, the government has announced a sharp reduction in university fees. It is not that universities are being required to slow their rate of expansion (in fact quite the contrary) but that the government had made it less financially attractive for them to expand on the backs of the fees-only students.

On the financial front, besides determining the overall level of its resource commitment, the major concern of the state is to ensure that the institutions of higher education act in a financially responsible manner. Parliamentary criticism of the universities' financial manage- ment, as well as that of the funding bodies themselves, has been particularly severe. The Public Accounts Committee made acerbic comments on events at University College at Cardiff, the manner in which some universities had conducted their redundancy pro- grammes, and on the way that – even after the passage of the

Education Reform Act, 1988 – several universities were running deficits and faced possible bankruptcy. This is as much, possibly even more of, a management question and as such falls mainly within the province of the funding councils. However, both the 1988 and 1992 Acts specify the need for careful audit and give the Secretary of State what can best be described as reserve powers *vis-à-vis* both funding councils and individual universities. The problem is that audit can be only an 'after-the-event' form of control, and Parliament has weakened the ministerial hand by refusing to permit specific conditions to be attached to grants made to individual institutions. Parliament probably feels that if university autonomy is to retain any meaning whatsoever, it is impossible to impose too many close conditions upon the making of a grant. Presumably the hope is that the controls are now sufficient to guarantee financial probity (not that there was much suspicion of widespread wrongdoing), and should there be shortcomings, the new legislative framework and administrative procedures will ensure that it is spotted quickly and acted upon swiftly.

Although the funding councils are expected to manage the universities, they do so within the framework of ministerial directives designed to ensure that the public receives value-for-money in return for the Exchequer's input. This is not simply a financial issue, but one that affects, in the broadest terms, the general direction of academic policy. As such we can see it as state influence, expressed both administratively and politically, upon the universities' academic development. Of course, universities have grown accustomed to ministerial exhortation to increase their commitment to science and technology ever since they started to receive tranches of public money. For example, when he was Secretary of State, Sir Keith Joseph made frequent statements to the effect that the central purpose of public investment in higher education was to assist economic growth. In concrete terms this again meant that the universities should expand their relative support for science and technology. There were specific programmes (the expansion of information technology, the 'new blood' appointments, and the Engineering and Technology Programme) which directed earmarked resources to this end. Although important in their own right, and as reflecting a general signal, their overall impact was limited. Either universities are autonomous institutions or they receive public money in a form which leaves them no option but to structure – significantly, rather than at the margins – their academic programmes in a manner consistent with ministerial imperatives.

Perhaps of greater significance is the clear ministerial support for the concentration of public resources donated for research. This has been reiterated frequently in recent years, and the funding councils have steadily implemented policies to fulfil it. It may be argued by government that more sharply defined separation of teaching and research roles will lead to better value for money – with the implication that the government's interest is financial in nature – but the intrusion has profound consequences both for the role of the individual academic as well as the functions of the universities. If universities are, overwhelmingly, publicly funded bodies, it is to be expected that the state would have a powerful interest in determining their academic character, and the tasks of their dons, but it does throw into question the traditional ideology of university autonomy. Historically the universities have operated within a value system that imagined that it was possible to separate funding from academic issues. Sooner or later it was inevitable that 'he who pays the piper would call the tune' and, to extend the metaphors, 'the chickens have come home to roost'!

The dimensions of ministerial guidance that we have considered above – control of the overall budget, projections of student numbers, the desire for a shift to science and technology, and the steady pressure in favour of the separation of the teaching and research functions – predate the 1988 *Education Reform Act*. But what that Act, reinforced subsequently by the 1992 *Further and Higher Education Act*, did was to place these various inputs into a statutory context which, besides extending them, greatly reinforced the hand of the Minister and Department against both the funding councils and the universities. As we have already dealt with the way in which legislation shaped the interaction between the Minister and the UFC/ PCFC, we will focus now upon the Department–HEFCs relationship as outlined in the 1992 Act, with particular reference to England. The Secretary of State appoints the members of the funding council, he makes grants to the council 'subject to such terms and conditions as he may determine' (Clause 68 [1]), he can require the repayment of sums if there is a failure to comply with the terms and conditions (Clause 68 [4]), and while the council can proffer advice and information 'as they think fit' (as well as being required to do so), they do so in a manner to be determined by the Secretary of State (Clause 69 [1]). Moreover, 'The Secretary of State may by order confer or impose on a council such supplementary functions relating to the provision of education as he thinks fit' (Clause 69 [5], and – presumably with University

College, Cardiff, in mind – 'If it appears to the Secretary of State that the financial affairs of any institution within the higher education sector have been or are being mismanaged he may, after consulting the council and the institution, give such directions to the council about the provision of financial support in respect of the activities carried on by the institution as he considers are necessary or expedient by reason of the mismanagement' (Clause 81 [3]).

While the legislation, supplemented by interpretation in the courts, imposes a binding framework upon the Minister and Department as well as the funding council and universities, it is a set of parameters that emerged from above rather than below. Although the universities were able to force concessions from the government, with reference to both the 1988 and the 1992 Acts, the present legislative framework is not one that the dominant university interests would have designed. Besides creating new guidelines, the legislation has inevitably led to the weakening – at the very least – of the traditional conventions that governed the old institutional nexus, with the consequence that the new conventions will emerge in a context that is less favourable to the interests of both the funding councils and the universities. Not only did the 1988 and the 1992 Acts give more formal authority to the Secretary of State than prevailed in the UGC years, but also the Acts have placed precise obligations upon the present funding councils which are quite clearly politically inspired. The funding councils not only have to relate to the state in a legislatively prescribed fashion, but the state places legal obligations upon them in the performance of their duties beyond the obvious need to fund the research and teaching activities of the universities.

Each council will be required, as the 1992 Act puts it, to assess 'the quality of education provided in institutions for whose activities they provide' (Clause 70 [1]), and to this end the funding councils have to 'establish a committee, to be known as the "Quality Assessment Committee", with the function of giving them advice on the discharge of their duty' (Clause 70 [1]). In recent years the quality of university research has come under scrutiny, and currently the institutions and procedures required to assess university teaching are being erected. As funding decisions have followed the evaluation of research, so we can expect a measure of discrimination in the funding of teaching to follow on from these further evaluative exercises. Finally, it needs to be pointed out that, although the legislative framework is not entirely under the control of the government, it cannot be modified without its sanction. So the state has put in place the current structures and procedures, and also determines whether they will be amended or not. Thus a very different situation exists from when such relationships were determined mainly by convention.

In the days before the HEFCs formally acquired responsibility for the funding of the universities (1 April 1993), there were protracted meetings between the UFC and the PCFC to determine the new council's funding procedures (our reference is to the HEFC for England). Clearly in a more diversified system of higher education there are a wider range of interests to be placated, and one can expect this to be reflected in the compromises that are reached. It is quite likely that, once the teething troubles are resolved, the procedures will be modified to reflect more clearly basic management principles as opposed to the need for political compromises. In the meantime the decisions have to be made in a context within which: 'In 1992–93, a total of £547.5M was distributed by the UFC for research to HEIs in England. The PCFC allocated £7M in the same year' (UFC-PCFC, 1992, 5). Moreover, in the UFC sector itself in the same year '25 institutions in England received some 75 per cent of the funding for research' (ibid.). In other words, research funding was becoming ever more selectively distributed. It is reasonable to expect at least some initial dilution of this trend in the early years of the amalgamation of the two funding bodies. The proposed new formula of the HEFC for England contains an element 'to encourage the development of research activity and to reward research potential in departments which do not receive substantial research funds' (ibid., 16), which could be said to favour the new universities but, as in the old UFC research funding formula, the overwhelming bulk of the monies (approximately 90 per cent according to some estimates) will follow volume and quality ratings. As much as the new formula may upset certain elements in the old university system, it seems a small genuflection in the direction of the new universities in view of the magnitude of the changed circumstances.

Given that, unlike research, both the former UFC and PCFC sectors were heavily involved in teaching, it has proved less controversial for the HEFC of England to create a formula for the distribution of its teaching funds. In its essentials it is closer to the model adopted by the PCFC: 'It is a core-plus-margin method with institutions guaranteed a very high percentage in real terms of their previous year's funding. In return for this guaranteed funding – the core – institutions will be expected to maintain home and EC enrolments. The remaining funds

– the margin – will be distributed on a competitive basis' (HEFCE, 1992, 3–4). Although the procedures for assessing teaching quality are not yet in place, the Funding Council has made it clear that those universities deemed to be providing high quality provision 'will be given an advantage in the competition for the allocation of new funded numbers' (ibid., 4), while departments (our term) judged to be making an unacceptably low quality of provision will be ineligible to compete for additional funded places, and could even have their support withdrawn if their quality fails to improve! Although the terms of the competition for additional funded places are at present unavailable, it seems likely, given the continuing expansionist pressures, that they will be constructed in such a way as to reward those institutions which take a disproportionate number of fees-only students, so following the prior example of the UFC, with the additional consideration of teaching quality built into the equation.

The former university and polytechnic sectors of higher education adopted different stances on the evaluation of teaching quality. The element of external intervention in such matters was inevitably higher in the polytechnics given that their degree programmes required the approval of the CNAA. Moreover, the polytechnics had admitted the HMIs to assess their teaching quality. By way of contrast, it is a powerful part of the traditional idea of a university that these are matters in which it is inappropriate for external parties to intervene, that teaching is the domain of the university don, and that standards can be guaranteed through the system of external examiners. In the face of political pressure, the CVCP established the Academic Audit Unit, in the belief that self-regulation was infinitely preferable to externally controlled monitoring. In a further move, designed in part to ward off the attentions of the HEFCE, the universities have now put into operation the Higher Education Quality Council (HEQC). While this is politically adroit, it still remains the responsibility of the funding councils to undertake the assessment of teaching quality. To this end the HEFCE has established a Quality Assessment Committee (QAC) and, while the specific procedures it intends to follow have yet to be finalised, the general principles which will govern its strategy are now known:

> There will be three distinct elements to the assessment process. Firstly, a set of performance indicators (PIs) will be collected and analysed. Secondly, institutions will be asked to provide a self-assessment of the quality of the education in the subject

concerned. Thirdly, the assessment team will visit the institution to assess the quality of education (HEFCE, 1992a, 7).

The final assessment outcome in each case appears as if it will be a combination of quantitative data and qualitative judgements. Regardless of the form it may finally take, the significance of the development cannot be overstated. It is not that a large measure of teaching incompetence is likely to be uncovered, but rather that it represents yet another level of managerial control to which critical funding decisions have been attached; a further plank in the new framework within which the universities are required to function.

The fourth set of managerial guidelines (after those governing the funding of teaching and of research, and of quality assessment) that the Funding Councils have to establish is a Financial Memorandum between themselves and the institutions they fund. This was taken a long way forward by the UFC, not surprisingly in view of the malaise surrounding the financial control – or rather the lack of it – exercised by the UGC. Institutions are now required to designate a principal officer with overall responsibility for ensuring that council funds are spent appropriately, to follow general guidelines in the management of their financial affairs, to present their accounts in an acceptable form, to ensure that they have in place a system of financial and managerial controls, and to accept that they are open to visits by the council's auditors who may be accompanied by DFE internal auditors (HEFCE, 1992b). Procedures *per se* cannot guarantee that financial irregularities will not occur, but these are such as to suggest that, should they occur, they will not be allowed to fester.

Are the managerial controls exercised by the funding councils over the individual institutions, and in turn the ministerial constraints upon the funding councils, so severe that to all intents and purposes there is no university autonomy? In effect, are the universities *de facto* part of the state? The answer to these questions depends upon how the slippery concept of autonomy is interpreted, how constraining the controls are perceived to be, and with what degree of rigour they will be enforced. It is a matter to be decided by both conceptual interpretation, and how the course of events evolves over time. We believe that it is still meaningful to see British universities as autonomous institutions, but their autonomy has a particular meaning. They are not constrained, as increasingly they were in the final years of the UGC, by a funding council which perceives itself as a planning body. The universities write their own mission statements, develop their own plans, and define their own strategies for achieving their goals. But, needless to say, they undertake these tasks in circumstances not of their own choosing. Moreover, they have to be sensitive to the fact that these circumstances may change, which could require them to modify their strategies. If diversity is the main characteristic of the new model university system, then the fluidity of its context is the main pressure to which it has to adjust.

There has been considerable pressure upon the universities to augment the income they obtain from the market as opposed to the Exchequer. While many universities have made moves in this direction, obviously this was a more viable option for some rather than others, with probably the Universities of Oxford and Cambridge in the most advantaged position. With the emphasis upon separating out research income from teaching income in the universities' recurrent grant, and the increasingly selective distribution of research income, the universities had to make key decisions as to how they would respond to this situation. If they perceived the need to maintain a high research income, they had to take steps to ensure that the work of their departments was rated highly in the research selectivity exercises. Very interestingly, the new University of Central England (UCE – formerly Birmingham Polytechnic) has made a conscious decision *not* to bid for research funding from the HEFCE:

> ... it has taken a policy decision to build on its strengths in near-market and applied research funded by industry, commerce and public authorities, rather than diversify simply because there is money on offer .... On the one hand, there will be the possibility of missing out on some public funding, but on the other, the board of governors has given the university a clear mission (Warner, 1992, 19).

Thus the UCE has made a purposeful decision not to move into the kinds of research fields traditionally supported by the funding councils. The UFC encouraged the expansion of student numbers by rewarding those universities which took on a disproportionate share of 'fees-only' students with additional 'fully-funded' undergraduates; a move that was enhanced by a sharp increase in the value of the fee. In view of recent cuts in that value, the expansion of 'fees-only' student numbers may appear a less attractive option. This is a perfect example of the manipulation of one of the parameters within which university decision-making takes place. It is not that the universities are being required either to act, or not to act, in a particular way, but that they need to re-evaluate past decisions in the light of changing circumstances. Again, one can expect the universities to move in different directions according to their own circumstances.

There has been significant external pressure upon how universities manage their internal affairs, with – almost as a direct consequence – the University of Cambridge undertaking the most radical changes in its structure of government and administration. It is undoubtedly true to say that the balance of power between university councils (often with strong lay representation) and senates (controlled by the academic faculty) has swung to the former, and that there has been renewed emphasis upon both the quality of university officials and the importance of their input into the policy-making process. It will be interesting to see whether these developments *per se* will result in the logic of the external pressures filtering down to change university policies and practices, or whether the state – either by modifying the parameters or bearing down more directly upon the funding councils – will have to exert a heavier hand. For example, it is true that the research income of the funding councils is being distributed more selectively to institutions, but it is more problematic as to how vigorously the institutions in turn are pursuing the selective internal distribution of those resources. It is within the old universities that the potency of the traditional values is strongest, and thus will prove most difficult to break down. Moreover, if the institutions themselves are apparently prepared to pay the price for what may seem from the outside irrational decisions, then – short of removing institutional autonomy altogether – there are limits to what the state can do.

If within the individual institutions the pressure has been for more lay representation in government, more administrative expertise and more flexible responses to changing parameters (aided by the steady erosion of tenure, the expansion of a more malleable work-force, and perhaps, eventually, local bargaining over pay and conditions of service), at the level of interaction between institutions the trend has been toward amalgamation and cooperation. In the more dramatic cases this has led to the merging of whole institutions and, less dramatically, the fusion of departments within differing institutions, the various bodies that conducted business for either the old university sector or the polytechnics (for example, UCCA and PCAS), or those organisations that represented specific interests within the two sectors (for example, the CVCP and the CDP), have either merged or are in the process of doing so. Inevitably this is a time of flux, and the

211

pace of change will take some time to slow down. However, if our analysis is correct, and this is indeed the age of the managed market, then change will be one of the permanent characteristics of the new model university system, even if the structures and principles that govern the system are now in place and set to last.

THE THEORY OF EDUCATIONAL CHANGE: THE INTERACTION OF THE STATE'S POLITICAL AND BUREAUCRATIC DYNAMICS

In our previous work we attempted to define the educational state (Salter and Tapper, 1985, 15–39), and emphasised the expanding role of the DES in forcing the pace of educational change (Salter and Tapper, 1981, 87–114). In this book we have examined the part played by the key institutions in the government of higher education, and have stressed the interaction of political and departmental pressures in bringing about a new model of higher education. Our heightened emphasis upon the importance of the political dynamic in forcing the process of educational change is a direct response to the new realities of the Thatcher years. In our opinion, if the consensual mould of government had continued into the 1980s, there is little doubt that the then DES would have exercised both a steadily expanding control of the educational service and an ever tighter hold over the process of educational change. The reality is, however, that when the first Thatcher government took office it contained powerful elements which claimed that the alleged failings of the British educational system were primarily the responsibility of a misguided educational establishment in which was included the DES. What the government believed it had to do was to break the power of this establishment and increase the authority of other parties – employers, governors and, above all, parents.

However, a quite different set of circumstances has been enacted. The significance of the input of what may be called the middle levels of power (most notably the local education authorities and the teachers' unions) has been undermined, while both the authority of the centre (the minister and department) and of the individual institutions has been increased substantially. With respect to higher education the government has retained an important role for the traditional institutional layer between itself and the individual institutions, but it has recast its character in an essentially managerial mould. While the funding councils may make representations on behalf of the universities to government, and indeed may have some policy influence, there can be little doubt that their main purpose is to perform a number of prescribed functions (the distribution of resources for teaching and research, the assessment of the quality of higher education, and the monitoring of the universities' financial probity) according to guidelines that are controlled at the centre both through legislation as well as by the minister and department. As in terms of schooling, the individual institutions – whose administration and government have been gradually reshaped – are granted a considerable measure of autonomy, with the obvious condition that they have to exercise it within the state's newly constructed boundaries. And it is at the level of the individual institutions that the government can claim to have genuflected to those political elements within its ranks that wanted to make the universities both more amenable to the pressures of their clients and competitive in their receipt of state funding. What we have called a managed market has been created.

The relationships between the various parties may be summarised diagrammatically as follows:

Level One: Defining the Parameters

Controlled by legislation, government policy and departmental action.

Level Two: The Managerial Functions

Functions decided at level one, but how these are to be implemented is determined at this level with some guidance, plus potential intervention, from above.

Level Three: The Universities

Autonomy in the context of boundaries established at Levels One and Two. Level One and Two institutions have powers that enable them to intervene directly in the affairs of the universities, but these are essentially of a reserve nature and, as such, will rarely be used.

The process of change in the relationship between the three levels is directed from above, although it may be true, as when the universities successfully resisted the UFC's attempt to impose a bidding system for student numbers, that the universities can resist measures designed to change their behaviour. In such situations one could imagine an appeal from Level Two to Level One institutions in order to buttress their authority and enforce compliance. But this would undermine some of the credibility vested in the middle-order institutions (and perhaps even threaten their own survival), and could prove a lengthy and costly process. It is much more likely that the Level Two institutions will adopt new strategies which make non-compliance less likely. Thus the UFC moved from a proposed bidding system to one that encouraged expansion and the cutting of unit costs by offering incentives to universities to take 'fees-only' students. In the same vein, it was widely mooted in the run-up to the replacement of the UGC by the UFC that the government's legislation would require the funding councils to make their resources available through contractual agreements between themselves and the universities. In the event neither the 1988 *Education Reform Act* nor the 1992 *Further and Higher Education Act* contains any reference to contracts. The universities lobbied to scotch this idea, and clearly demonstrated sufficient political support to warn the government that it was an idea that could not easily be enforced. Political discretion on the part of the government, therefore, led to a reshaping of the parameters. Although, therefore, the relationship between the three levels is directed from above, it is important not to overlook this element of struggle between, and within, levels in determining the nature of the boundaries, the management strategies, and indeed the development programmes of the individual universities.

Judgements as to whether the funding councils are to all intents and purposes part of the state apparatus and, as such, a mere appendage of the minister's authority, depend upon how significant you perceive their functions to be and the measure of discretion with which they can exercise them. It could be argued that their functions are mainly technical in nature and that their discretion is highly circumscribed by the parameters within which they most decidedly have to operate. This is not a view that we share. Although the controlling boundaries lay down the broad principles that the funding councils have to follow, how they are to be put into effect is by no means clearly defined. These are matters that will be determined by trial and error over time. This is a large arena waiting to be filled with new conventions in which all three levels will have a part to play. While the functions of the funding councils may be managerial in kind, demanding the evolution of technical expertise, they are none the less of critical importance. How to fund teaching and research, in what form quality control will be exercised, and the determination of financial probity may all be functions imposed on the councils, but this does not make the councils any less important. It could be fairly argued that, because of increased pressure from the state for the funding councils to exercise tighter supervision of university development, the role of the HEFCs has been considerably enhanced in comparison with the functions exercised by the now defunct, but still nostalgically remembered, UGC.

The framework within which the funding councils operate is regulated by a combination of legal, political and bureaucratic forces. For example, both legislation and the jurisdiction of university visitors is subject, within certain boundaries, to court rulings. Inevitably there is a considerable political input into many of the key ministerial decisions: the appointment of members to the councils, the issuing of the government's guidelines to the councils, the size of the Exchequer's input into higher education, and the form in which it is to be made available (for example, the balance between fee income and council funding). While these are political decisions, they are made within a departmental context and will be finalised on the advice of the pertinent civil servants. Moreover, there is a potentially strong departmental monitoring of university and funding council accounts. Perhaps more interesting, and more difficult to assess, is the relative weight of these varying inputs in changing the parameters of the state's control. We have already shown how the public sector of higher education received departmental favour from both the Ministry of Education and the DES, and that the wresting of control over public sector institutions from the local authorities owed much to the persistence of the DES. Ultimately, however, the most crucial decisions require government support. Thus, regardless of what the established position of the DES may have been, it was ultimately a political decision to create the NAB and to replace it with the PCFC. What the bureaucratic dynamic requires is favourable political circumstances to realise its policy goals. However, so long as no government can relinquish the links between the commitment of public resources, the need for public accountability, and the promotion of public policy, then its reliance on a strong and competent department is inevitable. Legal, political and bureaucratic interaction, combined with the manipulation of financial resources, are the ingredients of state power – past, present and future.

Appendix 1

Key Dates in the History of the Relations Between the State and Higher Education

1889 A Treasury Minute creates an *ad hoc* Committee on Grants to University Colleges in Great Britain.

1906 A Treasury Minute creates the Standing Advisory Committee on Grants to Colleges.

1911 A new Standing Advisory Committee on University Grants is established under the auspices of the Board of Education.

1916 The Department of Scientific and Industrial Research (DSIR) is created and made the responsibility of the Lord President of the Council.

1919 A Treasury Minute establishes the University Grants Committee (UGC).

1946 The University Grants Committee is given new, more *dirigiste* terms of reference.

1947 The Advisory Council on Scientific Policy (ACSP) is created.

1963 The Committee on Higher Education (Robbins) reports.

1964 The Department of Education and Science (DES) replaces the Ministry of Education and assumes responsibility for both the UGC and the research councils, including the ACSP.

1965 The Council for Scientific Policy (CSP) replaces the ACSP.

1965 The Secretary of State for the DES, Anthony Crosland, makes his famous Woolwich Polytechnic speech which leads to the creation of the polytechnics as an alternative tier of higher education to the universities.

1974 The Advisory Board for the Research Councils (ABRC) replaces the CSP.

1982 The National Advisory Board (NAB) for Local Authority Higher Education is created to assume broadly similar functions to the UGC for polytechnics and colleges.

1985 The remit of the NAB is extended to include the voluntary colleges and it is renamed the National Advisory Body for Public Sector Higher Education.

1988   The Education Reform Act creates the University Funding Council (UFC) which replaces the UGC (so placing, for the first time, the relationship between the state and the universities on a statutory basis). The Polytechnics and Colleges Funding Council (PCFC) replaces the NAB.

1992   The Further and Higher Education Act leads to the amalgamation of the UFC and the PCFC into the Higher Education Funding Councils (HEFCs). There will be separate funding councils for English, Scottish and Welsh institutions with the English funding council reporting to the Department for Education (DFE), the Scottish council to the Scottish Education Department, and the Welsh council to the Welsh Office.

1992   The DES becomes the DFE as its responsibilities for the ABRC and the science budget are transferred to the Office of Science and Technology (OST) in the Office of Public Service and Science (OPSS). A White Paper on Science and Technology is promised for 1993.

Appendix 2

The Changing Institutional Relations between the State and Higher Education

FIGURE 1

FROM THE CREATION OF THE UGC TO THE FORMATION OF THE DES, 1919–64

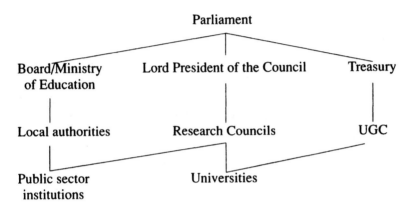

FIGURE 2

FROM THE CREATION OF THE DES TO THE 1988 EDUCATION REFORM ACT, 1964–88

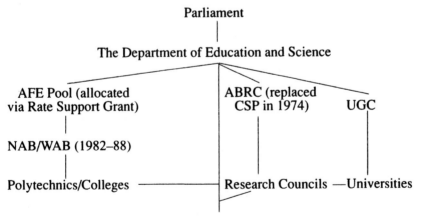

Open University, Cranfield, Royal College of Art
(funded by the DES until 1993)
The Voluntary Colleges
(post-1985 placed under the auspices of NAB/WAB)

Note: The Scottish Education Department funded directly the Scottish Central Institutions,
Scotland's equivalent to the polytechnics, an arrangement that continued until 1993.

FIGURE 3

FROM THE EDUCATION REFORM ACT, 1988, TO THE FURTHER AND
HIGHER EDUCATION ACT, 1992

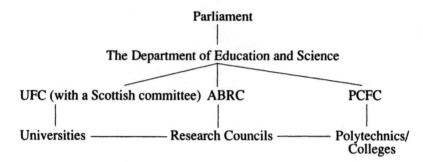

Note: Even after the passage of the 1988 Education Reform Act, the Welsh polytchnics and colleges remained under the auspices of their local authorities and the Wales Advisory Body.

FIGURE 4

FROM 1993

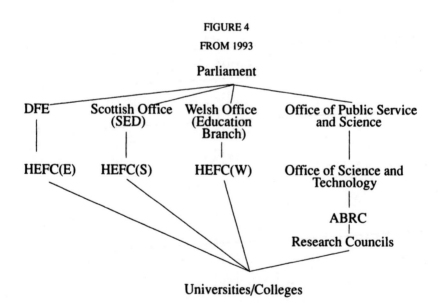

Appendix 3

Key Statistics

TABLE 1

UGC'S RECURRENT GRANT, FEE INCOME AND RESEARCH INCOME
AS A PERCENTAGE OF TOTAL UNIVERSITY INCOME (GREAT
BRITAIN)

	Recurrent Grant %	Fee Income %	Research Income %
1925/26	31.6	–	–
1939/40	33.1	–	–
1949/50	61.5	–	–
1959/60	70.5	10.0	7.9
1969/70	70.3	7.0	12.0
1979/80	63.1	15.9	13.6
1989/90	47.9	13.9	19.3

Sources: UGC Returns: 1925–26: Table 9; 1939–40: Table 5; 1949–50: Table 10; 1959–60: Table 11; 1970: Table 41; 1980a: Table 2; UFC, 1989–90a: Table 1.

We have included more information for 1959/60 onwards to demonstrate that the relative decline of the UGC's recurrent grant in the university income does not signify as dramatic a decline in dependence on state finance as the figures may suggest but rather an increase in the importance of fee and research income, most of which was provided by the Exchequer.

TABLE 2

TOTAL UNIVERSITY INCOME (GREAT BRITAIN)

	Total Income (£000s)	% Increase
1925/26	4,818	
1939/40	6,488	34.0
1949/50	22,010	239.2
1959/60	59,800	171.7
1969/70	269,585	350.8
1979/80	1,266,564	369.8
1989/90	3,900,000	207.9

Sources: As for Table 1.

TABLE 3
FULL-TIME UNIVERSITY STUDENT NUMBERS (GREAT BRITAIN)

	Total Numbers	% Increase
1922/23	36,404	
1938/39	42,323	16.3
1949/50	85,421	101.8
1959/60	104,009	21.8
1969/70	219,308	110.9
1979/80	292,738	33.5
1989/90	334,479	14.3

Sources: UGC Returns: 1922–23: Table 1; 1938/39: Table 1; 1949–50: Table 1; 1959–60: Table 1; 1970: Table 2; 1980: Table 2; UFC, 1989–90: Table 1.

TABLE 4
FULL-TIME AND PART-TIME UNIVERSITY STUDENTS IN HIGHER EDUCATION (UNITED KINGDOM)

	(thousands) 1956/66	1970/71	1980/81	1990/91
Universities				
Full-time	173	235	307	370
Part-time	13	43	101	154
Total	186	278	408	524
% Increases				
Full-time		35.8	30.6	20.5
Part-time		230.8	134.9	52.5
Total		49.5	46.8	28.4
Polytechnics/Colleges				
Full-time	133	222	228	378
Part-time	110	121	192	274
Total	243	343	420	652
% Increases				
Full-time		74.4	2.7	65.8
Part-time		10.0	58.7	42.7
Total		41.1	22.4	55.2

Source: Government Statistical Service, *Education Statistics for the United Kingdom*, Statistical Bulletin 2/93, January 1993, Table 5

APPENDIX 3: KEY STATISTICS

TABLE 5
EXPENDITURE ON ADULT, FURTHER AND PUBLIC SECTOR HIGHER EDUCATION (UNITED KINGDOM)

	£ millions	% Increase
1964/65	207.8	
1969/70	280.2	34.8
1979/80	1,393.6	379.4
1988/89	3,461.2	148.4

Sources: DES, *Statistics of Education, 1965, Part 1*, Table 37, 1968; Government Statistical Service: *Education Statistics for the United Kingdom, 1970*, Table 42, 1972; *Education Statistics for the United Kingdom, 1979/80*, Table 34, 1982; *Education Statistics for the United Kingdom, 1990*, Table 7, 1991

TABLE 6
GOVERNMENT EXPENDITURE ON SCIENTIFIC RESEARCH IN THE CIVILIAN FIELD BY SELECTED YEARS, 1900–50

Year	£000s
1900	62
1910	239
1920	1,291
1930	3,195
1939	3,993
1950	16,058

Source: ACSP, 1951, Appendix II

TABLE 7
RESEARCH COUNCIL'S EXPENDITURE AS PER CENT OF TOTAL GOVERNMENT EXPENDITURE ON RESEARCH AND DEVELOPMENT BY SELECTED YEARS (£m)

Year	Total government expenditure	Research council expenditure	Research councils as per cent of total government
1961–62	385	32	8
1970–71	584	107	18
1974–75	987	152	15
1978–79	1736	266	15
1985–86	4520	528	12
1990–91	4960	851	17

Sources: ACSP, 1964; ABRC, 1975; ABRC, 1979; Cabinet Office, 1987; Cabinet Office, 1992

Bibliography

Aitken, Sir Robert (1969), 'The Vice-Chancellors' Committee and the UGC', *Universities Quarterly*, Vol. 23, No. 2, 165–71.

Armytage, W.H.G. (1955), *Civic Universities*, London, Ernest Benn.

Barker, E. (1931), *Universities in Great Britain*, London, Student Christian Movement Press.

Barr, N. and Barnes, J. (1986), *Strategies for Higher Education: The Alternative White Paper*, Aberdeen University Press for the David Hume Institute and the Suntory-Toyota International Centre for Economics and Related Disciplines, London School of Economics.

Beloff, M. (1967), 'British Universities and the Public Purse', *Minerva*, Vol. 5, No. 4, Summer, 520–32.

Beloff, Lord (1990), 'Universities and the Public Purse: An Update', *Higher Education Quarterly*, Vol. 44, No. 1, 3–19.

Benn, R. and R. Fieldhouse (1993), 'Government Policies on University Expansion and Wider Access, 1945–51 and 1985–91 Compared', *Studies in Higher Education Review*, Vol. 18, No. 3, 229–313.

Berdahl, R.O. (1959), *British Universities and the State*, Cambridge University Press.

Booth, C. (1987), 'Central Government and Higher Education Planning, 1965–1986', *Higher Education Quarterly*, Vol. 41, No. 1, 57–72.

Bowden, Lord (1967), 'The Universities, the Government and the Public Accounts Committee', *Minerva*, Vol. 6, No. 1, Autumn, 28–42.

Boyle, E. (1966), 'Parliament and University Policy', *Minerva*, Vol. 5, No. 1, Autumn, 3–19.

Boyson, R. (1973), *Battle Lines for Education*, London, Conservative Political Centre.

Boyson, R. (1975), *Parental Choice*, London, Conservative Political Centre.

Carswell, J. (1985), *Government and the Universities in Britain*, Cambridge University Press.

Clokie, H.M. and J.W. Robinson (1937), *Royal Commissions of Inquiry*, Stanford, Stanford University Press.

Crequer, N. (1989), 'The Passing of the Education Reform Act', *Higher Education Quarterly*, Vol. 43, No. 1, 3–19.

Crowther-Hunt, Lord (1983), 'Policy-Making and Accountability in Higher Education' in M. Shattock (ed.), *The Structure and Governance of Higher Education*, Guildford, Society for Research in Higher Education, pp. 46–67.

Dodds, H.W. *et al.* (1952), *Government Assistance to Universities in Great Britain*, New York, Columbia University Press.

Engel, A.J. (1983), *From Clergyman to Don: The Rise of the Academic Profession in Nineteenth Century Oxford*, Oxford, Clarendon Press.

Farrant, J. (1987), 'Central Control of the University Sector', in T. Becher (ed.), *British Higher Education*, London, Allen & Unwin, pp. 29–52.

Farrell E. and Tapper, T. (1992), 'Student Loans: The Failure to Consolidate an Emerging Political Consensus', *Higher Education Quarterly*, Vol. 46, No. 3, Summer, 269–85.

Farrington, D. and Mattison, F. (eds.) (1990), *Universities and the Law*, Reading, Conference of University Administrators.

Ferns, H.S. (1969), *Towards an Independent University*, Occasional Paper No. 25, London, Institute of Economic Affairs.

Fry, M. (1948), 'The University Grants Committee. An Experiment in Administration', *Universities Quarterly*, Vol. 2, No. 3, May, 221–30.

Griffith, J. (1989), *Universities and the State: The Next Steps*, London, Council for Academic Freedom and Democracy.

Griffith, J.A.G. and Ryle M. with Wheeler-Booth, J.A.J. (1989), *Parliament: Functions, Practice and Procedures*, London, Sweet & Maxwell.

Hague, Sir Douglas (1991), *Beyond Universities: A New Republic of the Intellect*, Hobart Paper 115, London, Institute of Economic Affairs.

Hailsham, Lord (1963), *Science and Politics*, London.

Halsey, A.H. (1961), 'The Changing Functions of Universities' in A. Halsey, J. Floud, and C. Arnold (eds.), *Education, Economy and Society*, New York, Free Press, pp. 456–65.

Halsey, A.H. (1969), 'The Universities and the State', *Universities Quarterly*, Vol. 23, No. 2, 128–48.

Halsey, A.H. and Trow, M.A. (1971), *The British Academics*, London, Faber & Faber.

Hamilton, Sir William (1952), *Discussions on Philosophy and Literature, Education and University Reform*, Edinburgh, MacLachlan & Stewart.

Henderson, C. and Mattison, F. (1990), 'Universities and the Law', in D. Farrington and F. Mattison (eds), *Universities and the Law*, Reading, Conference of University Administrators, pp. 1–32.

Ince, M. (1986), *The Politics of British Science*, Brighton, Wheatsheaf Books.

Kedourie, E. (1988), *Diamonds into Glass*, London, Centre for Policy Studies.

Kerr, C. (1963), *The Uses of the University*, Cambridge, MA, Harvard University Press.

Knight, C. (1990), *The Making of Tory Educational Policy in Post-war Britain 1950–1986*, Barcombe, Falmer Press.

Kogan, M. (1987), 'The DES and Whitehall', *Higher Education Quarterly*, Vol. 41, No. 3, 225–40.

Kogan, M. (1987a), 'Review of the University Grants Committee: Report of a Committee under the Chairmanship of Lord Croham', *Higher Education Review*, Vol. 12, No. 3, 349–51.

Kogan, M. and Kogan, D. (1983), *The Attack on Higher Education*, London, Kogan Page.

Laurence, I. (1992), *Power and Politics at the DES*, London, Cassell.

Lawton, D. (1986), 'The Department of Education and Science: Policy-Making at the Centre', in A. Hartnett and M. Naish (eds), *Education and Society Today*, Barcombe, Falmer Press, pp. 19–36.

Letwin, O. *et al.* (1988), *Higher Education: Freedom and Finance*, London, Institute of Economic Affairs Education Unit.

Locke, M. (1974), 'Government' in J. Pratt and T. Burgess, *Polytechnics: A Report*, London, Pitman, pp. 149–71.

Locke, M., Pratt, J. and Burgess, T. (1985), *The Colleges of Higher Education, 1972–1982*, Croydon, Critical Press.

Maclure, S. (1982), 'British Higher Education Policy', *Political Quarterly*, Vol. 53, 259–72.

Maclure, S. (1987), 'The Political Context of Higher Education' in T. Becher (ed.), *British Higher Education*, London, Allen & Unwin, pp. 10–28.

Maclure, S. (1989), *Education Reformed: A Guide to the Education Reform Act*, London, Hodder & Stoughton.

BIBLIOGRAPHY

Mason, D. (1986), *University Challenge*, London, Adam Smith Institute.

Matterson, A. (1981), *Polytechnics and Colleges: Control and Administration in the Public Sector of Higher Education*, London, Longman.

Maynard, A. (1975), *Experiment with Choice in Education*, London, Institute of Economic Affairs.

Moberley, Sir Walter (1949), *Crisis in the University*, London, SCM Press.

Moodie, G. (1983), 'Buffer, Coupling and Broker: Reflections on 60 years of the UGC', *Higher Education*, Vol. 12, 331–47.

Moodie, G. (1987), 'Le Roi est Mort; Vive le Quoi? Croham and the Death of the UGC', *Higher Education Quarterly*, Vol. 41, No. 4, 25–41.

Moodie, G. and Eustace, R. (1974), *Power and Policy in British Universities*, London, Allen & Unwin.

Niblett, W.R. (1952), 'The Development of British Universities since 1945', *The Yearbook of Education*, London, Evans Institute of Education.

Nixon, N. (1987), 'Central Control of the Public Sector' in T. Becher (ed.), *British Higher Education*, London, Allen & Unwin, pp. 53–86.

Owen, T. (1980), 'The University Grants Committee', *Oxford Review of Education*, Vol. 6, No. 3, 225–278.

Peacock, A.T. and Wiseman, J. (1964), *Education for Democrats*, Hobart Paper 25, London, Institute of Economic Affairs.

Perkin, H.J. (1969), *Key Profession*, London, Routledge & Kegan Paul.

Pile, W. (1979), *The Department of Education and Science*, London, Allen & Unwin.

Pratt, J. and Burgess, T. (1974), *Polytechnics: A Report*, London, Pitman.

Prest, A.R. (1966), *Financing University Education*, Occasional Paper No. 12, London, Institute of Economic Affairs.

Price, G.L. (1978), 'The Expansion of British Universities and Their Struggle to Maintain Autonomy', *Minerva*, Vol. 16, No. 3, 357–81.

Ranson, S. (1985), 'Contradictions in the Government of Educational Change', *Political Studies*, Vol. 33, 56–72.

Robinson, E. (1970), *The New Polytechnics: The People's Universities*, London.

Rothblatt, S. (1968), *The Revolution of the Dons*, London, Faber & Faber.

Salter, B. and Tapper, T. (1981), *Education, Politics and the State*, London, Grant McIntyre.

Salter, B. and Tapper, T. (1985), *Power and Policy in Education: The Case of Independent Schooling*, Lewes, Falmer Press.

Salter, B. and Tapper, T. (1987a), 'DES: Steering a New Course', in T. Horton (ed.), *GCSE: Examining the New System*, London, Harper & Row, pp. 21–8.

Salter, B. and Tapper, T. (1987b), 'The Politics of Reversing the Ratchet in Secondary Education, 1969–86', *Educational Administration and History*.

Seldon, A. (1986), *The Riddle of the Voucher*, Hobart Paperback, No. 21, London, Institute of Economic Affairs.

Sharp, P. (1987), *The Creation of the Local Authority Sector of Higher Education*, Barcombe, Falmer Press.

Shattock, M. (1987), 'The Last Days of the University Grants Committee', *Minerva*, Vol., 25, No. 4, 471–85.

Shattock, M. and Berdahl, R. (1984), 'The British University Grants Committee 1919–83', *Higher Education*, Vol. 13, 471–99.

Shinn, C.H. (1986), *Paying the Piper, The Development of the UGC 1919–46*, Lewes, Falmer Press.

Sizer, J. (1987), 'Universities in Hard Times: Some Policy Implications and Managerial Guidelines', *Higher Education Quarterly*, Vol. 41, No. 4, 354–72.

Smith, P.M. (1981), 'The Exclusive Jurisdiction of the Visitor', *Law Quarterly Review*, Vol. 97, Oct., 610–47.

Tapper, T. and Salter, B. (1978), *Education and the Political Order*, London, Macmillan Education.

Tapper, T. and Salter, B. (1992), *Oxford, Cambridge and the Changing Idea of the University*, Buckingham, Open University Press.
Trustcot, B. (1943), *Redbrick University*, London, Faber & Faber.
Wade, E.C.S. and Bradley, A.W. (1986), *Constitutional and Administrative Law*, Harlow, Longman.
Woodhall, M. (1970), *Student Loans*, London, Harrap.

OFFICIAL PUBLICATIONS

Advisory Board for the Research Councils (1974) *First Report*, London, HMSO, Cmnd 5633.
Advisory Board for the Research Councils (1976) *Second Report 1974–75*, London, HMSO, Cmnd 6430.
Advisory Board for the Research Councils (1979) *Third Report 1976–78*, London, HMSO, Cmnd 7467.
Advisory Board for the Research Councils (1987) *A Strategy for the Science Base*, London, HMSO.
Advisory Council on Applied Research and Development (1980), *Biotechnology*, London, HMSO.
Advisory Council on Applied Research and Development (1980), *Information Technology*, London, HMSO.
Advisory Council on Applied Research and Development (1983), *Improving Research Links between Higher Education and Industry*, London, HMSO.
Advisory Council on Applied Research and Development and the Advisory Board of the Research Councils (1983), *Joint Report by the Chairmen of ACARD and ABRC*, London, HMSO, Cmnd 8957.
Advisory Council on Applied Research and Development (1986), *Exploitable Areas of Science*, London, HMSO.
Advisory Council on Scientific Policy (1950), *Third Annual Report 1949–50*, London, HMSO, Cmnd 7992.
Advisory Council on Scientific Policy (1951), *Government Scientific Organisation in the Civilian Field*, London, HMSO.
Advisory Council on Scientific Policy (1953), *Sixth Annual Report 1952–53*, London, HMSO, Cmnd 8874.
Advisory Council on Scientific Policy (1956), *Ninth Annual Report 1955–56*, London, HMSO, Cmnd 11.
Advisory Council on Scientific Policy (1957), *Annual Report 1956–57*, London, HMSO, Cmnd 278.
Advisory Council on Scientific Policy (1958), *Annual Report 1957–58*, London, HMSO, Cmnd 597.
Advisory Council on Scientific Policy (1959), *Annual Report 1958–59*, London, HMSO, Cmnd 893.
Advisory Council on Scientific Policy (1960), *Annual Report 1959–60*, London, HMSO, Cmnd 1167.
Advisory Council on Scientific Policy (1962), *Annual Report 1961–62*, London, HMSO, Cmnd 1920.
Advisory Council on Scientific Policy (1963), *Annual Report 1962–63*, London, HMSO, Cmnd 2163.
Advisory Council on Scientific Policy (1964), *Annual Report 1963–64*, London, HMSO, Cmnd 2538.
Agriculture and Food Research Council (1986), *Report 1985–86*, London, AFRC.
Agriculture and Food Research Council (1987), *Report 1986–87*, London, AFRC.

Barlow Report, Lord President of the Council (1946), *Scientific Manpower*, London, HMSO, Cmnd 6824.

Cabinet Office (1979), *Review of the Framework for Government Research and Development*, London, HMSO, Cmnd 7499.

Cabinet Office (1982), *Science and Government, Government Observations on the First Report of the House of Lords Select Committee on Science and Technology, Session 1981–82*, London, HMSO, Cmnd 8591.

Cabinet Office (1987), *Civil Research and Development*, London, HMSO, Cmnd 185.

Cabinet Office (1987), *Annual Review of Government Funded R and D*, London, HMSO.

Cabinet Office (1992), *Annual Review of Government Funded R and D*, London, HMSO.

Committee of Public Accounts (1947), *Third Report from the Committee of Public Accounts, Session 1946–47*, London, HMSO.

Committee of Public Accounts (1949), *Minutes of Evidence Taken Before the Committee of Public Accounts, Session 1948–49*, London, HMSO.

Committee of Public Accounts (1950), *Fourth Report from the Commitee of Public Accounts, Session 1950*, London, HMSO.

Committee of Public Accounts (1956), *Sixth Report from the Committee of Public Accounts, Session 1955–56*, London, HMSO.

Committee of Public Accounts (1967), *Parliament and Control of University Expenditure, Special Report from the Committee of Public Accounts together with the Proceedings of the Committee, Minutes of Evidence and Appendices, Session 1966–67*, HCP 290, London, HMSO.

Committee of Public Accounts (1973), *Eighth Report from the Committee of Public Accounts, Session 1972–73*, London, HCP385.

Committee of Public Accounts (1986), *41st Report from the Committee of Public Accounts, Session 1985–86, Redundancy Compensation Payments to University Staff*, London, HMSO.

Committee of Public Accounts (1988), *Financial Problems at Universities*, Minutes of Evidence DES, Sir David Hancock, UGC, Sir Peter Swinnerton Dyer, Session 1987–88, HCP499(I). HMSO.

Committee of Public Accounts (1990), *Financial Problems at Universities*, First Report, Session 1989–90, HCP136, London, HMSO.

Committee of Public Accounts (1990a), *Restructuring and Finances of Universities*, 36th Report, Session 1989–90, HCP258, London, HMSO.

Conservative Political Centre (1985), *No Turning Back*, London, Conservative Political Centre.

Conservative Research Department (1959), *Glossed Over: Socialist Plans Explained and Exposed*, London, Conservative Research Department.

Council for Scientific Policy (1966), *Report on Science Policy*, London, HMSO Cmnd 3007.

Council for Scientific Policy (1967a), *Report on Science Policy*, London, HMSO Cmnd 3420.

Council for Scientific Policy (1967b), *Report of the Working Party on Liaison Between Universities and Government Research Establishments*, London, HMSO Cmnd 3222.

Council for Scientific Policy (1971a), *Report of the Working Group on Biological Manpower*, London, HMSO Cmnd 4737.

Council for Scientific Policy (1971b), *Report of a Study on the Support of Scientific Research in the Universities*, London, HMSO Cmnd 4798.

Council for Scientific Policy (1971c), *The Future of the Research Council System*, London, HMSO.

Council for Scientific Policy (1972), *Third Report of the Council for Scientific Policy*, London, HMSO Cmnd 5117.

Dainton Report, Council for Scientific Policy (1968), *Enquiry into Flow of Candidates in Science and Technology into Higher Education*, London, HMSO.

Department of Education and Science (1966), *A Plan for Polytechnics and Other Colleges*, London, HMSO.

Department of Education and Science (1966a), *The Government of Colleges*, London, HMSO.

Department of Education and Science (1968), *Statistics of Education, 1965, Part One*, London, HMSO.

Department of Education and Science (1970), *Output Budgeting for the Department of Education and Science: Report of a Feasibility Study* (Educational Planning Paper No. 1), London, HMSO.

Department of Education and Science (1970a), *Student Numbers in Higher Education in England and Wales*, (Educational Planning Paper No. 2), London, HMSO.

Department of Education and Science (1972), *Education: A Framework for Expansion*, London, HMSO Cmnd 5174.

Department of Education and Science (1981), *Annual Report 1981*, London, HMSO.

Department of Education and Science (1985), *The Development of Higher Education into the 1990s*, London, HMSO Cmnd 9524.

Department of Education and Science (1987), *Higher Education: Meeting the Challenge*, London, HMSO.

Education Reform Act (1988), *Public General Acts and Measures*, Elizabeth II, London, HMSO.

Education, Science and Arts Committee (1980), *The Funding and Organisation of Courses in Higher Education*, Session 1979–80, 5th Report, HCP787(I), London, HMSO.

Education Science and Arts Committee (1982), *Expenditure Cuts in Higher Education: The Effects on the 'Robbins Principle' and the Universities*, Session 1981–82, First Report, HCP82, London, HMSO.

Education Science and Arts Committee (1985), *The Future of the Science Budget*, Session 1984–85, First Report, HCP46(I), London, HMSO.

Estimates Committee (1965), *Grants to Universities and Colleges*, Fifth Report from the Estimates Committee together with the Minutes of Evidence taken before Subcommittee B and Apendices, Session 1964–65, HCP283, London, HMSO.

Further and Higher Education Act (1992), *Public General Acts and Measures*, Elizabeth II, London, HMSO.

Gater Report, University Grants Committee (1956), *Methods used by Universities of Contracting and of Recording and Controlling Expenditure*, London, HMSO, Cmnd 9, London, HMSO.

Government Statistical Service (1982), *Education Statistics for the United Kingdom, 1979–80*, London, HMSO.

Government Statistical Service (1991), *Education Statistics for the United Kingdom, 1990*, London, HMSO.

Government Statistical Service (January 1993), *Education Statistics for the United Kingdom*, Statistical Bulletin 2/93, HMSO.

Haldane Report, Ministry of Reconstruction (1918), *Report of the Machinery of Government Committee*, London, HMSO.

Hansard (Commons) (1967) 26 July, Vol. 751.

Hansard (Commons) (1992) 11 Feb., Vol. 203.

Higher Education Funding Council for England (1992), *The Funding of Teaching by the HEFCE in 1993–94*, (Circular 1/92) Bristol, HEFCE.

Higher Education Funding Council for England (1992a), *Quality Assessment*, (Consultation Paper) Bristol, HEFCE.

Higher Education Funding Council for England (1992b), *Draft Financial Memorandum with Institutions*, (Consultation Paper) Bristol, HEFCE.

James Report, Committee of Inquiry into Teacher Education and Training (1972), *Teacher Education and Training*, London, HMSO.

Jones Report, Committee on Manpower Resources for Science and Technology (1967), *The Brain Drain, Report of the Working Group on Migration*, London, HMSO.

Mason Report, Advisory Board for the Research Councils (1983), *A Study of Commissioned Research*, London, HMSO.

Medical Research Council (1985), *Annual Report 1984–85*, London MRC.

Medical Research Council (1986), *Annual Report 1985–86*, London MRC.

Medical Research Council (1987), *Annual Report 1986–87*, London MRC.

Merrison Report, Advisory Board for the Research Councils and the University Grants Committee (1982), *Report of a Joint Working Party on the Support of University Scientific Research*, London, HMSO, Cmnd 8567.

Ministry of Education (1956), *Technical Education*, London, HMSO.

Ministry of Education (1958), *Education in 1958*, London, HMSO.

Ministry of Education (1963), *Education in 1963*, London, HMSO.

Muir-Wood Report, Advisory Board for the Research Councils/Advisory Council on Applied Research and Development (1983), *Improving Links between Higher Education and Industry*, London, HMSO, Cmnd 8957.

National Audit Office (1991), *Polytechnics and Colleges Funding Council*, London, HMSO.

Natural Environment Research Council (1982), *Annual Report 1981–82*, London, NERC.

Natural Environment Research Council (1983), *Annual Report 1982–83*, London, NERC.

Natural Environment Research Council (1985), *Annual Report 1984–85*, London, NERC.

Niblett Report, University Grants Committee (1957), *Report of the Sub-Committee on Halls of Residence*, London, HMSO.

Oakes Report, Department of Education and Science (1978), *Report of the Working Group on the Management of Higher Education in the Maintained Sector*, London, HMSO, Cmnd 7130.

OECD (1975), *Educational Development Strategy in England and Wales*, Paris, OECD.

Percy Report, Ministry of Education (1945), *Higher Technological Education*, London, HMSO.

Polytechnics and Colleges Funding Council (1989), *Funding Choices: Methods of Funding Higher Education in Polytechnics and Colleges*, PCFC.

Polytechnics and Colleges Funding Council (1990), *Performance Indicators*, Committee of Inquiry chaired by Mr Alfred Morris.

Polytechnics and Colleges Funding Council (1991), *Annual Report, 1990–91*, PCFC.

Polytechnics and Colleges Funding Council (1991a), *Parliamentary Accountability*, Circular 91/A/40.

Polytechnics and Colleges Funding Council (1991b), *Strategic Planning, 1992–93*, PCFC.

Public General Statutes (1923), 13 and 14 Geo V, London, Eyre and Spottiswoode, Ch. 33.

Regina v. Lord President of the Privy Council, Ex parte Page (3 December 1992) as reported in *The Times*, Law Report, 15 December, 1992.

Robbins, Committee on Higher Education (1963), *Report on Higher Education 6–7*, London, HMSO, Cmnd 2154.

Rothschild, Lord (1971), *A Framework for Government Research and Development*, London, HMSO, Cmnd 4814.

Royal Commission on Oxford and Cambridge Universities (1922), *Appendices to the Report of the Commission*, London, HMSO.

Rucker Report, University Grants Committee (1960), *Methods used by Universities of Contracting and of Recording and Controlling Expenditure*, London, HMSO, Cmnd 1235, London, HMSO.

Science and Engineering Research Council (1981), *Report 1980–81*, London, SERC.

Science and Engineering Research Council (1985a), *Corporate Plan*, London, SERC.

Science and Engineering Research Council (1985b), *Report 1985*, London, SERC.

Select Committee on Education and Science (1969), *Student Relations, Vol. 1. Report*, London, HMSO.

Select Committee on Education and Science (1972), *First Report from the Select Committee on Science and Technology, Session 1971–72*, London, HMSO.

Select Committee on Education and Science (1979–80), *Funding and Organisation of Courses in Higher Education: Interim Report of Overseas Students' Fees* (Volume II, Minutes of Evidence), HC363, London, HMSO.

Select Committee on Estimates (1952), *Fifth Report from the Select Committee on Estimates, Session 1951–52*, London, HMSO.

Select Committee on Estimates (1965), *Fifth Report from the Select Committee on Estimates, Session 1964–65*, London, HMSO.

Select Committee on Expenditure (1973), *Postgraduate Education*, Third Report, Session 1973–74, HC96(I).

Select Committee on Expenditure (1975–6), *Policy Making in the Department of Education and Science* (Tenth Report), London, HC621.

Select Committee on Procedure (1978), *First Report*, Session 1977–78, HC588(I), London, HMSO.

Select Committee on Science and Technology (1972), *Fourth Report from the Select Committee on Science and Technology, Session 1971–72*, London, HMSO.

Select Committee on Science and Technology (1973), *Research and Development*, Session 1972–73, HC421, London, HMSO.

Select Committee on Science and Technology (1975), *Scientific Research in British Universities*, Second Report, Session 1974–75, HC504, London, HMSO.

Select Committee on Science and Technology (1976), *University – Industry Relations*, Third Report, Session 1975–76, HC680, London, HMSO.

Select Committee on Science and Technology (1981), *Science and Government*, Session 1980–81, HLP20(I), London, HMSO.

Select Committee on Science and Technology (1987), *Civil Research and Development*, First Report, Session 1986–87, HLP20, London, HMSO.

Select Committee on Science and Technology (1988), *Priorities in Medical Research*, Session 1987–88, HLP54, London, HMSO.

Select Committee on Science and Technology (1989), *Civil Research and Development*, Third Report, Session 1988–89, HLP24, London, HMSO.

Swann Report, Committee on Manpower Resources for Science and Technology (1968), *The Flow into Employment of Scientists, Engineers and Technologists*, London, HMSO.

Trend Report, Committee of Enquiry into the Organisation of Civil Science (1963), *Report*, London, HMSO.

Universities Funding Council (1989), *Circular Letter, 39–89*, 12 Dec.

Universities Funding Council (1989/90), *University Statistics, Volume 1, Students and Staff*, Cheltenham, Universities Statistical Record.

Universities Funding Council (1989/90a), *University Statistics, Volume 3, Students and Staff*, Cheltenham, Universities Statistical Record.

Universities Funding Council (1992), *The Funding of Research by the Higher Education Funding Council for England*, (Consultation Paper) Bristol.

University Grants Committee (1921), *Report*, London, HMSO, Cmnd 1163.

University Grants Committee (1922/23), *Returns from Universities and Colleges in Receipt of Treasury Grant*, London, HMSO.

BIBLIOGRAPHY

University Grants Committee (1925/26), *Returns from Universities and Colleges in Receipt of Treasury Grant*, London, HMSO.

University Grants Committee (1925), *Report*, London, HMSO.

University Grants Committee (1930), *Report*, London, HMSO.

University Grants Committee (1936), *Report, 1929–30 to 1934–35*, London, HMSO.

University Grants Committee (1938/39), *Returns from Universities and Colleges in Receipt of Treasury Grant*, London, HMSO.

University Grants Committee (1939/40), *Returns from Universities and Colleges in Receipt of Treasury Grant*, London, HMSO.

University Grants Committee (1948), *University Development 1935 to 1946*, London, HMSO.

University Grants Committee (1949/50), *Returns from Universities and Colleges in Receipt of Treasury Grant*, London, HMSO.

University Grants Committee (1953), *University Development 1947 to 1952*, London, HMSO, Cmnd 8875.

University Grants Committee (1958), *University Development 1952 to 1957*, London, HMSO, Cmnd 534.

University Grants Committee (1959/60), *Returns from Universities and Colleges in Receipt of Treasury Grant*, London, HMSO.

University Grants Committee (1963), *University Development 1957–1962*, London, HMSO, Cmnd 2267.

University Grants Committee (1968), *University Development 1962–1967*, London, HMSO, Cmnd 3820.

University Grants Committee (1970), *Statistics of Education Volume 6: Universities*, London, HMSO.

University Grants Committee (1974), *University Development 1967 to 1972*, London, HMSO, Cmnd 5728.

University Grants Committee (1980), *University Statistics, Volume 1: Students and Staff*, Cheltenham, Universities Statistical Record.

University Grants Committee (1980a), *University Statistics, Volume 3: Finance*, Cheltenham, Universities Statistical Record.

University Grants Committee (1984), *Annual Survey 1982–83*, London, HMSO, Cmnd 9234.

University Grants Committee (1984a), *A Strategy for Higher Education into the 1990s*, London, HMSO.

Zuckerman Report, Office of the Minister for Science (1961), *Report of the Committee on the Management and Control of Research and Development*, London, HMSO.

OTHER PUBLICATIONS

Akker, J., 'Tenure: The Constitutional Position' (constructed title) Nov. 1984, *Bulletin*, No. 122, p. 7.

Association of University Teachers, Sept. 1982, *Bulletin*, 101.

Association of University Teachers, March 1983, *Bulletin*, 106.

Association of University Teachers, (1992) *Higher Education Politics for the 1990s* (LA/4630a) London, AUT. Further and Higher Education Act, 1992.

Booth, C. (1985), 'The Rise and Fall of Science Policy', Paper delivered to the conference *Educational Policy Making*, Cambridge University.

Calder, R. (1949), *Science and Socialism*, Towards Tomorrow, No. 3. London, Labour Publications Department.

Chamberlain, N. (1936), Letter to Lord Crawford, *Times Educational Supplement*, 7th March.

THE STATE AND HIGHER EDUCATION

Committee of Vice-Chancellors and Principals (1985), *Report of the Steering Committee for Efficiency Studies in Universities*, London, Committee of Vice-Chancellors and Principals (Jarratt Report).
Conservative Party (1979), *General Election Manifesto*, London, Conservative Party.
Crosland, A. (1965), Speech at Woolwich Polytechnic, 27 April.
Labour Party (1949), *New Deal for Science*, Labour Discussion Series, London, Labour Party.
Labour Party (1953), *Challenge to Britain, A Programme of Action for the Next Labour Government*, London, Labour Party.
Labour Party (1958), *Learning to Live, A Policy for Education from Nursery School to University*, London, Labour Party.
Labour Party (1961), *Science and the Future of Britain*, London, Labour Party.
Labour Party (1961a), *Signposts for the Sixties*, London, Labour Party.
Labour Party (1963), *The Years of Crisis*, Report of a Labour Party Study Group on Higher Education, London, Labour Party.
Labour Party (1972), *Labour's Programme for Britain*.
Labour Party (1973), *Higher and Further Education*, Report of a Labour Party Study Group, London, Labour Party.
Labour Party (1974), *Manifesto*, London, Labour Party.
Labour Party (1976), *Labour's Programme*, London, Labour Party.
Labour Party (1979), *Manifesto, The Labour Way is the Better Way*, London, Labour Party.
Labour Party (1982), *16–19 Learning for Life*, London, Labour Party.
Labour Party (1982a), *Education After 18: Expansion with Change*, London, Labour Party.
Labour Party (1986), *Education Throughout Life: A Statement on Continuing and Higher Education*, London, Labour Party.
Saville, C. (1983), 'The Department of Education and Science', paper presented to seminar on The Department of Education and Science, Christ's College, Cambridge.
Wilson, H. (1963), *Labour's Plan for Science*, Speech, Annual Conference, Scarborough, 1 Oct., London, Labour Party Reprint.

THE TIMES

The Times (1991), 6 Aug., 'Lecturers' tenure subject to terms of contract', p. 28.
The Times (1992), 15 Dec., 'Decision that cannot be challenged', p. 20.

TIMES HIGHER EDUCATION SUPPLEMENT

Anon. (1975), 7 March, 15.
Anon. (1976), 26 Nov., 17.
Anon. (1981), 'DES plans revolutionary new body', 30 Jan., 1.
Anon. (1982), 'NAB abandons course control for national plan', 28 May, 1.
Anon. (1986), 'Cold war or compromise', 20 June, 36.
Anon. (1986a), 'Defiant Labour to erase binary line', 3 Oct., 3.
Anon. (1987), 'Fabians reveal Labour's policy rift', 16 Jan., 1.
Anon. (1988), 'The PCFC personality', 9 Dec., 36.
Anon. (1989), 'Labour unveils plans to tempt extra students', 5 May, 2.
Anon. (1990), 30 March.
Anon. (1990), 14 Sept.
Anon. (1992), 19 June.

BIBLIOGRAPHY

David, P. (1981), 'Public body politic', 7 Aug., 7.

David, P. and O'Leary, J. (1981), 'National body: worst suspicions confirmed by Minister's memo', 7 Feb., 1.

Farrant, J. (24 Feb. 1992), *Interview*.

Flather, P. (1980), 'New status demanded for polys', 4 April, 1.

Flather, P. (1980a), 'Poly chiefs unveil funding plans', 25 April, 32.

Gold, K. (1984), 'CNAA stakes claim to influence and planning', 27 Jan., 1.

Gold, K. (1984a), 'Watching and listening', 10 Aug., 11.

Gold, K. (1985), 'Two-tier plan gets thumbs down from polys', 8 Feb., 1.

Gold, K. (1986), 'Polys are denied freedom as CNAA faces cuts', 21 March, 1.

Millar, F. (1992), 'An Open Letter to the UFC', 10 Jan., 14.

O'Leary, J. (1981), 'A perfect political solution', 6 Nov., 9.

O'Leary, J. (1982), 'Survey reveals huge college spending gaps', 6 Nov., 1.

O'Leary, J. (1984), '£40 increase is double what NAB expected', 5 Oct., 1.

O'Leary, J. (1986), 'NAB delays college shake-up for a year', 12 Dec., 1.

O'Leary, J. and Gold, K. (1983), 'NAB rethinks its plan as CNAA joins the critics', 23 Sept., 1.

Warner, D. (1992), 'Strength in going your own way', 9 Oct., 19.

Yarde, R. (1989), 'PCFC rejects Baker line on funding', 20 Jan., 1.

Index

237

Weaver, T., 97–8
Wilkinson, E., 76–7
Williams, D., 63
Wilson government, 78, 80, 188
Wilson, Harold, 24
Wiseman, J., 31

Workers' Education Association, 26

Yarde, R., 152

Zuckerman Report, *see* Office of the
Minister for Science

Printed in the United Kingdom
by Lightning Source UK Ltd.
120087UK00001B/22